The European Union in International Affairs

This Book Series aims to be a central resource for the growing community of scholars and policy-makers who engage with the evolving interface between the EU and international affairs. It provides in-depth, cutting edge and original contributions of world-class research on the EU in international affairs by highlighting new developments, insights, challenges and opportunities. It encompasses analyses of the EU's international role, as mediated by its own Member States, in international institutions and in its strategic bilateral and regional partnerships. Books in the Series examine evolving EU internal policies that have external implications and the ways in which these are both driven by, and feed back into, international developments. Grounded in Political Science, International Relations, International Political Economy, Law, Sociology and History, the Series reflects a commitment to interdisciplinary scholarship. We welcome book proposals relating to the changing role of the EU in international affairs across policies and the Union's relations with different parts of the world, as well as relations with states and multilateral institutions. We are interested in research on values and norms, interests and global governance and welcome both theory-informed studies and studies comparing the EU with other major global actors. To submit a proposal, please contact Commissioning Editor Ambra Finotello ambra.finotello@palgrave.com. This series is indexed by Scopus.

Irina Mützelburg

Transferring Asylum Norms to EU Neighbours

Multi-Scalar Policies and Practices in Ukraine

palgrave
macmillan

Irina Mützelburg
Centre for East European
and International Studies
Berlin, Germany

ISSN 2662-5911 ISSN 2662-592X (electronic)
The European Union in International Affairs
ISBN 978-3-031-04527-1 ISBN 978-3-031-04528-8 (eBook)
https://doi.org/10.1007/978-3-031-04528-8

Cover credit: Image Source/Getty Images

This Palgrave Macmillan imprint is published by the registered company Springer Nature Switzerland AG
The registered company address is: Gewerbestrasse 11, 6330 Cham, Switzerland

Preface

How to publish a book on Ukraine in 2022? Since the beginning of the full-scale Russian invasion on 24 February, our understanding of Ukraine and the whole region has been shaken. It's tempting to believe that everything that we knew or thought we knew about pre-2022 Ukraine has become obsolete. And indeed, we cannot predict what the Ukrainian state and society will be like when this war hopefully ends. A large share of the population will have been displaced—some to other countries, some within Ukraine. Many will have participated directly or indirectly in the war, and many more will have experienced fighting and feared for their own lives and those of people close to them. Many will have lost their jobs, companies and property, their psychological and physical health, their relatives and friends. Large parts of Ukrainian infrastructure, housing, private and state-owned buildings and land will have been destroyed or made unusable by landmines. All those who stayed in Ukraine will have lived through a prolonged phase of martial law. Some of the inhabitants of Ukraine will have lived under Russian occupation, subject to severe repression of civic and political rights, political propaganda, and at least in some regions, the kidnapping, rape, torture, and killing of civilians. When this book gets published, we do not know which territory will be under the control of the Ukrainian state, or how the institutions of this state will work.

So why still read a book about pre-invasion Ukraine?

First, knowing the history and recent past of a society and state will allow us to better understand the present and future even if war and displacement violently upturn the existing structures. Even if we do not yet know which ones, certain structures and historical legacies remain. Understanding asylum and xenophobia in pre-invasion Ukraine also helps us understand the beliefs and practices of Ukrainians who fled the war in 2022 and now find themselves labelled 'refugees' in other countries. For instance, some of the Ukrainians abroad do not wish to be called 'refugees', partly because they insist on their plan to return to Ukraine very soon, partly because they have negative associations with the term.

Second, this book is not only about pre-invasion Ukraine but also about transfer processes. It is about the ways certain actors try to shape policies and practices in other states. It is about how internationally weaker states respond to requests, incentives, and pressure from more powerful states or international organisations. It is about how state actors in these weaker countries introduce, implement, or pretend to implement laws and policies that they did not see as important or beneficial to their own country but were requested by international organisations. It is about how more powerful, bigger, and wealthier organisations fund smaller organisations in the target country to spread ideas and practices. These questions remain relevant—definitely in a lot of countries surrounding the European Union, probably also in Ukraine, which was granted candidate status together with Moldova in June 2022. The transfer processes in the context of conditionality for a visa-free regime described in this book bear many similarities with those in the context of EU accession.

The recent granting of EU candidate status to Ukraine is typical of a pattern of EU external action also visible in the granting of the visa-free regime. In the 2010s, the European Commission regularly published monitoring reports, which kept track of progress and outstanding problems in different policy areas that were subject to EU conditionality. From 2010 until 2015, the European Commission consistently pointed to the deficiencies that needed to be addressed before Ukraine could be granted visa freedom. Then in December 2015, under the influence of the change in political leadership in the aftermath of the Maidan protests, the Russian annexation of Crimea, and the war in Donbas, the European Commission declared that Ukraine had fulfilled all requirements for the visa-free regime—even though many of the changes requested by the

Commission had not yet been made. In the context of Russian aggression, the EU sought to support the Ukrainian state and its new political leadership by granting visa freedom. Similarly, the granting of candidate status in June 2022 was an expression of the EU's wish to symbolically support Ukraine. This despite the fact that until 2022, EU officials had insisted that they would not make any promises concerning Ukraine's membership prospects. In both cases, the EU made sudden concessions in the political context of Russian aggression and the EU's wish to show solidarity with Ukraine.

Studying the policy and norm promotion activities of the EU and international organisations does not mean supporting Russian propaganda about the supposedly totalitarian imperialism of a collective West, which Russian politicians and state media use to legitimise Russian military invasions. The use of soft power and diplomacy by the EU cannot justify the use of warfare by the Russian Federation. A 'normative Empire Europe' (Del Sarto) cannot be equated with a military Empire Russia.

Even in a context where there is a risk of academic research being used and distorted for state propaganda, it seems to me that it is the researcher's professional, ethical, and political duty to continue critically studying the foreign policies of the EU, its member states, and other international organisations and actors. For the sake of democracy and freedom of research, it remains important to point to power asymmetries in the relations between the EU and its neighbouring states as well as the EU's use of its power to impose its interests and norms abroad. Yet, despite such power asymmetries, actors in the neighbouring states are not passive recipients of EU domination. In contrast to Russian propaganda, this book takes Ukrainian state and non-state actors seriously, analysing how they make choices according to their own interests and beliefs and exercise their leeway in policies and practices.

Berlin, Germany
October 2022

Irina Mützelburg

Acknowledgements

First of all, I would like to thank Kathy Rousselet and Anne de Tinguy for accepting the supervision of my PhD. I am very grateful for their trust and support, the freedom they have given me, and their attentive and constructive proofreading and feedback. I am also extremely thankful to my tutors at the Centre Marc Bloch in Berlin, Mathilde Darley, Fabien Jobard, Joël Glasman, Elsa Tulmets, and Béatrice von Hirschhausen for all their time, energy, patience, and kindness in reading and commenting on parts of this book at various stages of its production. It was a great relief to know I could come and see you in an office next door. This book would not have been possible without the company, advice, proofreading, encouragement, and chocolate of my colleagues, office mates, and/or friends at the Centre Marc Bloch and later the ZOiS, among others Bénédicte Laumond, Caroline Garrido, Chloé Risbourque, Christina Reimann, Denis Eckert, Claudia Eggart, Emeline Fourment, Gesine Wallem, Jérémy Geeraert, Mélina Germes, Noa Levin, Sabine von Löwis, Salima Naït Ahmed, Sarah Kiani, Serge Reuby, Sophie Lambroschini, and Ulrike Zeigermann.

I am grateful to the Centre Marc Bloch's and ZOiS' management and administrative teams for such a stimulating and comfortable workplace and for their continuous efforts to make the institute even more pleasant and enriching. Funding from Sciences Po Paris, the Fazit Stiftung, and the Centre Marc Bloch made this research possible and funding from

Sciences Po Lyon, Triangle, and the Centre Marc Bloch made the English language editing possible.

Many people have contributed to this multilingual scientific undertaking with their native language skills. Anne, Jeffrey, Jill, and Noa have greatly improved the readability of the English text. I am very grateful to Olesia, Svitlana, Vasyl, and Yana for their tremendous help with their Russian and Ukrainian skills. I thank all those who have helped me in this adventure of conducting research in two languages and writing a thesis and then a book in two others, none of the four being my mother tongue.

I am deeply indebted to all those who have supported me in my fieldwork. My numerous interlocutors have granted me, some of them repeatedly, their precious time and trust without gaining anything in return, apart from my undivided attention and lasting gratefulness. I am particularly obliged to those who agreed to share their network with me and helped me organise interviews and observation sessions. Antonina, Katharina, Mariya, Natalia, Pierre, Vera, and several CouchSurfing hosts housed me, fed me, advised me, and kept me company in Brussels and in various parts of Ukraine. My warmest thoughts and wishes go to those who were and are in zones of fighting and those who had to flee.

This book as well as my mental and physical health owe a lot to my family and my friends outside of academia, whom I cannot list here. They have learnt to refrain from asking me whether I have *finally* handed in my thesis or submitted my book manuscript. Through their presence, their own interests, problems, and joys, their insisting on my company, including for holidays, they have kept me from drifting up into the mad ivory towers. Cécile has saved me numerous times with her comforting presence, her sofa, her tea, and her unlimited readiness to help me with logistical problems in Paris. I cannot thank Joé enough for everything he has done for me and the serenity with which he has surrounded me.

Contents

List of Figures

List of Tables

CHAPTER 1

Introduction

Until the full-scale Russian invasion in February 2022, the European Union (EU) had refused to grant Ukraine a membership perspective.[1] Nonetheless, the EU tried to shape laws, policies, and practices in Ukraine in different ways, including by offering other incentives, such as visa freedom for Ukrainian tourists in exchange for reforms, and funding the activities of international and non-governmental organisations in Ukraine. While the situation in Ukraine during and after the war is likely to differ in many ways from the situation in the 2010s, understanding EU conditionality and processes of norm and policy transfer will be more relevant than ever.

As this book shows, since the beginning of the war in Donbas in 2014, the loss of a geopolitical alternative, that Russia had represented, strengthened the normative influence of the EU in Ukraine. Ukrainian political decision-makers increasingly prioritised the cooperation with the EU. Indirectly, these macro-developments also enhanced the position and political influence of the Ukraine-based offices of international organisations and NGOs. The full-scale Russian invasion in February 2022 has further increased Ukraine's need for international military, financial, and

[1] In the EU-Ukraine Association Agreement, 'the European Union acknowledges the European aspirations of Ukraine and welcomes its European choice' without any concrete commitments to enlargement (2014).

I. Mützelburg, *Transferring Asylum Norms to EU Neighbours*, The European Union in International Affairs, https://doi.org/10.1007/978-3-031-04528-8_1

political support—and its corresponding dependence on North American and European states as well as organisations like the EU and the United Nations (UN). In June 2022, the EU granted Ukraine and Moldova candidate status. Similar to the process to achieve the visa-free regime studied in the present book, the road to EU accession is defined by EU conditionality and monitoring of reforms in various areas, namely fighting corruption, limiting the power of oligarchs, strengthening the rule of law, supporting free media, and protecting national minorities. This book's insights will help readers understand the transfer processes in the accession phase of Ukraine and other candidate countries, such as Moldova and Georgia.

Since the independence of the Ukrainian state in 1991, international organisations have promoted their norms and policies in the country. But how and why did change, desired by international organisations, take place in practice? This book examines the influence of the EU and other international organisations, such as the UN and the Council of Europe (CoE), on political and societal developments in Ukraine. International organisations requested changes in policies and state practices during negotiations and promoted them via projects, which they either implemented themselves or paid Ukrainian non-governmental organisations (NGOs) to carry out. Through this type of delegation, a diverse set of actors intervened across scales in the transfer regime. This book analyses these actors' practices and strategies for transferring international asylum norms and policies to Ukraine. It also looks at practices of resistance, contestation, and translation among local and national actors. Furthermore, it explores the intended and unintended normative and social effects of these transfer activities.

Asylum Norms and Policies

Fundamental Asylum Norms

While asylum, understood broadly as fugitives' protection from persecution, has existed for thousands of years, contemporary asylum is more specific (Schuster, 2004b). Even though asylum norms and treaties have been developed by various organisations (e.g. the Bangkok Principles on Status and Treatment of Refugees by the Asian-African Legal Consultative Organisation, 1966), what European and North American scholars and regional organisations commonly refer to as contemporary "international" asylum norms originated in post-World War II Western Europe and were formalised in the United Nations Universal Declaration of Human Rights (1948). They were then further specified in the Convention Relating to the Status of Refugees, approved at a United Nations conference in 1951. This political context shaped norm production, including the belief that fleeing people are a temporary exception and that humans should live in their own state, meaning that migrants should be either brought back to their state of origin or regularised. Contemporary asylum norms follow principles of state sovereignty and non-interventionism, based on a state-centric perspective—as opposed to migrant-centric—creating a right for states to grant asylum, rather than a right for migrants to be granted asylum (Schuster, 2004b).

In the context of the Cold War, the Convention was finalised without the Soviet Union and enabled Western states to grant protection status to those who fled the USSR due to their ideological support to the West. Article 1 of the Refugee Convention defines the criteria to categorise a migrant as a refugee: a person with "well-founded fear of being persecuted for reasons of race, religion, nationality, membership of a particular social group or political opinion". These criteria correspond to the values of the Western block, that is, individualism (to be recognised as a refugee, a person needs to be individually persecuted (Gorman, 2019)), as well as political and civic rights, while neglecting economic and social rights (Schuster, 2004a). These basic principles continue to define the normative framework of the international asylum regime.

Terminology

The terminology referring to migrants is highly contested and politicised. Right-wing politicians call all migrants "illegal" and pro-migrant activists call all migrants "refugees". While the discursive categorisation of migrants can be debated on political and ethical grounds, to understand state policies, laws, actors' practices, and migrants' experiences, it is necessary to make some distinctions in wording, following the categories of international and Ukrainian law. In this book, I use the term "migrant" to refer to non-Ukrainian citizens who left their country of origin to move to other countries for a longer period of time. "Migrant" thus encompasses here all types of legal statuses, places of origin, and motives of migration. I do not use it to distinguish "migrants" from "refugees"; I include asylum seekers and refugees in the category of migrants. Asylum seekers are migrants who applied formally for a protection status (e.g. in Ukraine). In theory, they receive a document from the administration, which certifies that they applied and which serves as proof of their temporary legal status in Ukraine. I use the term "refugee" as the legal status of a person who has been granted a protection status from state authorities. In Ukraine, there are theoretically three types of protection statuses, of which two are practically attributed by the administration: "refugee" and "person in need of complementary protection". For the sake of readability, I use the term "refugee" to refer to both types of persons who have received such a protection status. I only distinguish between the two statuses when their treatment differs.

The European Production of Asylum Norms and Policies

Various actors, such as the United Nations High Commissioner for Refugees, the European Union, and states have continued producing formalised asylum norms in the form of treaties, directives, regulations, and laws. Shaped by the negotiations among various actors with diverging beliefs and interests (Fresia, 2014), asylum norms have, on the one hand, been extended, for example to include additional groups of migrants or additional rights for asylum seekers. The EU Qualification Directive (2004, recast in 2011) created the status of subsidiary protection for people who do not fulfil the criteria for the refugee status according to the Refugee Convention but who face a risk of "serious harm" in their country of origin (death penalty, persecution, torture, inhuman or degrading treatment, threat to life) including due to war, violence, and massive violations of human rights (Article 2). The EU Reception Conditions Directive (2003, recast in 2013) established minimum standards for the treatment of asylum seekers, including certain social benefits, healthcare, access to the labour market, and education (Chetail et al., 2016).

On the other hand, the production of asylum norms and policies has been shaped by an increasing securitisation of migration (i.e. the representation of migrants as an existential threat (Bigo, 2006; Bourbeau, 2011)) and the objective of keeping unwanted migrants out. Taking up principles from national law, the Council of the EU decided on the Asylum Procedures Directive (2005, recast in 2013), which introduced the concepts of safe country of origin and safe third country. The concept of safe third country (STC) enables destination states to "transfer responsibility of asylum applications to a 'safe third country', providing that a 'connection exists between the applicant and the STC" (Hunt, 2014, p. 502). The concept of safe country of origin enables destination states to reject asylum applications without deeper examination. Both legal concepts facilitate restrictive asylum policies (Engelmann, 2014; Hunt, 2014).

Most scholars agree that the EU and its member states claim to respect human rights and asylum principles while in practice pursuing increasingly restrictive anti-migrant policies (Lavenex, 2018). Since the 1980s immigration in Europe has become more and more politicised and constructed as a major political problem (Boswell, 2003). States tend to criminalise migration and detain asylum seekers (Bosworth & Vannier, 2020). Scholars have demystified national asylum policies claimed to aim at supporting the most threatened migrants in need of protection. National asylum authorities may recognise asylum claims to condemn foreign governments when this is geopolitically desirable (Gorman, 2019). Yet, most of the time asylum administration staff works under political and institutional pressure to process applications quickly and to keep the number of recognised refugees as low as possible (Miaz, 2019; Spire, 2008). Officials and judges reject asylum applications of migrants perceived as undesirable or too numerous, using the law to justify rejections (Gorman, 2019). Studies have highlighted the role of street-level bureaucrats' value judgements of migrants, favouring applicants who comply with the procedure and dominant norms of deservingness, who manage to tell a story that resonates with the normative framework and personal representations of the state agents with whom they interact (Darley, 2010).

Since the 1990s, law and order officials, primarily from the ministries of the interior, have shaped the emerging asylum and migration policies at the EU venue and have sought to curtail unwanted immigration and asylum (Guiraudon, 2018). Struggling to agree on common internal immigration and asylum policies, EU member states have mainly opted for the lowest common denominator—the external dimension of migration policies. European states and the EU have increasingly extra-territorialised migration control, moving it to the high seas and to countries of origin or transit (El Qadim, 2021; Frelick et al., 2016). Extra-territorialisation refers to the "spatial transfer of control activities" (Bruns, 2019, p. 514), that is, "EU attempts to push back the

EU's external borders or rather to police them at a distance in order to control unwanted migration flows" (Rijpma & Cremona, 2007, p. 12). Hindering migrants from reaching EU territory allows states to prevent migrants from benefiting from the rights that are enshrined in national European law and to avoid oversight by NGOs and other migrant rights defending groups—while at the same time claiming to uphold European rule of law and asylum principles. In addition, European states have externalised migration control, that is, they have shifted control towards external actors (Bruns, 2019, p. 514). What is more, European states have partly privatised migration policies, shifting traditional state tasks, such as controlling access to the territory or running asylum or detention facilities, to private actors, for example airlines, shipping companies, and private security companies (Baird & Spijkerboer, 2019; Gammeltoft-Hansen & Sørensen, 2013). Extra-territorialisation, externalisation, and privatisation allow European actors to reject responsibility and avoid blame for human rights violations (Menz, 2013).

Concretely, states selectively attribute visas, shifting the border to the consulates (Alpes & Spire, 2014; Infantino, 2019). EU member states, Frontex, and—by delegation—neighbouring states have also increasingly strengthened border control, border fortifications, and sea patrols (including interceptions and pushbacks). Indeed, since the 1990s EU member states have called for combining foreign policy and immigration policies with the goal of limiting the influx of immigrants, including asylum seekers. They have sought to shift the task of migration control to countries of the region of origin as well as to EU neighbouring states. Neighbouring states are encouraged to increase the control of their own borders and mobility on their territory, penalise irregular (e)migration, prevent irregular border crossing into the EU, build detention facilities, and sign readmission agreements with their neighbours, forcing them to take back their own citizens as well as third-country citizens who had transited through the country to enter EU territory irregularly (Crane, 2020). In addition, EU states have used readmission agreements with third countries to send back asylum seekers (Coleman, 2009; Peshkopia, 2005).

The EU has tried to transform in particular the neighbouring countries in the East, including by training staff of state authorities, non-state actors, migrants, and people willing to migrate (Marung, 2015). Since the late 1990s, seeking to shift the responsibility for asylum to third countries, the EU has tried to spread international asylum norms in (potential) transit countries (Lavenex, 2006) and has supported them in building up their "reception capacities" and asylum systems (Hertog, 2014). The underlying expectations are that asylum seekers might voluntarily stay in these countries instead of further migrating to the EU. Alternatively, if transit countries respect international asylum norms, EU states may appear legitimate in sending back asylum seekers to the transit country, according to the safe third country principle, because their rights are supposedly guaranteed there. For instance, the EU has tried (and largely failed) to push Turkey to comply with international and EU asylum norms, hoping to be able to outsource asylum policies to its neighbour (Aydin & Kirişci, 2013; Kirişci, 2007). Similarly, since 2003, the EU has sought short-term restrictive migration control and "long-term normative alignment" in its eastern neighbourhood (Makaryan, 2015, p. 225), including in Ukraine. Even if with the new phase of the Russian-Ukrainian war since February 2022 the EU and its member states are unlikely to try to externalise the reception of asylum seekers to Ukraine in the short term, the general patterns of EU external asylum policies remain relevant.

The unusually welcoming reception of Ukrainian protection seekers in the EU in 2022 might be interpreted as a sign of change in EU asylum policies. Indeed, the EU did not try to outsource the reception of Ukrainians but even greatly facilitated their entry and transit across the EU as well as many procedures required to obtain the temporary protection status, social benefits, and the right to work. However, this favourable treatment seems so far to remain an exception, based on the activation of the Temporary Protection Directive (2001/55EG) by the European Council on 4 March 2022 and limited to people fleeing from Ukraine, and mostly to Ukrainian citizens.

In regard to people fleeing from other countries, the EU asylum policies have not changed and the EU continues to try to externalise asylum to other countries. In April 2022, post-Brexit UK signed an Asylum Partnership Agreement with Rwanda, foreseeing that the UK would deport migrants to Rwanda where their asylum applications would be processed and where they would be encouraged to stay. The EU and its member states pursue similar objectives and have set up agreements and programmes with other states to keep migrants from moving on to the EU or take migrants back. For instance, in 2017 and 2020, the governments of Italy and Libya signed the Memorandum of Understanding on

Migration according to which Italy and the EU support the Libyan coastguard so that it intercepts migrants in the sea and transfers them to Libyan detention centres.

How Asylum Came to Ukraine Without Asylum Seekers

Various actors tried to change the practices of the Ukrainian state towards asylum seekers and refugees so that they would correspond to international asylum norms. Despite the low number of asylum seekers in Ukraine and Ukraine's uncertain status as a transit country (Düvell, 2012; İçduygu & Yükseker, 2012), the European Union continued to try to spread international asylum norms in this state (Bruns, 2019). Indeed, the number of official asylum seekers in Ukraine was low (1000–2000 applicants per year)[2] in comparison to most Western European states.[3] This upholding of the efforts can be explained, apart from bureaucratic path dependence at EU institutions, by the fear that migration routes might change (as was the case in the Balkans in 2014), which could turn Ukraine into a veritable country of asylum and transit. Furthermore, the EU tried out new instruments of migration control in the countries of the Eastern Partnership, a region that was seen as presenting little migratory risk for the EU, to then use the results of the experiment in negotiations with other states (Brouillette, 2018, p. 6). UNHCR also had an interest in keeping the EU involved in Ukraine as EU funding for asylum programmes was primarily (and in recent years exclusively) channelled through the office of UNHCR in Kyiv.

However, studies have usually found that these foreign attempts to influence Ukrainian asylum policies did not trigger the desired results. Scholars have observed that the Ukrainian state provided minimal support to asylum seekers and refugees (Rechitsky, 2016; Zhyznomirska, 2006, p. 48) and took decisions on the refugee status in a slow and opaque

[2] Rechitsky argued that the actual numbers of foreign fugitives in Ukraine was much higher because many foreign citizens fear to approach the Ukrainian state authorities and UNHCR due to "lack of faith in the asylum procedure or concerns for their security" (Rechitsky, 2016, p. 173).

[3] For instance, the Office français de protection des réfugiés et apatrides under the French Ministry of Interior registered between 60 000 and 140 000 new asylum applications per year from 2012 to 2021 in France.

way (Geiger, 2011, pp. 208–210). Academics and international and non-governmental organisations (Amnesty International, 2013; Border Monitoring Project Ukraine, 2011; Human Rights Watch, 2010; No Borders, 2011; UNHCR, 2013) mostly found that Ukrainian asylum policies strongly diverged in practice from the adopted national asylum laws and international standards (Bruns, 2019; Freyburg et al., 2009, p. 927; Shevel, 2011; Wunderlich, 2012; Zimmer, 2010). Scholars explained this divergence by the Ukrainian "state's lack of resources and institutional capacities" (Zhyznomirska, 2006, p. 48), "insufficient legislation, implementation, procedures, resources, staffing and training" (Düvell, 2008, p. 5), and by the fact that asylum policies were mainly pushed by external actors whereas the Ukrainian government remained indifferent to such policies (Zimmer, 2008, p. 1).

Yet, Anne Wetzel argued in 2016 that the Ukrainian asylum legislation and policies had been rapidly harmonised with EU demands since 2010 (Wetzel, 2016). The European Commission claimed in its last visa liberalisation progress report from 2015 that in the sector of asylum "substantial progress" had been made and that "[t]he asylum benchmark is deemed to have been achieved" (European Commission, 2015, pp. 4–5). This book shows that changes did take place due to EU conditionality but were less radical than what the last EU progress report suggested.[4]

It is the aim of this book to scrutinise the transfer of asylum norms and policies in Ukraine. A norm is understood as "a standard of appropriate behavior for actors with a given identity" (Finnemore & Sikkink, 1998, p. 891). In practice, norm promoters do not only deal with norms in a strict sense. They try to influence policy making (goals, content, instruments) (Dolowitz & Marsh, 2000, p. 9), legislation, administrative structures, beliefs and practices. Norm promoters try to spread both soft norms (general principles and ideas, values, beliefs, objectives, guidelines, "good practices", ways of doing) and hard norms (formal and technical rules, e.g. standards, laws, directives, treaties, regulations) (Delcour & Tulmets, 2019, pp. 4–5). They spread, for instance, concepts, categories, and definitions, such as "refugees", "persons in need of complementary protection", and "unaccompanied minors". Moreover, they shape

[4] The last European Commission progress report was the result of EU actors' political decision to overlook remaining lacunas in the requested reforms in order to introduce the visa-free regime as a sign of support to the Ukrainian regime and state that was under Russian attack.

normative distinctions in legitimate and illegitimate persons (for example opposing refugees and other migrants). Promoters of asylum norms transfer legal principles, for example the rights that recognised refugees should enjoy. They also promote working methods, procedures, and templates, and teach domestic state officials how to write an evaluation of an asylum application or how to conduct a refugee status determination interview. For instance, the EU funded "Regional Protection Programme" claimed to enhance the reception and protection capacities in Sub-Saharan Africa and in the Western Newly Independent States, including Ukraine. Thanks to EU funding, Ukrainian state bodies were intended to learn to work in accordance with UN and EU asylum norms, following "hard" norms, such as the respect of the refugee definition, but also of "soft" norms, such as pursuing the objective of refugees' self-reliance by offering support to employment or vocational education (Bruns, 2019). These attempts to transfer asylum norms to Ukraine were part of the overall EU-Ukraine relations and broader EU attempts to impose its norms, policies, and interests in its neighbourhood.

The Political Context in Ukraine and the European Neighbourhood Policy

The EU pursues its own interests in its neighbourhood. After decades of gradual and halting progress in developing a common European foreign policy, and more specifically after the EU accession of several Central and Eastern European states in the 2000s, the EU launched the European Neighbourhood Policy (ENP) in 2004. Many EU member states saw the ENP as a way to avoid further enlargements while fostering good relations between the EU and its neighbours, thus preventing the development of new dividing lines between the enlarged EU and its neighbours (Faustini-Torres, 2020). The Council of the EU claimed it was building prosperity and security in the neighbourhood in order to 'promote a ring of well-governed countries to the East of the European Union and on the borders of the Mediterranean with whom [the EU] can enjoy close and cooperative relations' (Council of the European Union, 2003). Despite emerging narratives about 'local ownership' in the neighbouring countries, the EU's policies have remained focused on the EU's own interests, especially its security (Petrova & Delcour, 2020). The EU perceives its neighbours as a source of threats, including migratory ones (Cianciara, 2020; Delcour, 2013). It thus seeks to protect itself from outside threats by triggering change in its neighbourhood, thus making it more stable and more similar to itself. The EU has sought to enhance its own security and prevent unwanted migration by spreading its rules beyond its borders.

Until the mid-2010s, Ukraine was frequently presented as an apple of discord between Russia and the EU (Samokhvalov, 2015). However, to understand the Western influences on Ukrainian policy making, one needs to look beyond Ukraine as a passive object between the hands of the two major geopolitical players in the region and to take into consideration the agency of domestic actors.

Since the EU enlargements of 2004 and 2007, Ukraine has been a direct neighbour of the EU, bordering Poland, Slovakia, Hungary, and Romania. Researchers have frequently presented Ukraine as a likely case (a "frontrunner") for Europeanisation in the Eastern EU neighbourhood (Delcour & Wolczuk, 2015; Franke et al., 2010, pp. 155–156; Freyburg et al., 2009). Ukraine has usually been among the first post-Soviet countries to join EU assistance programmes and to sign agreements with the EU (Partnership and Cooperation Agreement (1998), European Neighbourhood Policy (2004), visa-facilitation and readmission agreements (2007), Visa-Liberalisation Action Plan (2010), Association Agreement including a Deep and Comprehensive Free Trade Area (2014–2017), visa-free travel to the Schengen Area (2017), candidate status to EU accession (2022)) (Delcour, 2016b, pp. 50–53). Scholars have depicted Ukraine as willing to cooperate, interested in becoming an EU member state, and relying on the EU in terms of economy and security (Melnykovska & Schweickert, 2008, p. 456). Nevertheless, until 2014, research often presented the influence of the EU as limited by the relations between Ukraine and Russia.

The impact of the Russian Federation on Western norm transfer to Ukraine depended on the policy sector and the period, or more specifically, the relations between Ukraine and Russia. Since Ukraine's independence in 1991, its policies reacted to economic difficulties and shifted between democratisation and authoritarianism (Pleines, 2016b). The successive presidents redefined their preferences in the relations with the Western and Eastern neighbours of Ukraine, though this was long less radical than often assumed. Ukrainian oligarchs, pursuing certain economic interests, including in regard to Ukrainian foreign policy, predominantly supported the winning political actors, thus acting as catalysts for ongoing change rather than as initiators of radical change

(Pleines, 2016a). Until the Maidan protests in 2014 and the war with Russia, Ukrainian politicians tried to maintain and deepen the cooperation with both Russia and the EU. Until 2014 and in the sectors in which the EU's and Russia's policies and conditionalities diverged and competed, the Russian influence hindered EU norm promotion, for example in the energy sector (Delcour, 2018; Dimitrova & Dragneva, 2009; Langbein, 2013; Tulmets et al., 2018).

Since 2014, Russia's aggression towards Ukraine has strengthened Ukrainian politicians' interest in political and economic rapprochement with the EU (Bátora & Navrátil, 2016; Langbein, 2015). Trade with Russia has decreased since 2014 and Ukrainian business interests in the EU further increased (Delcour, 2016a, p. 60). Interactions between Ukrainian and EU authorities have become more frequent (Bátora & Rieker, 2018). This trend is likely to be even more prevalent following the 2022 Russian-Ukrainian war and the granting of EU candidate status to Ukraine in June 2022.

Scholars have controversially debated the impact of the European Neighbourhood Policy (ENP) in the region, and specifically in Ukraine. Some have judged the ENP against its declared objective of building a stable "ring of friends" and security through democracy, which failed, as illustrated by the war in the eastern parts of Ukraine (Nilsson & Silander, 2016). Some have argued that the ENP has been weakened by its own design, pointing to the lack of membership perspectives (Schimmelfennig, 2015), contradictions among its objectives, namely between democratisation and stability (Börzel & Hüllen, 2014), and by the lack of coordination among the numerous actors involved (Bátora & Rieker, 2018). Studies have highlighted obstacles to ENP-induced change in Ukraine's domestic structures, for instance diverging interests among elites, high adoption costs, and weak state capacities (Dimitrova & Dragneva, 2009). Others have pointed to the disappointed expectations among actors in Ukraine, in particular concerning security and lacking support in the conflict with Russia (Delcour & Wolczuk, 2015; Samokhvalov, 2015, pp. 1383–1384). In addition, Ukrainians were disillusioned in regard to democracy promotion, the lack of differentiation of the "one-size-fits-all" approach to the EU neighbours, and the top-down approach despite a partnership rhetoric (Dekanozishvili, 2020).

Nevertheless, some scholars have insisted on legislative and policy changes in specific policy areas (Ademmer & Börzel, 2013). In addition, EU action after the Maidan protests in 2013 was praised for its efforts to support profound state building by creating "reform enclaves" within the Ukrainian public administration. These were defined as "dedicated reform units" of domestic staff, often recruited externally, committed to achieve change from within the state apparatus (Wolczuk, 2019). The role of the EU in domestic policy change as well as in institutional restructuring is hence still debated. The present case study contributes to these debates by providing a nuanced picture of the effects of EU policies in its neighbourhood. In particular, it underlines that the EU was only one of several (international and national) norm promoters in Ukraine and it shows how these activities were interconnected. It also draws attention to the role of domestic allies, most of whom were produced by the international organisations.

The case selected for this investigation, the spreading of international asylum norms in Ukraine, is specific due to the absence of strong domestic interest and prior traditions in the area. The international asylum norms from the 1951 Refugee Convention had little impact on the Soviet Union. This book demonstrates that the emergence of asylum norms in post-Soviet Ukraine, as in the other former communist countries beginning in the early 1990s, was a result of transfer. Furthermore, Russian state actors were not interested in the sector of asylum in Ukraine and did therefore not compete with Western norm promoters (Wetzel, 2016). Asylum in Ukraine therefore makes it possible to study external Western influences without strong a priori domestic positions and to clearly identify the consequences of active transfer endeavours—in contrast to fields in which domestic interest may cause the import of international norms. Indeed, as I will show, asylum did not attract the interest of domestic elites and was not framed as a public policy problem in Ukrainian media, political debates, or street demonstrations. While no major domestic political actors supported the import of international asylum norms, they also rarely opposed it actively. Hence, this research investigates the paradox of the establishment of international asylum norms in Ukraine and, thus fills a gap of research on Europeanisation and policy transfer, which, so far, has paid little attention to scenarios in which there is neither strong domestic opposition nor strong support of international norms. I will demonstrate that despite the absence of domestic interests in the policy area, various domestic actors participated in shaping the transfer process.

Transfer of Norms and Policies

The actors involved in transferring international asylum norms to Ukraine framed their activities in different terms. These differences in terminology reflect how differently the actors perceived and presented the sense of their activities and their own position in relation to others.

EU actors wrote about Ukraine's "harmonisation", "approximation", "compliance", "conformity", "convergence", "fulfilling commitments", "alignment to EU standards and legislation", "adaptation", "implementation", "modernisation", or more concretely the "development of a functioning asylum system according to international standards", while the EU carried out "capacity building", "support to reforms", "monitoring", and "assessments of approximation of Ukraine's legislation to the EU acts".

UNHCR referred to its own activities as "addressing problems", "protecting rights", "monitoring implementation", "assessment of the Ukrainian asylum system", "support to capacity building", "develop institutions and structures to protect refugees", being "consulted", "lobbying for adherence to international and European standards", "shar[ing] with the authorities comparative tables showing how Ukrainian asylum legislation falls seriously short of European standards, as well as proposals for amendments to the country's Refugee Law", "drafting relevant implementing instructions". About Ukraine, UNHCR commented that national law was (or not) "in line with international standards", or was being "brought in line". It evaluated Ukraine's "legislative and administrative reforms", "commitment to meeting international and European standards in the area of asylum law", "compliance with international human rights and refugee instruments", or "observance of basic recognized human rights standards for the treatment of asylum seekers and refugees".

Employees of asylum NGOs in Ukraine said that they "help refugees get their rights respected", "assist" migrants and the authorities, "discuss" and "communicate" with state officials, "educate", "train" or "teach" them, try to "change the state", try to "get officials to care for refugees", and "to respect the law and international standards".

Ukrainian subordinate state officials explained that they "learn to do the work" or "how to work with refugees", that they "participate in trainings", "perfect their skills", "receive advice", "information", or "help" from colleagues, NGOs, or UNHCR.

While the actors involved employed various expressions to describe their own and others' practices (translating their activities for different audiences), for the analysis I have chosen the term transfer. David Dolowitz and David Marsh have defined transfer as a "process by which knowledge about policies, administrative arrangements, institutions and ideas in one political system (past or present) is used in the development of policies, administrative arrangements, institutions and ideas in another political system" (D. Dolowitz & Marsh, 2000, p. 5).

In contrast to more diffuse phenomena of norm circulation or diffusion, I refer to "transfer" to indicate that one set of actors actively promotes certain norms among another set of actors (Evans & Davies, 1999). I will show that the transfer of asylum norms to Ukraine was initiated and driven by certain actors, mainly the EU and international and non-governmental organisations—rather than being the result of Ukrainian policy-makers' search for a solution to a perceived public policy problem.

Indeed, policy makers in Ukraine showed little interest in actively shaping asylum policies. This is why, the analysed transfer of asylum policies to Ukraine turned out to be largely unidirectional or a "one-way transaction" (Stone et al., 2020, p. 10). In recent years, scholars have insisted on the existence of reverse influences, that is, the repatriation of local feedback from domestic actors to international actors (Acharya, 2015). While minor reverse influences can be noticed (for instance, the Kyiv office of UNHCR adapted its working methods to the reactions it observed among its Ukrainian state targets), the overall transfer process was strongly driven and shaped by the international actors. Hence, without denying the relevance of research that highlights the existence of reverse influences and South-North or South-South learning, the present study suggests that such phenomena are not always significant, but depend on the domestic actors' interest in the issue and the power relations between the actors involved in the transfer undertaking.

This study develops the analytical tool of a "transfer chain" (Fig. 1.1). Drawing upon research on development aid with the concepts of aid chain (Wallace et al., 2007) or chain of donors (Sampson, 2004), the transfer chain points to the power relations between actors and logics of delegation from norm promoters to norm addressees, which involve predominantly unidirectional flows of money, control, and norms. The EU delegates transfer tasks to international organisations who, in turn, transfer norms and delegate activities to NGOs. All these actors try

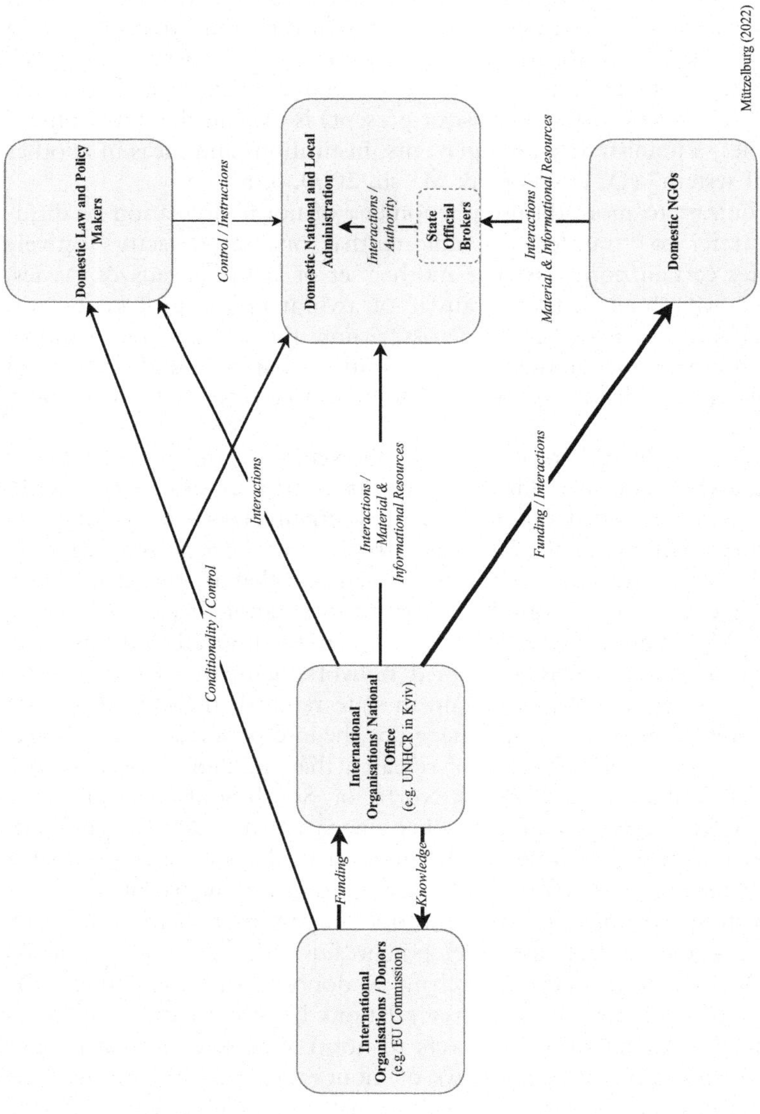

Fig. 1.1 Schematised transfer chain

to delegate transfer tasks to the domestic state officials charged with spreading international asylum norms among their colleagues. The actors are not limited to a single role: From norm addressee they may become norm promoter. In particular, transfer brokers occupy an intermediary position. They are multi-positioned; that is, they interact with distinct spheres whose language and codes they master (Mützelburg, 2020b). Linking these different spheres, brokers act as both norm addressees and promoters. For instance, certain Ukrainian state officials become brokers who interact with NGO workers, adopt international norms, and actively promote them among their colleagues. As an analytical tool, the transfer chain makes it possible to grasp the fluidity of the various involved roles and to look beyond the binary classification between norm promoters and norm addressees.

Transfer as Multi-Actor Translation and Resistance

Transfer research has been primarily interested in the normative outcome of transfer attempts. Scholars often wonder to what extent the transfer initiators' declared objectives have been fulfilled. Has the illiberal state adopted laws that prohibit the discrimination of sexual, ethnic, religious, or political minorities? And does it effectively and fully implement them in practice? The answer is often yes to the first question and no to the second. Transfer scholars diagnose an "implementation gap", "theatre or pantomime" (Hadjiisky et al., 2017), "façade change", "change on paper", "formal change", "partial" or "fake" compliance (Noutcheva, 2009), "decoupling" (Zimmermann, 2016), "shallow Europeanization" (Goetz, 2005, p. 262), or "Potemkin harmonization" (Jacoby, 1999). All of these terms designate a lack of implementation following the formal adoption of international norms. Scholars have explained this gap with filters and structures, including the normative fit (i.e. the convergence between the transferred norms and the domestic normative framework), lacking state capacities, informal institutions (Sedelmeier, 2006, p. 13), characteristics of the domestic political and administrative systems such as poor coordination among state institutions (Wolczuk, 2008, p. 104, 2009, p. 207), inertia and the hierarchical system of instructions (Langbein & Wolczuk, 2012, p. 870), inter-institutional struggles (Wetzel, 2016), understaffing as well as rent-seeking practices and interpenetration of economic and political interests (Delcour, 2016b, pp. 122; 126). The present book takes into consideration how xenophobia, unstable and hierarchically structured state institutions with partly unclear lines of authority, lack of resources, low salaries and the high turnover at the administration, informality and the importance of personalised relations shape transfer processes.

Yet, the focus on structures only provides a static explanation of the frequently diagnosed gap between formal adoption and practical implementation of imported norms. It is essential to also study the role of actors in the transfer processes (Dandashly & Kourtelis, 2020). Some researchers argue that policy-makers seek to obtain the benefits associated with formal adoption (i.e. international recognition or incentives), while having no interest in the practical application (Schimmelfennig & Sedelmeier, 2004, p. 663). In the case of Ukraine, I lend credence to this idea: Ukrainian politicians included international asylum norms in legislation in order to obtain incentives from the Council of Europe and the EU and in order to gain international recognition by conforming to norms of "democratic" and "modern" European states. Their lack of interest in the substance of asylum explains some of the top-down obstacles to implementation.

Many studies that have taken into account the role of actors in transfer have limited themselves to elites, namely powerful political and economic veto players (Dimitrova & Dragneva, 2013). However, this book shows that various actors participate in shaping the transfer process and its outcomes. It includes state and non-state actors, local, national, and international actors, elite, intermediate, and subordinate actors.[5] Transfer researchers focusing on domestic politicians' interests implicitly assume that the central government has control over policy implementation. Public policy studies—in particular, microsociological studies that examine the role of street-level bureaucrats—highlight the importance of the "implementation gap" between formal policies and rules and practical implementation (Dubois, 1999; Lipsky, 1980). These studies show that central government actors do not fully control policy implementation. However, most transfer scholars have paid little attention to the role of non-elite actors. Dandashly and Kourtelis (2020) underlined the importance of local actors for policy transfer, as they make the difference between "thin" and "thick" implementation. Yet, the role of

[5] The boundaries between these identification categories can be blurred and actors play with them (Wedel, 2004), as discussed, among others, in the section on multi-scalar transfer.

non-elite actors and especially street-level bureaucrats in the translation of transferred policies remains understudied (Baker et al., 2020; Hadjiisky et al., 2017). Applying micro-approaches to transfer goes well beyond the simple diagnosis of weak implementation as a way of understanding the reasons and processes underlying the "implementation gap".

Indeed, I will show that actors involved in transfer do not mechanically execute transfer activities but translate and resist—depending on their social position, their relations of power and of interdependence with other actors, their collective and individual interests and beliefs. Translation refers to the modification of norms, concepts, ideas, knowledge, policies, instruments, organisational templates, and objects as they travel; it means in particular their adaptation to "local socio-economic, political and normative contexts" (Capie, 2008; Kluczewska, 2019, p. 359) and the target actors' beliefs, norms, or interests (Acharya, 2004; Berger & Esguerra, 2018; Freeman, 2009; Mukhtarov, 2014; Stone, 2012). Actors translate norms into discourse, law, and implementation, reinterpreting them, modifying their meaning, adding, or leaving parts out (Zimmermann, 2016). Translation is further used to reformulate a problem in order to make it acceptable, create alliances, and mobilise actors (Callon, 1986). Translation thus implies negotiation between different actors and strategic adaptation in order to achieve objectives that could not be achieved when insisting on the initial norm (Sigman, 2013). The actors of the transfer chain translate the norms, which they try to spread, to adapt them to the new context (Clarke et al., 2015; Hassenteufel & Maillard, 2013). I distinguish between reframing and adaptation. While reframing is a rhetorical process to make a project, norm, or policy acceptable to different audiences without changing its substance (Fröhlich, 2010, p. 86), adaptation involves substantial changes (Clavier, 2013; Sigman, 2013; Smith, 2013).

Actors also resist, that is, they hinder transfer in practice. "[R]esistance refers to active and passive opposition to the transposition and implementation of […] norms (passive resistance being also known as inertia)." (Saurugger & Terpan, 2013, p. 4). Antipreneurs, actors who "defend the entrenched status quo against challengers" (Bloomfield, 2015, p. 12), may openly obstruct transfer activities, refuse to interact with norm promoters, or try to renegotiate power relations. In a more discreet way, they can circumvent norm transfer (e.g. by avoiding the application of norms or appropriating them for another purpose (Saurugger & Terpan, 2013, pp. 23–25)), pretend to comply or contribute to norm transfer while avoiding doing so substantially (Koven, 2019, p. 29), or delay norm transfer (Bloomfield, 2015). While most transfer scholars have focused on elite resistance (Bloomfield, 2015; Casier, 2011, p. 972), others have argued that resistance is the weapon of the weak (Bache & Taylor, 2003). I will demonstrate that resistance may occur at all scales even if actors use different techniques of resistance depending on their position and their resources. For instance, I show that the national parliament, while apparently adopting international norms, discreetly resists norm transfer through delayed, selective, and superficial legislative adoption. Parliaments have not yet been studied as actors of resistance. Furthermore, I argue that, depending on the power relations between norm promoters and resisters, resistance and translation is carried out in a more or less hidden way (Scott, 1990). Practices of translation and resistance hence differ among actors, and over time.

Going beyond linear visions that evaluate transfer outcomes only in terms of their deviance from the exported model and therefore observe the deficiency of the outcomes (Dimitrova & Dragneva, 2009; Freyburg et al., 2009), this book follows the idea that full adoption or full rejection of travelling norms are exceptions, whereas most situations lie in between (Zimmermann, 2016). Norms are constantly renegotiated (Zwingel, 2012, p. 126) and policy implementation involves various actors with discretionary powers (Lipsky, 1980). I show that actors who participate in norm transfer always translate and sometimes resist. As a result, transfer is never completed and homogeneous, but rather is a process that is unstable and heterogeneous across actors, space, and time.

Transfer as (Power) Relations and Practices

The understanding of transfer can be enriched by analysing it as practices and relations among actors. These practices and relations affect the target country normatively and socially. Research on transfer has focused on normative changes while overlooking other effects. Yet, research on development aid has pointed to the changes caused by foreign money and interventions (Eade, 2007; Wallace et al., 2007). The study of policy transfer, in particular in respect to the social effects produced by transfer undertakings on the targeted society, can benefit from the literature on development aid. Indeed, transfer endeavours produce norm promoters—organisations, individuals, and networks. International organisations, acting as donors, delegate transfer activities to smaller organisations—some of which reorganise their work and their structures to fit the donors' expectations while others are set up for this purpose. In the course of their transfer endeavour, international actors produce transfer organisations, partly from scratch (Delpeuch & Vassileva, 2017). These organisations turn individuals into norm promoters. First, they turn their own employees into norm promoters by employing, training, and socialising them. Second, they attempt to turn other actors into norm promoters, especially state officials, whom they "teach" and with whom they try to interact regularly to build up personalised relations and to persuade them to adopt the norms. Due to the transfer initiators' activities, pressure, and incentives, various actors—state and non-state ones—have formed networks (Evans & Davies, 1999; Saguin & Howlett, 2019). These networks tend to favour iterative policy transfer (Legrand, 2016, p. 451) and, more generally, further interactions among these same actors. For instance, endeavours to transfer asylum norms to Ukraine have established networks between certain NGO workers and state officials that have since 2014 shaped the support for internally displaced people.

Transfer undertakings affect (power) relations between actors and are affected by them. On the one hand, international funding for asylum-related activities confers resources to certain NGOs, thereby altering relations between the NGOs and state authorities. For instance, these NGOs have the means to fund interpretation for the communication with asylum seekers—a service that state migration officers need but lack. They therefore depend on NGO support to do their work. On the other hand, the existing power relations between norm promoters and norm addressees and their respective resources shape the norm promoters' capacity to transfer norms and the methods they may use (Dolowitz et al., 2019). For example, when officials dominate relations with NGO workers, controlling their access to migrant detention facilities, NGO workers refrain from public criticism and use conciliatory rhetoric when trying to persuade officials to change their work practices. While most transfer research has focused on normative effects, I stress the importance of analysing transfer as a social practice.

Understanding transfer as a social practice and relations among different actors also sheds light on the normative effects of transfer. Some organisations, such as the EU and the Council of Europe, can, in certain contexts, exercise coercive conditionality "where the conditions associated with a reluctance to adopt recommended policies are such as to leave a government with little choice but to implement them" (Ellison, 2017,

p. 19). In the present case, the EU used the incentive of abolishing visa requirements for Ukrainian tourists to obtain reforms in Ukraine, including in the area of asylum. The EU threatens to withhold incentives and uses monitoring for control (Dolowitz & Marsh, 2000). The power that international organisations can derive from their incentives depends on the attractiveness of the incentives in the eyes of the domestic policy-makers, the existence of alternative offers, the credibility of the threat to withhold the incentives, and the organisations' capacity of monitoring (Langbein, 2015, p. XXI; Lavenex & Schimmelfennig, 2009; Vachudová, 2005). In line with the literature, I confirm the importance of conditionality and monitoring by the EU and the Council of Europe; I specify that it has direct effects on politicians, triggering deeper legislative adoption and implementation. In a less coercive way, UNHCR in Ukraine temporarily managed to increase its capacity to transfer norms through an exchange of favours with the authorities.

Certain organisations, such as UNHCR, produce norms, standards, narratives, and knowledge, and monitor, criticise, and shame, shaping what is perceived as normal or legitimate (Barnett & Finnemore, 1999; Geiger & Pécoud, 2013). Indeed, in the years after Ukraine's independence, the politicians' discourse indicates that they sought to adopt the norms produced by UNHCR as they tried to correspond to the standards of Western, democratic states and pursued international recognition.

In addition, I have identified factors that become visible via micro- and meso-perspectives. Researchers have claimed that transfer can occur via socialisation, (social) learning, or persuasion, but empirical operationalisation has often remained limited. Indeed, processes occurring within actors' minds are difficult to document (Schimmelfennig & Sedelmeier, 2005, pp. 9–10). Instead, I investigate interactions as transfer practices. Norm promoters use their interactions with norm addressees in the hopes of furthering transfer objectives through information provision, persuasion, threats, and personalised relations. Interactions between norm promoters and norm addressees at the state authorities can be formal and rare, as through trainings and seminars, or informal and frequent. UNHCR benefits from the uninterrupted presence of an office in Kyiv, to regularly lobby and to establish personal contacts among the main official decision makers.

Norm promoters try to compensate for their own limits by cooperating with other actors to take advantage of these actors' resources or legitimacy. UNHCR and the EU benefit from each other's resources.

This logic also applies to the transfer chain, as dominant actors delegate transfer activities to dominated actors, who benefit from more specific expertise, geographic proximity, monitoring capacities, local legitimacy, and a better network in the targeted sphere. In addition to the delegation from international donors to Ukrainian NGOs, NGOs and IOs turn domestic officials into allies and even norm promoters to benefit from their contacts and legitimacy among their peers or towards subordinate officials.

Multi-Scalar Transfer Practices

While top-down approaches, focusing on national political elites who would determine policies, have been dominant in transfer studies for a long time, scholars have only recently begun to investigate the role of scales (also called levels) in the transfer of norms and policies. Multi-scalar or multi-level approaches uncover that different actors participate in transfer at different levels (Lavenex, 2008). Transfer is shaped by the relations between these different types of actors. For instance, looking at interactions between different actors located at different levels, scholars have shown that Swiss "cantons bypassed the national level to transfer [a] policy measure and committed to the supranationally agreed-upon standards" (Mavrot, 2017, p. 101). Moreover, multi-level approaches draw attention to the direction in which transfer occurs (top-down, bottom-up, or within levels). They also highlight that the way transfer takes place differs depending on the level (Hadjiisky et al., 2017; Marshall, 2005).

However, so far, most multi-level transfer studies have used the term scale or level without further conceptualisation: they have either used it implicitly in the sense of perspectives (see section below) or adopted its meaning from the literature on multi-level governance—or they used it with both meanings (D. Dolowitz & Marsh, 2000; Evans, 2010; Evans & Davies, 1999; Hadjiisky et al., 2017). Multi-level governance research, while defining multi-level governance, has made little effort to explicitly conceptualise levels. Rather, research has tended to use them implicitly as institutionalised hierarchical juridical or administrative arenas, for instance to examine subnational, national, and European levels of authority or of government (Marks, 1993).

These multi-level transfer studies take levels and scales as pre-existing (Dufour & Goyer, 2010). For instance, Mark Evans and Jonathan Davies argued: "Five levels of political spatiality are commonly referred to in political science: transnational, international, national, regional and local. International policy transfer might conceivably take place at and between any of these levels" (Evans & Davies, 1999, p. 368). However, as debated in the work of human geography since the 1980s, scales are socially produced and are often the result of socio-political struggles (Moore, 2008). I understand scales as vertically differentiated spaces where power relations are renegotiated (Swyngedouw, 1997, p. 140). They can correspond to administrative tiers (e.g. districts, cantons, regions, states) but do not always (Hameiri & Scarpello, 2018, pp. 146, 150): Actors sometimes construct scales in relation to state institutions, and sometimes independently or in opposition to them (Dufour & Goyer, 2010). Scales and the relations among them are constantly contested and renegotiated as different arrangements privilege different actors (Brenner, 2001; Smith, 2004). Failing to analyse scales as categories of practice leads scholars to short-sighted conclusions similar to treating actor-produced categories, such as ethnicity or nations, as "things out there" (Kaiser & Nikiforova, 2008; Moore, 2008).

Rather than treating scales as given, I analyse how actors, in the course of their activities to further or hinder transfer, produce, and renegotiate scales, and how they use (and hence confirm) scales produced before and by others. Scales matter for transfer in two ways: First, by engaging in transfer, actors produce and renegotiate scales, hence affecting social relations more broadly, beyond the norms they seek to spread. Second, scales that have been produced and institutionalised prior to the transfer endeavours shape the transfer activities by defining power relations among norm promoters and addressees, and, consequently by defining legitimate and illegitimate transfer channels.

Certain scales have become more institutionalised than others. This book shows that actors in Ukraine take scales of the state for granted and do not question them, meaning that top-down transfer across state hierarchies is perceived by all actors as legitimate. Such path-dependent scalar fixes (Brenner, 2001, p. 607) are less contested and modified than other scales. However, the relations between the state scales and others, for example those of international and non-governmental organisations, are constantly renegotiated. The production and renegotiation of scales in the course of transfer activities means the (re-)negotiation of power relations among actors through discourse and practices around questions, such as

- Who is legitimate to make decisions over a certain issue / policy area?
- Who is legitimate to make decisions over a certain space?
- Who has authority over whom?
- Who can legitimately criticise or teach whom?
- Who controls resources?

More specifically, I investigate how actors of the transfer network use and produce scales through:

Framing:

- Actors self-define and get assigned what I call a scalar identity, that is, the scale at which they present themselves and at which they are perceived by others as legitimate, for example through qualifications like "international" organisations.[6] Actors produce and use this scalar identity for instance by claiming authority over a large geographical stretch (sometimes the entire world) and vertical legitimacy (over states).[7] UNHCR, for example, claims a global scale identity, which legitimises its involvement in Ukrainian asylum policies. Actors can also use others' scalar identities to delegitimise their involvement in a certain matter. For example, certain Ukrainian MPs criticised EU attempts to shape Ukrainian migration policies, arguing that the EU was acting in its own interests rather than in Ukrainian interests. They framed migration policies as a national matter—a framing that delegitimised the involvement of the EU, which was attributed a European scale identity (which in this case excluded Ukraine from the European space). Actors may also derive legitimacy from their "location" or "rootedness" (Stone et al., 2020, p. 6) so that NGOs framed as "local" can legitimise norm transfer that had been initiated by international actors.

[6] While this may reify actors in their scalar identity, I use these terms in my writing for the sake of readability, for instance "international organisation" as a short form for an organisation that presents itself as or is perceived by others as an organisation with an international scale identity.

[7] Beyond framing, this scalar identity is produced through various processes. For instance, by intervening on certain sites or judging phenomena across a certain space (e.g. by publishing reports about Ukrainian asylum policies), actors produce their scalar identity.

- Actors promoting or resisting norm transfer "construct problems and solutions as pertinent to a certain geographical scale" (Mukhtarov et al., 2013). For instance, to counter certain Ukrainian state practices, asylum NGOs present some issues as human rights violations that are so severe that they matter "beyond" the national scale, so that the debates about them can be shifted to a European or global scale and involve the EU, the CoE, or the ECHR.

Addressing an issue at a certain scale: Norm promoters try to shift the decision-making to the scale where they are the most likely to be influential (Mukhtarov, 2014). NGOs and UNHCR sometimes turn to staff of the central State Migration Service to address a problem faced by asylum seekers at various regional Migration Services throughout Ukraine. On other occasions, they "jump scales" and directly target international institutions (Stubbs, 2005), for example by taking asylum and refoulement cases to the European Court of Human Rights. They hence produce the respective scale as the relevant one, as hierarchically superior to other scales, and signal that they consider the contacted actor to be in a legitimate position to make a decision.

Networking and alliance building: Norm promoters try to build up a network of allies who will be helpful for their norm transfer activities.

- Norm promoters seek alliances with actors whom they see as influential and able to spread norms at their own scale or at the scales below. In this way, they participate in producing scales and actors' scalar identities. Indeed, they show that they recognise the other actors as legitimate to decide on certain matters at a certain geographical scope. For example, NGO workers try to establish contact with the heads of the asylum departments of regional Migration Services, considering that these officials can shape asylum practices at the regional scale. NGOs co-produce a regional scale by building up a network around administrative units of the regional Migration Services and addressing issues at this scale.
- Norm promoters "engage in networking and coalition-building that span scales of governance" (Mukhtarov et al., 2013, p. 117). They often try to establish a network which encompasses actors with different scalar identities. For example, Kyiv-based NGOs have allies at the central Migration Service and some ministries (national scale

identity) as well as at the Kyiv city Migration Service (city scale identity), and the office of UNHCR in Kyiv (partly national scale partly international scale identity). Such a multi-scalar network gives norm promoters the flexibility to shift their activities from one scale to another, adapting to the framing of a certain issue or to obstacles they may face on a certain scale. If, for instance, the Kyiv Migration Service refuses to comply with the NGO's demands to change its practices, the NGO turns to allies at the central Migration Service to ask them to exercise "top-down" pressure.

Defining their hierarchical relations to other actors through various routine practices and in particular by teaching, criticising, controlling other actors or by accepting / refusing to be taught, criticised, or controlled. Depending on the actors' respective scalar identities, norm promoters try to teach, criticise, or control norm addressees—or decide to refrain from such practices. Conversely, norm addressees, often state officials, resist or accept such endeavours, which defines their position in relation to the norm promoters. Within the state apparatus, hierarchies are overall well defined and scales largely accepted. Nevertheless, scales are constantly reperformed, for instance as the central State Migration Service tries to maintain its control over the regional Migration Services' practices. Scales between state and non-state actors are fuzzier and are the object of constant struggles. The question of which non-state actor is allowed to teach, criticise, and control which Ukrainian state officials is constantly renegotiated and may depend on several factors, including personal relations, actors' resources, and the larger political context. Overall, NGO workers explain that they are not in a legitimate position to intervene as trainers in seminars for state officials. Employees of the UNHCR office in Kyiv may act as trainers, but even more legitimate are trainers from international organisations who live and work abroad. EU conditionality temporarily affected the relations between the scales of state and non-state actors. In a context in which local officials were under pressure to fulfil EU requirements but lacked necessary resources, they became more open to the criticism of NGOs. The results of the negotiations between EU officials and members of the Ukrainian government can affect norm transfer between NGO workers and employees of a regional Migration Service.

Norm promoters often resort to multi-scalar action to favour norm transfer, in particular by making use of their alliances and by shifting an issue to a different scale to be addressed. Norm promoters often count on the hierarchical structure of the Ukrainian state apparatus, hoping that orders from higher state scales will affect the practices of lower state scales. Due to the state officials' discretionary powers, this does not always come to fruition.

Within the state apparatus, multi-scalar approaches depend on actors' legal authority. Following Weber, I find that non-state actors' appeals to a higher state body are only effective when the latter exercises legitimate domination (*Herrschaft*) over the subordinate state body—that is, when subordinate officials obey the superordinate officials' orders as they consider them legitimate to exercise authority (Weber, 1922, pt. I; Chapter III). Legitimate domination is based here on legal authority (*legale Herrschaft*); that is, the belief in the superordinate state body's legal right to give orders to the subordinate state body and the threat of legal punishment in case of non-compliance. This means that scales are most effective among state officials within the same state institution. While officials believe in scales outside their own institution, they only follow their requests for action if they have the formal right to give orders and sanction deviant practices.

Multi-scalar action can entail "geographical dilemmas" (Masson, 2009, p. 126). As argued by Masson, what seems strategic to defend at one scale may negatively affect activities at another. For instance, NGOs and the office of UNHCR in Kyiv sometimes turn to the European Court of Human Rights to counter forceful extradition of asylum seekers from Ukraine, shifting the decision-making and the power struggle from the national to a European scale, where they have better chances to succeed. Yet, shifting to a European scale and criticising Ukrainian state practices to an international audience often causes a deterioration of the relations between the NGO or UNHCR and the Ukrainian officials at the national scale.

Furthermore, depending on the scale, issues, activities, and demands need to be redefined and reframed. Indeed, different scales follow different logics and norms. Actors active across scales need to cope with tensions and contradictions among these logics. For example, NGO workers primarily care about individual migrants' situations, whereas their indirect donor, the European Commission, cares about the "sustainability" of systemic changes of asylum policies at the national scale. Actors therefore translate their activities and objectives depending on the scale.

Finally, actors may find themselves "locked in" a certain scalar identity even when a different identity would be more useful in a certain context or for certain undertakings. For example, an international identity can be used to discredit actors as uninformed about the local situation, as pursuing foreign values, or as having interests or loyalties that diverge from the local ones. In these cases, actors may benefit from allies who have another scalar identity. For example, the office of UNHCR in Kyiv has allies with a local scale identity (NGO subcontractors) and allies with a European scale identity (UNHCR in Geneva, the EU, the Council of Europe). Occasionally, a norm promoter may actively produce an organisation with another scalar identity. UNHCR triggered the emergence of NGO subcontractors in Ukraine (Mützelburg, 2018). The "Hebrew Immigrant Aid Society" (HIAS), which works on different continents, including in Ukraine, created the NGO "Right to Protection / Право на захист" (R2P) in Ukraine—an organisation that shares the same staff and premises as HIAS but that has a national Ukrainian status. Such close allies or substantially identical organisations make it possible to benefit from different formal categories (e.g. from certain funding requirements only open to a certain type of organisation) and from multiple scalar identities.

In short, this case study contributes to the field of transfer studies by explaining how and why the effects of transfer attempts are unstable and heterogeneous across actors, space, and time. It demonstrates the role of the agency of the different actors involved in the transfer process, highlights the multi-scalar nature of the transfer activities, and shows that transfer practices have social effects beyond the intended normative ones.

Multiple Perspectives and Sources to Grasp the Complexity of Transfer

Diversifying the perspectives of observation allows the researcher to gain complementary insights and to question established research categories and ideas (Boulay, 2019). I understand perspectives as the lens adopted when zooming in or out to investigate a phenomenon (Grossetti, 2006). Depending on how much we zoom in, we take into consideration a more or less large territorial and temporal scope (Bromberger, 2021), a more or less specific sector, more or fewer units of the same kind (e.g. of persons, organisations, states) (Grossetti, 2006) and different types of units (e.g. individual or collective actors). Each perspective sheds light on certain aspects while occulting others, so that combining different perspectives enriches the conclusions (Revel, 1996).

Much research on policy diffusion and transfer has been conducted with a macro perspective. Many diffusion scholars have used large-N comparative studies to identify structures affecting the reasons for and results of diffusion, for instance structures of the economy or of governments (Marsh & Sharman, 2009). Part of the transfer literature, while paying more attention to actors than the diffusion literature, investigates one or several entire states, concerning one or several large policy sectors, often for a short period of time (a given moment or a few years) (Ademmer & Börzel, 2013; Schimmelfennig & Sedelmeier, 2004). This has led scholars to conclude that political regime types, geopolitics, EU bargaining power, and political elites' interests matter most in shaping transfer outcomes—factors that are visible with the adopted perspective and with the sources used (e.g. official state documents, international organisations' reports).

Emerging micro perspective research has questioned the conclusions that have emerged due to the limitations of macro perspectives on transfer. Scholars adopting ethnographic methods, focusing on individual actors and small sites, have highlighted that norms change in the course of transfer processes because the actors—often ordinary individuals—involved in the norm circulation enjoy leeway, translating and adapting the norms to different contexts (Croix, 2013; Kluczewska, 2019).

Seeking to unite micro and macro in one consistent perspective, Janine Wedel adopted ethnographic methods to follow the policy and aid chain, looking at local phenomena and interactions that represent larger, non-local, systems (Wedel, 2004). Yet, empirical investigations do not always allow for an equal access to equivalent types of sources, such as ethnographic observation of all actors and at all sites. Given heterogeneous access to empirical material, it is often necessary to combine different types of sources and perspectives (Fanchette, 2019). Using different types of sources and methods, the present book links diverging strands of transfer research and combines different perspectives on transfer. Multiple perspectives are particularly relevant to study transnational transfer processes as the actors involved produce different scales and act across varying scopes of time and space (Fanchette, 2019).

Written Sources for Macro and Meso Perspectives

Written—often published—sources allowed for macro and meso perspectives. I have analysed Ukrainian law texts, especially the six versions of the Law on Refugees (and Persons in Need of Subsidiary and Temporary Protection), the Action Plan for the Integration of Refugees as well as the amended versions of the Law on the Legal Status of Foreign Citizens and Stateless Persons and other laws concerning asylum seekers and refugees (e.g. the Basic Law on Healthcare). This analysis shows how the legislation changed over time, at which moments and according to which principles. It also indicates which formulations were adopted directly from international law and which were adapted.

Another source under scrutiny was a collection of 45 debates of the Parliament of Ukraine, the Verkhovna Rada, on asylum laws between 1993 and early 2021.[8] Parliamentary debates reflect what members of the Parliament (MPs) and high officials of the administration discussed during recorded and formal debates in parliament. They thus indicate which norms and actors the MPs who took the floor considered legitimate and useful for their own public image. I have coded the relevant sections of the parliamentary debates with the help of the software MAXQDA which has allowed me to compare the arguments presented in favour or against asylum laws in the different debates and thus to grasp the changes which occurred over time in the arguments, that is, in the norms and actors considered legitimate in parliament.[9] Moreover, MPs and representatives of the high administration referred to contact with and criticism of

[8] I have selected the relevant parliament debates by searching through the parliament's online archives for the keywords 'біжен' and 'бежен'—the roots of the Ukrainian and the Russian word for refugee, without the suffix. These terms appear systematically in the debates on asylum laws. In contrast to a variety of terms meaning asylum seeker, the term refugee is less ambiguous (except for the period since 2014, which saw the emergence of internally displaced persons, who were also frequently referred to as refugees).

[9] Codes included the arguments mobilised to legitimise the need for the amendment (legal clarification, coherence with Ukrainian legislation, public policy problem, humanitarian need, migration control, international commitments of Ukraine, international reputation of Ukraine, Council of Europe demand, UNHCR demand or advice or approval, EU demand for visa liberalisation) and the arguments mobilised to criticise the amendment (too restrictive towards migrants, too liberal, West as a model of migration control, West as counter-model for lacking migration control, contradicting international standards, too high costs, not adapted to Ukrainian problems, need to care more for Ukrainians, exploitation by the EU as a buffer zone).

other actors such as the EU and UNHCR. Even though not exhaustive, these comments give an idea of the existence of interactions between state officials and international actors. References to international actors and comments reflecting their perception of legitimacy hint towards a certain influence of these actors on the legislative process.

Written documents produced by the European Union and international organisations such as evaluation reports about the situation of asylum in Ukraine reflect how these organisations evaluated the situation in Ukraine. Published reports have been the result of diplomatic filters and compromises within the organisations and have translated the message the organisations agreed to deliver in accordance with political and strategic considerations. The reports have allowed me to understand the norms which these organisations tried to transfer to Ukraine. They were produced with a certain goal and for a certain audience. In combination with other sources such as interviews with members of these organisations, they revealed the strategies and approaches of the organisations in regard to asylum in Ukraine—but also in regard to other issues such as their fundraising. Several requests under the Freedom of Information Act also allowed me to obtain internal documents from the European Commission about its activities and funding regarding asylum in Ukraine.

I have also used written sources to gather factual information about asylum in Ukraine in the last decades, for example the establishment and dissolution of state authorities or migration statistics. Given that academic research on asylum in Ukraine has to date been scarce, data needed to be collected from other knowledge producers. For certain issues and periods (e.g. in the 1990s and early 2000s), reports of international organisations were the only sources of information available to continuously trace the developments in Ukraine. Information from these reports was cross-checked and supplemented with other sources of information such as the Ukrainian state migration authorities' herald, *Міграція* (Migration).[10]

These written sources have allowed me to examine the period spanning 1993—year of the passing of the first law on refugees in Ukraine—to approximately 2017. The analysis of a long span of time such as this one makes it possible to grasp the evolution of the transfer process (Miao,

[10] All issues from 2009 onwards may be consulted on the website of the herald, http://migraciya.com.ua/. Earlier publications were published irregularly and cannot be found online. However, some publications may be consulted at the Vernadsky state library in Kyiv.

2018) and to question certain actors and factors taken for granted in much of the transfer literature. For instance, starting the analysis of legislative production in Ukraine before the EU became involved in the norm promotion process has enabled me to qualify the often-assumed dominant influence of the EU in norm transfer in its neighbourhood.

The analysis of these written sources also sheds light on a larger geographical scope, often the territory of the Ukrainian state. This corresponds to the way many of the actors conceive of their action: EU officials, Ukrainian MPs, and central state bodies' officials produce laws or projects officially aimed at the territory of an entire state. Nevertheless, some of the documents produced by these actors also refer to specific sites, for instance cities or migrant accommodation centres, hinting to the spatially differentiated nature of the activities.

These documents make it possible to identify the diverse actors involved in the transfer regime in Ukraine. Written sources refer both to a large number of actors and to actors of different types, including individual MPs, collective offices of international organisations located in Kyiv or Brussels, as well as international organisations or states presented as unified actors. Yet, the written official sources mostly shed light on collective actors, such as the State Migration Service of Ukraine, NGOs, UNHCR, and the European Commission. Looking at states and collective actors (organisations) are relevant perspectives when one considers that the actors involved present themselves and others in these terms (Amelina et al., 2012).

Such a perspective makes it possible to analyse collective actors' official discourses of legitimation, publicised activities, funding, and cooperation with other collective actors. This perspective is well suited to study formalised and documented processes, such as the legislative adoption of international norms. Their large geographical and temporal stretch allows for comparison. Yet, even well-documented activities, such as lawmaking, benefit from alternative perspectives that reveal informal processes. Indeed, macro and meso perspectives based on written sources are usefully complemented with micro and meso perspectives based on fieldwork research.

Multi-Sited Fieldwork for Micro and Meso Perspectives

To diversify my understanding of the transfer processes and the transfer regime, I carried out fieldwork at different sites in Ukraine and Brussels.

Fieldwork research is limited in the space and time that a researcher can cover. Transnational policies are multi-sited, meaning that a researcher needs to select a few sites and cannot cover all potentially relevant ones (Lendvai & Stubbs, 2007, p. 183). I conducted interviews and observation among a large range of actors involved in transfer: current and past representatives of EU institutions and of international organisations in Brussels and in Kyiv as well as of non-governmental organisations, of state institutions and migrants with different legal statuses in Ukraine (Table 1.1).

During the five months of fieldwork spent between 2013 and 2015 in Ukraine, I stayed in different cities and towns with significant numbers of asylum seekers. I focused primarily on Kyiv, the country's capital city, because most relevant actors were based there. In order to cover more actors and to include potential variations among different regional Migration Services, I also conducted fieldwork in other cities in the north, west, south, and east of Ukraine: in Chernihiv (a city with a detention centre for irregularised migrants), three cities and towns in Western Ukraine near the EU border, Lviv, Uzhhorod (close to the migrant detention centre Chop), and Mukachevo (where a temporary accommodation centre for

Table 1.1 Fieldwork research conducted in Brussels and in Ukraine

Type of actor	*Number of interviews*
Migrants	23
Ukrainian state actors	21
Out of which officials of regional Migration Services	11
NGOs in Ukraine	45
Observation (at NGOs and regional state authorities in Ukraine)	9
International Organisations	
-In Ukraine	19
-In Brussels	4
European Representations in Kyiv (esp. EU Delegation)	7
European Commission	12
European Parliament (MEPs, their assistants and the secretariat)	7
Other actors in Brussels (other EU institutions such as COEST of the Council and the EEAS, diplomatic representations)	5
Total	152

Source Author's production

Fig. 1.2 Map of the fieldwork conducted in Ukraine

refugee women and families is located), in Kharkiv, and Odesa (two cities with major immigrant communities) (Fig. 1.2).[11]

For fieldwork research in Ukraine, I chose specific sites from among the different sites and state bodies of the Ukrainian asylum policies. Indeed, asylum policies include as diverse aspects as border control, detention of irregularised immigrants, police controls, access to social benefits, housing, healthcare, education, and the administrative and judicial procedure of accessing a protection status. As I was interested primarily in transfer processes and not in an exhaustive picture of the Ukrainian asylum system, I selected the key actor of the Ukrainian asylum system: the asylum departments of the State Migration Service (SMS – Державна міграційна служба України). They deal with asylum seekers most often (in contrast to most other state bodies which only infrequently encounter

[11] Crimea as well as the Russia-backed so-called Donetsk People's Republic (DNR) and Luhansk People's Republic (LNR) have been excluded from the analysis as they were no longer under the control of the Ukrainian state. The files of the migration authorities in these regions have been moved to authorities under Ukrainian state control.

asylum seekers and refugees) and have a crucial role in asylum policies in Ukraine. These departments decide on the legal status of asylum seekers and are, at least theoretically, in charge of what they call the integration of refugees. Integration covers such areas as access to social rights, employment, language courses, and housing. Ukrainian political decision makers, such as MPs and high-level ministerial staff were difficult to access and when interviewed cautious and reticent to describe any details of their work practices, interactions, or biographies. This is why this research cannot provide a full sociological or micro perspective of the legislative processes and actors.

I intensively investigated the non-state sector of asylum in Ukraine that includes the most active and immediate norm promoters. This sector encompasses both the offices of international organisations in Ukraine (mostly located in Kyiv) and NGOs. Given that the non-state asylum sector in Ukraine is of limited scope, I managed to study most of its active participants. Among the international organisations I focused on UNHCR, the most powerful and active international organisation working on asylum in Ukraine. International non-governmental organisations (INGOs), an intermediary group of organisations, which sometimes act as Ukrainian NGOs and sometimes as donors,[12] as well as the Ukrainian asylum NGOs were also interviewed. The interviews with these organisations allowed me to grasp their practices, strategies, and relations (among themselves, with donors and with state authorities). In most cases I interviewed the head of the organisation and one or several other employees. This enabled me to see differences between the larger strategies concerning funding and influence onto state authorities, primarily formulated by the heads of the organisations, and the everyday practices and experiences of the majority of the staff.

In order to understand the production of EU policies in regard to asylum in Ukraine both within and among the EU bodies and in interaction with the offices of international organisations and country representations in Brussels, I spent a total of four weeks in Brussels speaking with representatives of the European Commission, the European Parliament, the European Council, and the European External Action Service, the representation of Ukraine to the European Union as well as the employees of lobbying offices of international organisations.

[12] The Hebrew Immigrant Aid Society (HIAS), the Danish Refugee Council (DRC), the Comité d'Aide Médicale (CAMZ), Caritas, and the Jesuit Refugee Service (JRS).

To diversify perspectives and to avoid perceiving Ukrainian asylum policies only through the eyes of implementers and norm promoters, I also talked to those most concerned: migrants of different legal statuses and length of stay in Ukraine. While most of them were either in the asylum procedure or had completed it—successfully or unsuccessfully –, a few interlocutors had never applied for asylum. Indeed, migrants often mistrusted the Ukrainian asylum procedure or did not believe they would find protection and prosperity in Ukraine. I asked migrants about their experience with state officials (border guards, police, State Migration Services, courts, hospitals, institutions of public education, etc.) and with non-state actors (IOs, NGOs, diaspora networks). As they had different statuses, had come to Ukraine at different times, and had different characteristics (e.g. Russian speakers and non-Russian speakers, migrants from CIS countries and non-CIS countries, non-European looking and European-looking migrants, men and women, those with a large compatriot community in Ukraine and those without, etc.), their experience of asylum practices gave important insights into the diversity of these practices. Communication with migrants was largely informal. Given the sensitivities of this group, I did not record the communication but took notes, did not collect data that would allow recognising them individually, and did not question them about their life in their home country or their journey before reaching Ukraine. Focusing on their situation in Ukraine and their experience with Ukrainian state officials and institutions allowed me to make my interlocutors feel comfortable and to avoid reopening wounds or increasing risks to their security or that of their close ones.

The topic of asylum and asylum-related activities in Ukraine was sensitive to many of my informants. While for asylum seekers their life could be at risk, for NGO workers critical comments might endanger their relations to domestic state authorities or to their donors. State officials might suffer sanctions at work if voicing criticism or describing practices that diverged from the law or official instructions. EU officials were cautious about diplomatic implications of their conversations with a researcher, in particular in politically sensitive contexts such as the negotiations around the visa-free regime for Ukraine. Some informants did not want to be recorded. To protect my interlocutors from negative repercussions, I have made sure to profoundly make anonymous the reference to individuals but also to certain organisations or departments of institutions.

For instance, I decided not to indicate the names of Ukrainian towns or cities as the sector of asylum NGOs in Ukraine is very small.

Interviews, informal conversations, and observation favour micro and meso perspectives. Individual practices and beliefs as well as inter- and intraorganisational dynamics become visible. Individual actors' discretionary powers and relations of friendship or dislike between individuals of different organisations affect transfer processes and practices. Informality, invisible when studying only written official documents, appears as an important factor. These perspectives uncover the often overlooked heterogeneity, fluidity, instability and uncertainty of transfer. For example, examining individual state officials' careers and their interactions at work, it becomes clear that the high turnover of staff at the administration destabilises norm transfer over time.

By combining different sources and perspectives, it is possible to uncover how certain phenomena, visible only from one perspective, are interrelated or affect each other. For instance, from a macro perspective and when studying parliamentary debates, I realised that in 2014/2015 the Ukrainian government sought intensively to fulfil EU demands in order to obtain the incentive of visa freedom. At meso perspectives, through interviews with EU and Ukrainian administrative officials, I found out that the EU Commission carried out regular monitoring missions and regular feedback reporting that increased pressure on the Ukrainian administration, including the asylum departments. Moreover, UNHCR and NGOs met with EU "experts" during monitoring missions to direct their attention to certain aspects they should criticise in their reports and comments to the Ukrainian administration. Through micro perspectives it became clear that these EU-Ukraine- and European Commission-administration-UNHCR-relations shaped the interactions between individuals working for the asylum administration and for asylum NGOs, as administrative staff became dependent on information and material support from NGO workers to fulfil hierarchical demands and report on their successful implementation of action plans. Micro and meso perspectives make it possible to uncover more complex power relations, asymmetric, interdependent and shifting, between NGO workers and administrative staff.

By combining different perspectives, we grasp relations between structure and agency, that is how actors act within but also upon structures. For instance, it can be seen how neoliberal, imperial, and bureaucratised structures constrain and direct NGOs' everyday practices and choices, but also how these NGOs co-define these structures through compliance, resistance, and coping (Mützelburg, 2020a).

Multiplying perspectives also helps to avoid presupposing who the relevant actors are—individuals, organisations, or states. Adopting macro perspectives directs the focus on international organisations, the European Union, or (European) states as the drivers of the transfer of norms and policies. Macro perspective studies often rely on sources produced by actors who initiate and dominate transfer processes, as they are frequently the only knowledge producers. Changing perspectives means including other sources and hence other views on transfer. When shifting between different perspectives, we see that all types of actors may shape transfer processes, including small organisations and individuals (Hadjiisky et al., 2017, pp. 273–274). We also remain open to grasping causality in different directions, instead of expecting them to flow from supposedly more powerful, bigger, or more international actors to supposedly weaker, smaller or more local actors. For example, small NGOs may participate in orienting EU evaluations. In diversifying the perspectives of analysis, I am able to propose a more complex understanding of multi-scalar transfer processes, practices, and actor relations.

Structure of the Book

This book investigates why and how norm transfer is undertaken and with which normative and social effects. I start off with a macro perspective, looking at political developments over nearly 30 years. The analysis is gradually expanded to include meso and micro perspectives on low-scale actors, to finally lead, especially in the final chapters, to a multi-perspective examination of multi-scalar transfer practices. The first part of this book shows that since the state's independence in 1991, due to international influences and despite unfavourable domestic conditions, the Ukrainian Parliament introduced international asylum norms into domestic law—initially in a shallow, selective, and delayed way. In light of this foot-dragging adoption, the second part examines the implementation of formal asylum norms, demonstrating that it is even more heterogeneous and unstable and needs to be investigated through the prism of a transfer chain involving international and domestic state and non-state actors shifting across scales.

Chapter 2 presents the context into which international asylum norms were imported, focusing on two factors that, according to transfer research, shape the effects of transfer attempts: domestic political interests and domestic social norms. It highlights the history of predominantly CIS migration in the Soviet Union and independent Ukraine, the prevailing xenophobia towards non-CIS foreigners, and the gradual development of restrictive immigration policies towards them. This makes for an unfavourable domestic setting for the development of asylum policies. Moreover, the lack of asylum as a traditional norm in the post-Soviet context, the low numbers of asylum seekers, competing political priorities regarding other social problems (perceived as more important and concerning Ukrainian citizens) and political ties with CIS states mean that domestic interests and normative misfit were likely to hinder the transfer of international asylum norms to Ukraine.

In Chapter 3, I observe that despite the obstacles sketched out in the previous chapter, most international asylum norms were integrated into Ukrainian law. However, when translating international asylum norms into Ukrainian law, domestic law and policy-makers exercised leeway. Delaying or selectively adopting and translating norms, decision makers resisted the import of norms that clashed with the objectives of restrictive migration control and cooperation with allied regimes. Indeed, in parallel to the concept of "shallow Europeanisation" I develop the notion of "shallow legislative adoption" to refer to the harmonisation of the most visible laws with international norms, while failing to adapt other relevant laws and secondary legislation, thus making full implementation impossible. Norms in line with or at least not contradicting domestic decision makers' objectives were adopted faster, more extensively, and more deeply than the others. In addition to timing, domestic politicians resisted the transfer when a norm was internationally weak. Norms are weakened by vague formulations, when exceptions are included in the text, when European states commonly violate the norm, and when an alternative norm coexists concerning the same issue.

Seeking to explain this import of international asylum norms into Ukrainian legislation, in Chapter 4, I analyse the domestic legislators' discourse on asylum as well as international organisations' transfer practices. I find that lesson drawing, the search for a policy solution from another context (Rose, 1991), cannot account for the convergence because lawmakers were aware of the fact that the asylum laws did not tackle existing public policy problems in Ukraine. Instead, in the first years after independence, domestic politicians stressed the international legitimacy and reputation associated with the adherence to refugee norms.

Moreover, they justified the adoption with the pre-accession conditionality of the Council of Europe and later, between 2010 and 2016, the EU conditionality related to the introduction of a visa-free regime. The coming to power of a pro-EU oriented political leadership in 2014, after the Maidan protests, further enhanced the position of the EU in Ukraine. The chapter contributes to the research on conditionality by exposing the workings of EU monitoring through macro and meso perspectives. UNHCR interacted directly with Ukrainian decision makers to shape the emerging asylum laws. These international organisations are interrelated and cooperate in their transfer attempts. While examining national legislative developments and politicians' debates, this chapter also takes into consideration factors visible from a meso perspective, for instance the role of resources enjoyed by the country offices of international organisations.

After showing in the first part that international influences and not domestic demand caused the gradual and uncertain formal adoption of international asylum norms in Ukraine, I investigate in the second part if, how, and why domestic state authorities carried out asylum policies in practice.

In Chapter 5 I scrutinise state practices of asylum. I find that top-down obstacles, such as reorganisations of the administrative bodies, political power struggles as well as lack of resources, information, and legislative coherence hindered the implementation of the introduced asylum laws. In addition, utilising the literature on public policy implementation, especially in West Africa, the chapter stresses street-level bureaucrats' crucial role, as some of these subordinate officials improvised to do their work despite top-down obstacles. I further explore the interactive dynamics between central authorities' attempts to control law and policy implementation and the regional bureaucrats' discretionary powers. While most transfer scholars only consider top-down factors, researchers analysing the implementation of public policies show that subordinate state officials are actually policy-makers who choose to apply and interpret certain formal rules according to social norms, emotions, and moral judgements. This constant translation of formal rules into everyday state practices implies that asylum policies were strongly heterogeneous across actors, space, and time.

Norm promoters tried to influence state practices through additional channels. These transfer attempts took place via a transfer chain. Chapter 6 shows that international donors produced NGOs as domestic norm promoters. International organisations' funding triggered the emergence of domestic asylum NGOs or the refocusing of existing NGOs' activities, as well as the transfer of skills, norms, knowledge, and standardised practices to the NGOs. In harmony with the literature's findings on development aid and donor-NGO relations, in this chapter, I highlight the unstable and donor-driven state of the non-state asylum sector in Ukraine. Despite rather close control from the main donor, NGO workers enjoyed some, though limited leeway and translate between the international donors' expectations, their organisations' needs, and their own appreciations and norms. As the next part of the transfer chain, non-state actors tried to transfer international asylum norms directly to Ukrainian state officials and thus to change their practices. NGOs tried to transmit international norms and standardised practices to domestic officials via personal contacts and interaction. This approach through interactions increased state officials' knowledge and awareness of international asylum norms and Ukrainian laws, as well as their legitimacy. However, officials' leeway, resistance, high number, and turnover meant that normative effects of transfer via interactions were heterogeneous across actors and space and unstable over time. Norm promoters tried to overcome the instability of the approach via brokers by using informal strategies to formalise procedures.

In Chapter 7 I show how norm promoters tried to adapt their transfer practices to norm addressees' resistance and structural obstacles. Tracing these practices reveals that when conciliatory transfer approaches failed or were unavailable, non-state actors tried to change state practices by denouncing them. If possible, they denounced lower scale authorities to brokers at key positions, benefiting from their legal authority over subordinate state actors to recommend or request changes. When non-state actors lacked such contacts, they directly confronted the implementing officials. In case of resistance they shifted across scales, complaining to superordinate officials or to courts. When a case could be framed as a particular salient violation of human rights or asylum norms, norm promoters turned to international organisations in the hopes that they would exert pressure on domestic politicians. However, contentious approaches depended in their effectiveness on the approached state actor's capacity to ignore the complaints. Furthermore, they caused geographical dilemmas, because they provoked resistance and damaged relations to officials, hence limiting the norm promoters' access to non-contentious transfer practices.

Chapter 8 summarises the contribution of this book to research on asylum policies, NGO-state relations, post-communist administration, and transfer. While this book confirms the widespread finding in the transfer literature of the importance of conditionality, it shows that this is only one of the transfer channels. Through multiple perspectives, it demonstrates how different, usually overlooked actors and transfer practices are interrelated and all participate in shaping the fluctuating transfer processes. The effects of these transfer activities, rather than completed transfer, are constantly shifting, heterogeneous across actors, space, and time. This research suggests that to understand transfer, it is necessary to analyse the various actors' roles, leeway, interactions, and (transfer) practices, including multi-scalar ones.

References

Acharya, A. (2004). How ideas spread: Whose norms matter? Norm localization and institutional change in Asian regionalism. *International Organization, 58*(2), 239–275.

Acharya, A. (2015). The responsibility to protect and a theory of norm circulation. In R. C. Thakur & W. Maley (Eds.), *Theorising the responsibility to protect* (pp. 59–78). Cambridge University Press.

Ademmer, E., & Börzel, T. A. (2013). Migration, energy and good governance in the EU's Eastern neighbourhood. *Europe-Asia Studies, 65*(4), 581–608.

Alpes, M. J., & Spire, A. (2014). Dealing with law in migration control: The powers of street-level bureaucrats at French consulates. *Social & Legal Studies, 23*(2), 261–274. https://doi.org/10.1177/0964663913510927

Amelina, A., Nergiz, D. D., Faist, T., & Glick Schiller, N. (2012). *Beyond methodological nationalism: Research methodologies for cross-border studies*. http://ebookcentral.proquest.com/lib/sciences-po/detail.action?docID=981719

Amnesty International. (2013). *Return to torture: Extradition, forcible returns and removals to Central Asia* (EUR 04/001/2013). https://www.amnesty.org/en/documents/eur04/001/2013/en/

Aydin, U., & Kirişci, K. (2013). With or without the EU: Europeanisation of Asylum and competition policies in Turkey. *South European Society and Politics, 18*(3), 375–395. https://doi.org/10.1080/13608746.2013.799729

Bache, I., & Taylor, A. (2003). The politics of policy resistance: Reconstructing higher education in Kosovo. *Journal of Public Policy, 23*(3), 279–300.

Baird, T., & Spijkerboer, T. (2019). Carrier sanctions and the conflicting legal obligations of carriers: Addressing human rights leakage. *Amsterdam Law Forum, 11*(1), 4–19.

Baker, T., McCann, E., & Temenos, C. (2020). Into the ordinary: Non-elite actors and the mobility of harm reduction policies. *Policy and Society, 39*(1), 129–145. https://doi.org/10.1080/14494035.2019.1626079

Barnett, M. N., & Finnemore, M. (1999). The politics, power, and pathologies of international organizations. *International Organization, 53*(04), 699–732. https://doi.org/10.1162/002081899551048

Bátora, J., & Navrátil, M. (2016). Extending the EU's security community amidst conflict: The case of Ukraine. In P. Rieker (Ed.), *External governance as security community building: The limits and potential of the European neighbourhood policy* (pp. 19–48). Palgrave Macmillan UK. https://doi.org/10.1057/978-1-137-56169-5

Bátora, J., & Rieker, P. (2018). EU-supported reforms in the EU neighbourhood as organized anarchies: The case of post-Maidan Ukraine. *Journal of European Integration, 40*(4), 461–478. https://doi.org/10.1080/07036337.2018.1467412

Berger, T., & Esguerra, A. (Eds.). (2018). *World politics in translation: Power, relationality, and difference in global cooperation*. Routledge.

Bigo, D. (2006). Sécurité et immigration: Vers une gouvernementalité par l'inquiétude ? *Cultures & Conflits, 31–32*. http://conflits.revues.org/index539.html

Bloomfield, A. (2015). Norm antipreneurs and theorising resistance to normative change. *Review of International Studies, 42*, 1–24.

Border Monitoring Project Ukraine. (2011). *'You want to be free? You pay money!'—Corruption in the immigration detention and Asylum system of Ukraine*. Pro Asyl Foundation. http://bordermonitoring-ukraine.eu/files/2012/01/corruption.pdf

Börzel, T. A., & van Hüllen, V. (2014). One voice, one message, but conflicting goals: Cohesiveness and consistency in the European neighbourhood policy. *Journal of European Public Policy, 21*(7), 1033–1049.

Boswell, C. (2003). The 'external dimension' of EU immigration and Asylum policy. *International Affairs, 79*(3), 619–638.

Bosworth, M., & Vannier, M. (2020). Blurred lines: Detaining asylum seekers in Britain and France. *Journal of Sociology, 56*(1), 53–68. https://doi.org/10.1177/1440783319882534

Boulay, S. (2019). Introduction—Questionner et pratiquer les échelles en sciences humaines et sociales. In S. Fanchette (Ed.), *La question des échelles en sciences humaines et sociales* (pp. 5–21). Éditions Quæ. http://books.openedition.org/quae/20482

Bourbeau, P. (2011). *The securitization of migration: A study of movement and order*. Routledge.

Brenner, N. (2001). The limits to scale? Methodological reflections on scalar structuration. *Progress in Human Geography, 25*(4), 591–614. https://doi.org/10.1191/030913201682688959

Bromberger, C. (2021). Échelles (d'analyse). *Ethnologie Francaise, 51*(1), 41–42.

Brouillette, M. (2018). From discourse to practice: The circulation of norms, ideas and practices of migration management through the implementation of the mobility partnerships in Moldova and Georgia. *Comparative Migration Studies, 6*(1), 5.

Bruns, B. (2019). Homogenous and extra-territorial border regime? Migrations and control efforts across the Eastern EU external border. *Journal of Borderlands Studies, 34*(4), 509–526. https://doi.org/10.1080/08865655.2017.1402194

Callon, M. (1986). Éléments pour une sociologie de la traduction: La domestication des coquilles St-Jacques et des marins pêcheurs dans la baie de St. Brieuc. *L'Année Sociologique, 36 numéro spécial La sociologie des Sciences et des Techniques*, 169–208.

Capie, D. (2008). Localization as resistance: The contested diffusion of small arms norms in Southeast Asia. *Security Dialogue, 39*(6), 637–658. JSTOR.

Casier, T. (2011). The EU's two-track approach to democracy promotion: The case of Ukraine. *Democratization, 18*(4), 956–977. https://doi.org/10.1080/13510347.2011.584734

Chetail, V., Bruycker, P. D., & Maiani, F. (2016). *Reforming the common European Asylum system: The new European refugee law*. BRILL.

Cianciara, A. K. (2020). *The politics of the European neighbourhood policy*. Routledge.

Clarke, J., Bainton, D., Lendvai, N., & Stubbs, P. (2015). *Making policy move: Towards a politics of translation and assemblage*. Policy Press.

Clavier, C. (2013). Les causes locales de la convergence. *Gouvernement Et Action Publique, 3*, 395–413.

Coleman, N. (2009). *European readmission policy: Third country interests and refugee rights*. BRILL.

Council of the European Union. (2003). *A Secure Europe in a Better World. European Security Strategy*.

Crane, A. (2020). The politics of development and humanitarianism in EU externalization: Managing migration in Ukraine. *Environment and Planning c: Politics and Space, 38*(1), 20–39. https://doi.org/10.1177/2399654419856908

de la Croix, J. F. (2013). How to build a better future? Kyrgyzstani development workers and the 'knowledge transfer' strategy. *Central Asian Survey, 32*(4), 448–461.

Dandashly, A., & Kourtelis, C. (2020). Classifying the implementation of the EU's normative power in its Southern Neighbourhood: The role of

local actors. *JCMS: Journal of Common Market Studies, 58*(6), 1523–1539. https://doi.org/10.1111/jcms.13051
Darley, M. (2010). Le pouvoir de la norme. *Déviance Et Société, 34*(2), 229–239. https://doi.org/10.3917/ds.342.0229
Dekanozishvili, M. (2020). The European union's credibility–expectations gap in its European neighbourhood policy: Perspectives from Georgia and Ukraine. *Southeast European and Black Sea Studies, 20*(2), 289–305. https://doi.org/10.1080/14683857.2020.1767467
Delcour, L. (2013). The EU: Shaping migration patterns in its neighbourhood and beyond. In D. Kochenov & F. Amtenbrink (Eds.), *The European Union's shaping of the international legal order* (pp. 261–282). Cambridge University Press. https://doi.org/10.1017/CBO9781139519625.015
Delcour, L. (2016a). Multiple external influences and domestic change in the contested neighborhood: The case of food safety. *Eurasian Geography and Economics, 57*(1), 43–65. https://doi.org/10.1080/15387216.2016.1183220
Delcour, L. (2016b). *The EU's policy transfer to the post-soviet space: Domestic responses, (post)-soviet legacies and Russia's policies* [HDR]. Institut d'études politiques de Paris.
Delcour, L. (2018). 'You can lead a horse to water, but you can't make it drink': The EU's and Russia's intersecting conditionalities and domestic responses in Georgia and Moldova. *European Politics and Society, 19*(4), 490–505. https://doi.org/10.1080/23745118.2018.1441699
Delcour, L., & Tulmets, E. (2019). *Policy transfer and Norm circulation: Towards an interdisciplinary and comparative approach.* Routledge. https://books.google.de/books?id=tVGdswEACAAJ
Delcour, L., & Wolczuk, K. (2015). Spoiler or facilitator of democratization? Russia's role in Georgia and Ukraine. *Democratization, 22*(3), 459–478. https://doi.org/10.1080/13510347.2014.996135
Delpeuch, T., & Vassileva, M. (2017). Judicial reforms as a political enterprise: American transfer entrepreneurs in post-Communist Bulgaria. In M. Hadjiisky, L. A. Pal & C. Walker (Eds.), *Public Policy Transfer* (pp. 29–50).
Dimitrova, A., & Dragneva, R. (2009). Constraining external governance: Interdependence with Russia and the CIS as limits to the EU's rule transfer in the Ukraine. *Journal of European Public Policy, 16*(6), 853–872. https://doi.org/10.1080/13501760903087894
Dimitrova, A., & Dragneva, R. (2013). Shaping convergence with the EU in foreign policy and state aid in post-orange Ukraine: Weak external incentives powerful veto players. *Europe-Asia Studies, 65*(4), 658–681.
Dolowitz, D., & Marsh, D. (2000). Learning from abroad: The role of policy transfer in contemporary policy-making. *Governance, 13*(1), 5–23.

Dolowitz, D. P., Plugaru, R., & Saurugger, S. (2019). The process of transfer: The micro-influences of power, time and learning. *Public Policy and Administration, 34*, 1–20.

Dubois, V. (1999). *La vie au guichet: Relation administrative et traitement de la misère* (3 (2010)). Economica.

Dufour, P., & Goyer, R. (2010). Analyse de la transnationalisation de l'action collective: Proposition pour une géographie des solidarités transnationales. *Sociologie Et Sociétés, 41*(2), 111–134. https://doi.org/10.7202/039261ar

Düvell, F. (2008). On the fringes of Europe: Refugees in Ukraine. *Research Resources Report: Country Profile, 2*, 1–9.

Düvell, F. (2012). Transit migration: A blurred and politicised concept. *Population, Space and Place, 18*(4), 415–427. https://doi.org/10.1002/psp.631

Eade, D. (2007). Capacity building: Who builds whose capacity? *Development in Practice, 17*(4–5), 630–639. https://doi.org/10.1080/09614520701469807

El Qadim, N. (2021). Les politiques migratoires européennes: À la recherche d'un impossible compromis ? *Migrations Société, 186*(4), 11–27.

Ellison, N. (2017). Politics, power and policy transfer. *Journal of Asian Public Policy, 10*(1), 8–24. https://doi.org/10.1080/17516234.2016.1258519

Engelmann, C. (2014). Convergence against the odds: The development of safe country of origin policies in EU member states (1990–2013). *European Journal of Migration and Law, 16*(2), 277–302. https://doi.org/10.1163/15718166-12342056

European Commission. (2015). *Sixth progress report on the implementation by Ukraine of the action plan on Visa liberalisation* (COM(2015) 905 final). http://ec.europa.eu/transparency/regdoc/rep/1/2015/EN/1-2015-905-EN-F1-1.PDF

Evans, M. (Ed.). (2010). *New directions in the study of policy transfer*. Routledge.

Evans, M., & Davies, J. (1999). Understanding policy transfer: A multi-level, multi-disciplinary perspective. *Public Administration, 77*(2), 361–385. https://doi.org/10.1111/1467-9299.00158

Fanchette, S. (2019). Conclusion. In S. Boulay & S. Fanchette (Eds.), *La question des échelles en sciences humaines et sociales*.

Faustini-Torres, L. (2020). Another nexus? Exploring narratives on the linkage between EU external migration policies and the democratization of the southern Mediterranean neighbourhood. *Comparative Migration Studies, 8*(1), 9. https://doi.org/10.1186/s40878-019-0165-z

Finnemore, M., & Sikkink, K. (1998). International norm dynamics and political change. *International Organization, 52*(04), 887–917.

Franke, A., Gawrich, A., Melnykovska, I., & Schweickert, R. (2010). The European Union's relations with Ukraine and Azerbaijan. *Post-Soviet Affairs, 26*(2), 149–183.

Freeman, R. (2009). What is 'translation'? *Evidence & Policy, 5*(4), 429–447.
Frelick, B., Kysel, I. M., & Podkul, J. (2016). The impact of externalization of migration controls on the rights of Asylum seekers and other migrants. *Journal on Migration and Human Security, 4*(4), 190–220. https://doi.org/10.1177/233150241600400402
Fresia, M. (2014). Building consensus within UNHCR's executive committee: Global refugee norms in the making. *Journal of Refugee Studies, 27*(4), 514–533. https://doi.org/10.1093/jrs/feu025
Freyburg, T., Lavenex, S., Schimmelfennig, F., Skripka, T., & Wetzel, A. (2009). EU promotion of democratic governance in the neighbourhood. *Journal of European Public Policy, 16*(6), 916–934. https://doi.org/10.1080/13501760903088405
Fröhlich, C. (2010). Walking the tightrope. Russian disability NGOs' struggle with international and domestic demands. In S. Fischer & H. Pleines (Eds.), *Civil society in central and Eastern Europe* (pp. 77–87). ibidem-Verlag.
Gammeltoft-Hansen, T., & Sørensen, N. N. (2013). *The migration industry and the commercialization of international migration*. Routledge.
Geiger, M. (2011). *Europäische Migrationspolitik und Raumproduktion. Internationale Regierungsorganisationen im Management von Migration in Albanien, Bosnien-Herzegowina und der Ukraine*. Nomos.
Geiger, M., & Pécoud, A. (2013). International organisations and the politics of migration. *Journal of Ethnic and Migration Studies, 40*(6), 865–887. https://doi.org/10.1080/1369183X.2013.855071
Goetz, K. H. (2005). The new member states and the EU: Responding to Europe. In S. Bulmer & C. Lequesne (Eds.), *The member states of the European Union* (pp. 254–280). OUP Oxford.
Gorman, C. S. (2019). Singled out: Scaling violence and social groups as legal borderwork in U.S. Asylum law. *Geographical Review, 109*(4), 487–506. https://doi.org/10.1111/gere.12311
Grossetti, M. (2006). Trois échelles d'action et d'analyse L'abstraction Comme Opérateur D'échelle. *L'année Sociologique, 56*(2), 285–307.
Guiraudon, V. (2018). the 2015 refugee crisis was not a turning point: Explaining policy inertia in EU border control. *European Political Science, 17*(1), 151–160. https://doi.org/10.1057/s41304-017-0123-x
Hadjiisky, M., Pal, L. A., & Walker, C. (Eds.). (2017). *Public policy transfer: Micro-dynamics and macro effects*. Edward Elgar Publishing.
Hameiri, S., & Scarpello, F. (2018). International development aid and the politics of scale. *Review of International Political Economy, 25*(2), 145–168. https://doi.org/10.1080/09692290.2018.1431560
Hassenteufel, P., & de Maillard, J. (2013). Convergence, transferts et traduction. *Gouvernement Et Action Publique, 3*, 377–393.

Hertog, L. den. (2014). *The rule of law in the external dimension of EU migration and asylum policy: Organisational dynamics between legitimation and constraint*. Wolf Legal Publishers.

Human Rights Watch. (2010). *Buffeted in the borderland: The treatment of migrants and Asylum seekers in Ukraine*. http://www.hrw.org/sites/default/files/reports/ukraine1210WebVersion.pdf

Hunt, M. (2014). The safe country of origin concept in European Asylum law: Past, present and future. *International Journal of Refugee Law, 26*(4), 500–535. https://doi.org/10.1093/ijrl/eeu052

İçduygu, A., & Yükseker, D. (2012). Rethinking transit migration in Turkey: Reality and re-presentation in the creation of a migratory phenomenon. *Population, Space and Place, 18*(4), 441–456. https://doi.org/10.1002/psp.633

Infantino, F. (2019). *Schengen visa implementation and transnational policy-making—Bordering Europe*. Palgrave. https://www.palgrave.com/gp/book/9783030106461

Jacoby, W. (1999). Priest and penitent: The EU as a force in the domestic politics of Eastern Europe. *East European Constitutional Review, 8*(1–2), 62–67.

Kaiser, R., & Nikiforova, E. (2008). The Performativity of scale: The social construction of scale effects in Narva, Estonia. *Environment and Planning d: Society and Space, 26*(3), 537–562. https://doi.org/10.1068/d3307

Kirişci, K. (2007, May). *The limits of conditionality and Europeanization: Turkey's dilemmas in adopting the EU acquis on asylum*. http://aei.pitt.edu/7936/

Kluczewska, K. (2019). How to translate 'good governance' into Tajik? An American good governance fund and norm localisation in Tajikistan. *Journal of Intervention and Statebuilding, 13*(3), 357–376.

Koven, S. (2019). *The case against bureaucratic discretion*. Palgrave Macmillan.

Langbein, J. (2013). Unpacking the Russian and EU impact on policy change in the Eastern neighbourhood: The case of Ukraine's telecommunications and food safety. *Europe-Asia Studies, 65*(4), 631–657.

Langbein, J. (2015). *Transnationalization and regulatory change in the EU's Eastern neighbourhood* (Routledge/UACES Contemporary European Studies).

Langbein, J., & Wolczuk, K. (2012). Convergence without membership? The impact of the European Union in the neighbourhood: Evidence from Ukraine. *Journal of European Public Policy, 19*(6), 863–881.

Lavenex, S. (2006). Shifting up and out: The foreign policy of European immigration control. *West European Politics, 29*(2), 329–350.

Lavenex, S. (2008). A governance perspective on the European neighbourhood policy: Integration beyond conditionality? *Journal of European Public Policy, 6*(15). https://www-tandfonline-com.acces-distant.sciences-po.fr/doi/full/10.1080/13501760802196879

Lavenex, S. (2018). 'Failing forward' towards Which Europe? Organized hypocrisy in the Common European Asylum system. *Journal of Common Market Studies, 56*(5), 1195.

Lavenex, S., & Schimmelfennig, F. (2009). EU rules beyond EU borders: Theorizing external governance in European politics. *Journal of European Public Policy, 16*(6), 791–812.

Legrand, T. (2016). Elite, exclusive and elusive: Transgovernmental policy networks and iterative policy transfer in the Anglosphere. *Policy Studies, 37*(5), 440–455. https://doi.org/10.1080/01442872.2016.1188912

Lendvai, N., & Stubbs, P. (2007). Policy reconsidered: Meanings, politics and practices. In S. M. Hodgson & Z. Irving (Eds.), *Policies as translation: Situating transnational social policies*. Policy Press.

Lipsky, M. (1980). *Street-level bureaucracy: The dilemmas of the individual in public service*. Russell Sage Foundation.

Makaryan, S. (2015). Construction of migration policies in the Eastern neighbourhood of the European union. *Journal of Contemporary European Studies, 23*(2), 222–237. https://doi.org/10.1080/14782804.2015.1029241

Marks, G. (1993). Structural policy and multi-level governance in the EC. In A. W. Cafruny & G. G. Rosenthal (Eds.), *The state of the European community: The Maastricht Debate and beyond* (pp. 391–411). Lynne Rienner.

Marsh, D., & Sharman, J. C. (2009). Policy diffusion and policy transfer. *Policy Studies, 30*(3), 269–288. https://doi.org/10.1080/01442870902863851

Marshall, A. (2005). Europeanization at the urban level: Local actors, institutions and the dynamics of multi-level interaction. *Journal of European Public Policy, 12*(4), 668–686. https://doi.org/10.1080/13501760500160292

Marung, S. (2015). Die wandernde Grenze. Territorialisierungsentwürfe nach der EU-Osterweiterung 2004. In U. Jureit & N. Tietze (Eds.), *Postsouveräne Territorialität: Die Europäische Union und ihr Raum* (1. Auflage). Hamburger Edition.

Masson, D. (2009). Politique(s) des échelles et transnationalisation: Perspectives géographiques. *Politique Et Sociétés, 28*(1), 113–133. https://doi.org/10.7202/001727ar

Mavrot, C. (2017). Concerted horizontal policy transfer: How local action can drive national compliance to international norms. In M. Hadjiisky, L. A. Pal, & C. Walker (Eds.), *Public policy transfer: Micro-dynamics and macro effects* (pp. 101–124). Edward Elgar Publishing.

Melnykovska, I., & Schweickert, R. (2008). Bottom-up or top-down: What drives the convergence of Ukraine's institutions towards European standards? *Southeast European and Black Sea Studies, 8*(4), 445–468. https://doi.org/10.1080/14683850802556426

Menz, G. (2013). The neoliberalized state and the growth of the migration industry. In T. Gammeltoft-Hansen & N. N. Sørensen (Eds.), *The migration industry and the commercialization of international migration* (pp. 108–127). Routledge.

Miao, J. T. (2018). Parallelism and evolution in transnational policy transfer networks: The case of Sino-Singapore Suzhou Industrial Park (SIP). *Regional Studies, 52*(9), 1191–1200. https://doi.org/10.1080/00343404.2017.1418979

Miaz, J. (2019). Entre examen individuel et gestion collective: Ce que les injonctions à la productivité font à l'instruction des demandes d'asile. *Lien Social Et Politiques, 83*, 144–166. https://doi.org/10.7202/1066088ar

Moore, A. (2008). Rethinking scale as a geographical category: From analysis to practice. *Progress in Human Geography, 32*(2), 203–225. https://doi.org/10.1177/0309132507087647

Mukhtarov, F. (2014). Rethinking the travel of ideas: Policy translation in the water sector. *Policy & Politics, 42*(1), 71–88.

Mukhtarov, F., Brock, A., Janssen, S., & Guignier, A. (2013). Actors and strategies in translating global conservation narratives to Vietnam: An agency perspective. *Policy and Society, 32*(2), 113–124. https://doi.org/10.1016/j.polsoc.2013.05.006

Mützelburg, I. (2018). L'empowerment par des financements internationaux ? Comment les donateurs créent un secteur non étatique en Ukraine. *Revue Gouvernance, 15*(1), 63–85.

Mützelburg, I. (2020a). Remote management of the European neighbourhood policy. The neoliberal bureaucratisation of a non-governmental sector in Ukraine. *Revue D'études Comparatives Est-Ouest, 4*, 45–75.

Mützelburg, I. (2020b). Produire des passeurs: Une stratégie de transfert de normes internationales. *Revue Française De Science Politique, 70*(5), 595–615.

Nilsson, M., & Silander, D. (2016). Democracy and security in the EU's Eastern neighborhood? Assessing the ENP in Georgia, Moldova, and Ukraine. *Democracy and Security, 12*(1), 44–61. https://doi.org/10.1080/17419166.2015.1135744

No Borders. (2011). *Annual Report 2011.* No Borders. http://noborders.org.ua/en/files/2012/04/annual-report-2011.pdf

Noutcheva, G. (2009). Fake, partial and imposed compliance: The limits of the EU's normative power in the Western Balkans. *Journal of European Public Policy, 16*(7), 1065–1084.

Peshkopia, R. (2005). Asylum in the Balkans: European Union and United Nations High Commissioner for Refugees assistance to Balkan countries for establishing asylum systems. *Southeast European and Black Sea Studies, 5*(2), 213–241. https://doi.org/10.1080/14683850500122869

Petrova, I., & Delcour, L. (2020). From principle to practice? The resilience–local ownership nexus in the EU Eastern Partnership policy. *Contemporary*

Security Policy, 41(2), 336–360. https://doi.org/10.1080/13523260.2019.1678280
Pleines, H. (2016a). Oligarchs and politics in Ukraine. *Demokratizatsiya: The Journal of Post-Soviet Democratization, 24*(1), 105–127.
Pleines, H. (2016b). From competitive authoritarianism to defective democracy: Political regimes in Ukraine before and after the orange Revolution. In M. Klein, H.-H. Schröder, & S. Stewart (Eds.), *Presidents, oligarchs and bureaucrats: Forms of rule in the post-soviet space* (pp. 125–137). Routledge.
Rechitsky, R. (2016). Global migration and extraterritorial controls: The case of international refugee policy in Ukraine. *International Journal of Sociology, 46*(3), 169–188. https://doi.org/10.1080/00207659.2016.1163990
Revel, J. (Ed.). (1996). *Jeux d'échelles. La micro-analyse à l'expérience*. Seuil.
Rijpma, J. J., & Cremona, M. (2007). *The extra-territorialisation of EU migration policies and the rule of law* [Working Paper]. European University Institute. https://cadmus.eui.eu//handle/1814/6690
Rose, R. (1991). What is lesson-drawing? *Journal of Public Policy, 11*(01), 3–30. https://doi.org/10.1017/S0143814X00004918
Saguin, K., & Howlett, M. (2019). Policy transfer and instrument constituency: Explaining the adoption of conditional cash transfer in the Philippines. *Asia & the Pacific Policy Studies, 6*(3), 352–366. https://doi.org/10.1002/app5.280
Samokhvalov, V. (2015). Ukraine between Russia and the European union: Triangle revisited. *Europe-Asia Studies, 67*(9), 1371–1393. https://doi.org/10.1080/09668136.2015.1088513
Sampson, S. (2004). Too much civil society? Donor-driven human rights NGOs in the balkans. In L. Dhundale (Ed.), *Revisiting the role of civil society in the promotion of human rights*. Danish Institute for Human Rights.
Saurugger, S., & Terpan, F. (2013). Resisting EU norms. A framework for analysis. *Sciences Po Grenoble Working Paper, n°2.*
Schimmelfennig, F. (2015). Europeanization beyond Europe. *Living Revue European Governance, 10*(1). http://www.europeangovernance-livingreviews.org/Articles/lreg-2015-1/
Schimmelfennig, F., & Sedelmeier, U. (2004). Governance by conditionality: EU rule transfer to the candidate countries of Central and Eastern Europe. *Journal of European Public Policy, 11*(4), 661–679. https://doi.org/10.1080/1350176042000248089
Schimmelfennig, F., & Sedelmeier, U. (2005). Conceptualizing the Europeanization of Central And Eastern Europe. In *The Europeanization Of Central And Eastern Europe* (pp. 1–28). Cornell University Press.
Schuster, L. (2004a). Chapter 3: Constructions of the refugee problem since the second world war. In *The use and abuse of political Asylum in Britain and Germany* (pp. 97–129). Routledge.

Schuster, L. (2004b). *The use and abuse of political Asylum in Britain and Germany*. Routledge.

Scott, J. C. (1990). *Domination and the arts of resistance: Hidden transcripts*. Yale University Press.

Sedelmeier, U. (2006). Europeanisation in new member and candidate states. *Living Rev. Euro. Gov., 1*. http://europeangovernance.livingreviews.org/Articles/lreg-2006-3/

Shevel, O. (2011). *Migration, refugee policy, and state building in postcommunist Europe*. Cambridge University Press.

Sigman, C. (2013). Le « nouveau management public » en Russie. *Gouvernement Et Action Publique, 3*, 441–460.

Smith, A. (2013). Transferts institutionnels et politiques de concurrence. *Gouvernement Et Action Publique, 3*, 415–440.

Smith, N. (2004). Scale bending and the fate of the national. In E. Sheppard & R. B. McMaster (Eds.), *Scale and geographic inquiry: Nature, society, and method* (pp. 192–212). Wiley-Blackwell.

Spire, A. (2008). *Accueillir ou reconduire: Enquête sur les guichets de l'immigration*. Raisons d'agir.

Stone, D. (2012). Transfer and translation of policy. *Policy Studies, 33*(6), 483–499.

Stone, D., Porto de Oliveira, O., & Pal, L. A. (2020). Transnational policy transfer: The circulation of ideas, power and development models. *Policy and Society, 39*(1), 1–18. https://doi.org/10.1080/14494035.2019.1619325

Stubbs, P. (2005). Stretching concepts too far? Multi-level governance, policy transfer and the politics of scale in South-eastern Europe. *South East European Politics, 6*(2), 66–87.

Tulmets, E., Vieira, A., & Ferreira-Pereira, L. C. (2018). Introduction: Competing conditionalities? Eastern Europe and the South Caucasus between the European Union and Russia. *European Politics and Society, 19*(4), 451–470. https://doi.org/10.1080/23745118.2018.1456745

UNHCR. (2013). *Ukraine as a country of asylum. Observations on the situation of asylum-seekers and refugees in Ukraine*.

Vachudová, M. A. (2005). *Europe undivided: Democracy, leverage, and integration after communism*. Oxford University Press.

Wallace, T., Bonstein, L., & Chapman, J. (2007). *The aid chain: Coercion and commitment in development NGOs*. Practical Action.

Weber, M. (1922). *Wirtschaft und Gesellschaft—Grundriß der verstehenden Soziologie (Economy and society—An outline of interpretative sociology)* (G. Roth & C. Wittich, Eds.). University of California Press.

Wedel, J. (2004). Studying through' a globalizing world: Building method through aidnographies. In J. Gould & H. Secher (Eds.),

Ethnographies of aid: Exploring development texts and encounters (pp. 149–174). Roskilde University IDS Occasional Paper 24. ojs.ruc.dk/index.php/ocpa/article/viewFile/3883/2058

Wetzel, A. (2016). From halt to hurry: External and domestic influences on Ukrainian asylum policy. *Eurasian Geography and Economics, 57*(1), 66–88.

Wolczuk, K. (2008). Ukraine and its relations with the EU in the context of the European neighbourhood policy. In S. Fischer (Ed.), *Ukraine: Quo Vadis?* (Institute for Security Studies, pp. 87–118). www.iss.europa.eu/uploads/media/cp108.pdf

Wolczuk, K. (2009). Implementation without coordination: The impact of EU conditionality on Ukraine under the European neighbourhood policy. *Europe-Asia Studies, 61*(2), 187–211.

Wolczuk, K. (2019). State building and European integration in Ukraine. *Eurasian Geography and Economics, 60*(6), 736–754. https://doi.org/10.1080/15387216.2019.1655463

Wunderlich, D. (2012). The limits of external governance: Implementing EU external migration policy. *Journal of European Public Policy, 19*(9), 1414–1433. https://doi.org/10.1080/13501763.2012.672106

Zhyznomirska, L. (2006). Externalities of the EU immigration and Asylum policy: The case of Ukraine. *Review of European and Russian Affairs, 2.*

Zimmer, K. (2008). Migrants and refugees in the buffer zone: Asylum policy in Ukraine. *Migrationonline.Cz*, 1–9.

Zimmer, K. (2010). The implementation of migration policy in Ukraine: Autonomous or directed? *SEER: Journal for Labour and Social Affairs in Eastern Europe, 13*(3), 343–353.

Zimmermann, L. (2016). Same same or different? Norm diffusion between resistance, compliance, and localization in post-conflict states. *International Studies Perspectives, 17*(1), 98–115.

Zwingel, S. (2012). How do norms travel? Theorizing international women's rights in transnational perspective1. *International Studies Quarterly, 56*(1), 115–129. https://doi.org/10.1111/j.1468-2478.2011.00701.x

PART I

The Legislative Adoption of Asylum Norms in Ukraine: A Process Driven by International Actors

The introduction of external norms into a country's domestic legislation has often been analysed as a result, rather than as a process. This result-oriented perspective has obscured important factors shaping the transfer of norms. It has caused the norms' legislative adoption process to appear as unproblematic, entailing low material and political costs. The first part of this research challenges the view that the adoption of external norms in EU neighbouring states has been smooth and complete. Instead of assuming from the very beginning that the transfer of norms truly happened, this research investigates the reasons for and the process of adoption of international asylum norms. Tracing the developments of the Ukrainian asylum legislation back to its origins in the early 1990s, I bring to light the complexity of the underlying reasons for the adoption and the diversity of the involved actors. This first part challenges the widespread binary classification opposing adoption and the absence of adoption of international norms. It shows that the translation of international norms into Ukrainian law was gradual, partial, and heterogeneous.

Law-making and transfer activities via law-making use and confirm the national scale as the relevant one to define asylum policies. They confer actors with a national scale identity legitimacy to shape the process. Fashioning asylum policies via law-making means that the development of these policies is affected by national institutions and national political elites' interests and beliefs. Beginning with macro-perspectives and gradually moving to meso perspectives on the legislative establishment of asylum in Ukraine, this part will shed light on the role of the domestic context, the volatile phases of the recent Ukrainian history, and different actors' beliefs, interests, and strategies.

CHAPTER 2

An Unfavourable Domestic Context for Asylum Policies

This chapter presents the context into which international asylum norms have been imported, focusing on two factors that, according to transfer research, shape the effects of transfer attempts: domestic political interests and domestic social norms. It highlights the history of migration predominantly from the Commonwealth of Independent States (CIS), the prevailing xenophobia towards non-CIS foreigners, and the gradual development of restrictive immigration policies towards them. Moreover, the lack of asylum as a traditional norm in the post-Soviet context, and competing political priorities favouring Ukrainian citizens and political ties with CIS states mean that domestic interests and normative misfit have been likely to hinder the transfer of international asylum norms to Ukraine.

Unwelcoming Treatment of "Non-Traditional" Immigrants: From Soviet Immigration Control to Restrictive Contemporary Ukrainian Immigration Policies

A young man from Sri Lanka told me how he was caught by policemen on a train in Ukraine without a proof of legal status. He explained to them

I. Mützelburg, *Transferring Asylum Norms to EU Neighbours*, The European Union in International Affairs, https://doi.org/10.1007/978-3-031-04528-8_2

that he wanted to apply for asylum but was arrested, brought to the police station, and beaten up there the whole night. (May 2014)

A Somali man who spoke fluent Russian reported that "Sometimes there are police controls but with a document it's better. If the policeman already knows this document then there is no difficulty. [...] But I can speak the language. I can explain my situation and so on... then it's ok." (April 2014)

An Iranian middle-aged man told me that it took him three years to obtain status as a refugee. He had to go through the procedure four times as a result of needing to start over for various reasons. "I was controlled by the militia: usually I preferred to pay 40 or 50 UAH and get away. If you don't pay, you are taken to the militia office. And then they let you wait one or two days before you can call the Migration Service. The Migration Service doesn't work on Saturdays or Sundays. Also they generally don't pick up the phone. So it's better to pay. [...] It's better now with the militia, though. Three to four years ago you could be stopped ten times on one day by the militia. The militia saw you are a foreigner and stopped you. [...] If I have documents there are no problems. I think the militia feels that you are afraid when you don't have documents and so they stop you for a control. What helped me were the documents and wearing a tie. I told my friends to wear a tie against the police. [...] Black people walk around in groups for their safety. It's more difficult for them because Ukrainians don't like black people." (May 2014)

Foreign-looking migrants in Ukraine regularly report spontaneous police controls in the street, the need to bribe to avoid being arrested, and sometimes physical and verbal abuse from police. They usually describe the asylum procedure as long, complicated, and arbitrary. These micro-accounts hint to racist police behaviour, irregular administrative practices in treating asylum applications, and migrants' partial agency in dealing with officials. They can be better understood when combined with macro-contextualisation, taking into account the Soviet and post-Soviet Ukrainian history of migration policies.

Oxana Shevel has argued that after independence in 1991, Ukraine had to build up its asylum policies "from scratch" (Shevel, 2011, p. 3). While it is true that the newly independent Ukrainian state had little legal or institutional basis in the area of migration, asylum policies did not appear ex nihilo. The political context in which these policies and instruments were developed was shaped by historical experiences and norms, such as Soviet xenophobia and categorisations of migrants.

The first protection seekers in Ukraine in the late 1980s and early 1990s had fled conflict-ridden (former) Soviet Republics (namely Azerbaijan, Uzbekistan, Transnistria, Abkhazia, and Chechnya); they were largely perceived as domestic and not as foreign. However, the composition of the asylum flows evolved in the following years, shifting towards an influx of migrants from more distant countries. Since the mid-1990s, the number of asylum seekers from Azerbaijan, Georgia, and Russia (especially from Chechnya), Kyrgyzstan, Uzbekistan, Armenia, and Belarus decreased. Instead, most asylum seekers came from outside the former USSR. Afghans were the major group because of ties and networks which dated back to the Soviet Union.

Due to conflicts and crises in their home countries, the influx of asylum seekers of other nationalities, namely those from Syria, Somalia, Congo, Iraq, and Palestine, fluctuated. Congolese immigrants were present in relatively large numbers since 1997. Between 2008 and 2013, Somalia was one of the major countries of origin. Since 2011, a large number of Syrians arrived in Ukraine. Between 2007 and 2009, a significant portion of asylum seekers came from Pakistan and India. In more fluctuating proportions since 1998 came asylum seekers from Iraq and Sudan. Minor countries of origin were Bangladesh, Iran, and Ethiopia.

The treatment of asylum seekers in Ukraine has been shaped by the treatment of immigrants more generally. Indeed, the Soviet legacy of xenophobia and the gradual elaboration of selective immigration policies have constituted an unwelcoming context for asylum seekers in Ukraine.

The Soviet Legacy of Xenophobia in Post-Soviet Ukraine

Soviet-era experience has shaped the perception of foreigners in contemporary Ukraine. While tsarist immigration policies had actively recruited immigrants, the Soviet Union halted immigration (e.g. of Korean and Chinese populations) and expelled many of its foreign residents (Light, 2012, p. 401). The Soviet Union controlled and restricted immigration and emigration. The regime attempted to shelter its population from foreign influences which might have destabilised the state. It therefore strongly limited foreign travel of its own citizens abroad as well as foreign tourism to the USSR. Emigration of Soviet citizens was equally restricted (especially until the 1970s, but even then remained limited) and immigration to the Soviet Union was an exception. The USSR did not have official immigration objectives, quotas, or laws. Instead, immigration was only permitted in exceptional cases, primarily via ad hoc political decisions and agreements with some foreign governments of socialist and allied "developing" countries (e.g. Cuba and Vietnam) that could send a limited number of "guest workers" and students (Katsakioris, 2016; Light, 2012, p. 402; Mellakh, 2016). Moreover, the demand to immigrate to the USSR was modest.

Soviet citizens therefore primarily encountered Soviet migrants. Both despite and because of the Soviet government's attempts to regulate internal migration (e.g. via resettlement), Soviet citizens moved from one republic to another. Soviet citizens came to Ukraine primarily from Central Asian republics (especially Kazakhstan), the North Caucasus, Transcaucasia, and the Central Black Earth Region of the Russian Soviet Federative Socialist Republic (Pribytkova, 2011; Vollmer & Malynovska, 2016, pp. 17, 21). Direct contact with non-Soviet citizens was an exception, which might partly account for xenophobia in the Soviet Union.

Moreover, Soviet policies institutionalised national territories, that is, bounded subunits of the Soviet state, each named after a titular nation whose inhabitants benefited from affirmative action and preferential treatment in addition to Russians (Brubaker, 1994). The tension between this ethnoterritorial federalism and the attribution of nationalities to individuals by descent as well as major migratory movements (especially of "ethnic Russians") fuelled fears in various areas that the titular nation could become "denationalised", that is, that it could become a minority in its "own" republic (Brubaker, 1992). While the situation was much less controversial in Ukraine than in the Baltic republics, Soviet internal migratory policies may have contributed more generally to producing foreigners as a threatening "other".

By denying the existence of racism in the USSR, and thus excluding any debate for decades, Soviet authorities fostered hostile attitudes towards foreigners. The official narrative maintained that racism did not exist and could not exist in the Soviet Union. Such a discourse was based on the contention that socialism excluded racism while racism in the West (e.g. in the shape of colonialism) was condemned (Zakharov, 2015, p. 34). Race was often framed "as a socio-historical backwardness, not biological inferiority, with some ethnoracial groups seen as doomed to extinction and others persecuted for having the 'wrong' ethnic origins and claims to group identity" (Law, 2012, p. 144). An example of this was Soviet anti-Muslim policies and violations of Muslim rights. African and Asian people were often considered inferior and backward, which also served to justify the Soviet civilising mission (Zakharov, 2015, p. 34). Soviet popular culture depicted Africans as racially or culturally different (e.g. as not worrying about the future and never working). Paternalistic and condescending attitudes towards Africans turned into hostility and racist aggression against African students in the USSR at the time of the perestroika, when Soviet citizens suffered economic hardship and felt that the USSR was "feeding" Africa and paying for African students (Matusevich, 2009).

In post-Soviet Ukraine, society tends to distinguish between Slavic and non-Slavic immigrants. Nataliia Pribytkova pointed out the discrepancies between the treatment of fellow post-Soviet citizens (especially Slavic ones) and others, "Ukrainian society is friendly and tolerant primarily to the ethnic groups that traditionally live in such countries as Ukraine, Russia, Belarus, but the attitude is worse towards people of other nationalities and races, and those who live in countries which are poorer than Ukraine" (Aleksynska, 2011; Pribytkova, 2015, p. 163). Since the beginning of the full-scale Russian invasion in February 2022, these statements about friendly attitudes towards Russians certainly need to be qualified. Nativist patriotism has spread and become normalised in post-Soviet Ukraine, for example through schoolbooks and politicians' speeches (Gorbach & Budraitskis, 2017). Scholars as well as international and non-governmental organisations have reported regular incidents of discrimination and violence against persons of foreign appearance, including among state authorities and namely the police (European Commission Against Racism and Intolerance—Council of Europe, 2012, pp. 7–8; Ghosh, 2010, pp. 28–31; Rechitsky, 2016, p. 177). Asylum seekers have often needed to bribe officials in order for their documents to be processed, and foreign-looking people have faced racial profiling by the police, also leading to bribes (Düvell, 2008; Kazmierkiewicz, 2011, p. 60). Xenophobia and corruption of state authorities have thus reinforced each other—especially in the case of non-Slavic immigrants.

Ukrainian policies and attitudes towards immigrants have been shaped by a distinction between three groups: "traditional" and "non-traditional" migrants, and "ethnic Ukrainians". Indeed, contemporary Ukrainian migration policies, societal attitudes and many Ukrainian scholars distinguish between "traditional" immigrants (that is, citizens from other former Soviet republics, who are not considered Ukrainians) and "non-traditional" immigrants (a vague group defined negatively: people who are not from Europe, North America, or the post-Soviet space—primarily people from African and Asian countries) (Braichevska et al., 2004; Popson, 2000). This reflects the persistence of Soviet categories of thought and of a logic of proximity, according to which immigrants from former Soviet republics are perceived and treated differently than other immigrants. For instance, the category of traditional immigrants does not include Afghans, notwithstanding the fact that their presence and regular immigration flows to Ukraine date back to the Soviet Union when Afghans came to pursue their studies.

"Non-traditional" immigrants have been present in lower numbers than "traditional" immigrants and have often been in more precarious situations in contemporary Ukraine. In the 2000s, the number of immigrants who were not from CIS countries increased, but stayed lower than that of CIS citizens—at least in terms of immigrants with formal status (Kazmierkiewicz, 2011, p. 24). Vietnamese, Chinese, Pakistani, Indian, Israeli, Afghan, Iranian, Nigerian, Somali, and Turkish immigrants were the major groups in Ukraine who were not from the CIS. They came to Ukraine to work or study—some of them during the USSR (Braichevska et al., 2004, pp. 1–2). Foreign students have represented an important and increasing share among the immigrant population in Ukraine and most of them have come from non-CIS countries. However, many foreign students have encountered difficulties during their studies in Ukraine (linguistic problems, discrimination, lack of financial means, the necessity to work in irregular and poorly paid jobs in parallel to their studies, higher costs due to corruption, agents' deceit, etc.). Many have therefore been forced to drop out of their studies, which meant that they lost their legal status and often remained in Ukraine under precarious conditions (The "Social Action" Centre—"No Borders" project & Minority Rights Group International, 2011, pp. 67–69). Far more non-traditional, unofficialised immigrants are estimated to live in Ukraine than what statistics suggest. Numbers are very controversial and estimations vary between 60,000 and 1.6 million. "Non-traditional migrants" apprehended without regular status were primarily from China, India, Pakistan, Vietnam, Afghanistan and Somalia (Düvell & Vollmer, 2009, pp. 20–22; Tolstokorova, 2011,

p. 14). The media and policy-oriented research have reinforced xenophobia in Ukrainian society by associating irregular immigration with criminality and violence and depicting it in a negative light.

Building up a Ukrainian State and Establishing Selective Immigration Policies

In the course of its state-building process, the Ukrainian state has increasingly sought to control migration movements. It has elaborated differential immigration policies for different groups of migrants, has tried to strengthen its borders, and has joined European agreements to control migration.

The Ukrainian state has facilitated the immigration of "traditional" immigrants and of "ethnic Ukrainians". From the early 1990s until the early 2000s, several million people moved from the former Soviet Union to Ukraine, which is mostly attributed to "return migration", though a share of the migrants had never lived in Ukraine but were descendants of inhabitants of Ukraine (Vollmer et al., 2010, p. 23). These "return migrations" or migrations of "ethnic affinity" (Brubaker, 1992) are the tributaries of Soviet migration policies and deportations. In the course of the migratory history of the USSR, persons considered ethnic Ukrainians but also other groups living in Ukraine (for example Crimean Tatars, Greek, Bulgarians, Armenians, and Germans) were deported to other regions of the Soviet Union. These groups partly returned to Ukraine in the aftermath of independence and made up the majority of the immigrants who moved to Ukraine at this time (Malynovska, 2006). These five million "ethnic Ukrainians", born in other Soviet Socialist Republics, have rarely been seen as immigrants in Ukraine. Migration policies of the new Ukrainian state actively encouraged the return of these "ethnic Ukrainians", and to a lesser degree, of traditional ethnic minorities from Ukraine, especially Crimean Tatars (OSCE, 2007).

In addition to this encouraged "ethnic" or "return" migration, CIS citizens have been able to move easily to Ukraine. At least until the full-scale Russian invasion in 2022, citizens of the Russian Federation and, to a lesser extent, from Moldova, Belarus, Armenia, Georgia, Kazakhstan, Azerbaijan, and Uzbekistan, represented by far the largest group among the legal and permanent immigrants in Ukraine. The visa regime and the largely open borders within the CIS facilitated this mobility. Indeed, after the collapse of the Soviet Union, borders which had been internal, administrative borders became state borders. De facto, however, these borders at the north and east of Ukraine remained largely uncontrolled and open to the movement of foreign citizens (Chindea et al., 2008, p. 33). After the beginning of the war in the Donbas in 2014, Ukraine's Eastern borders became more uncertain, subject to military fights, but also more controlled through the establishment of checkpoints between the Russia-backed republics and the government-controlled areas. The Belarusian state also increasingly marked and controlled the border with Ukraine (Eckert, 2017; Eckert & Lambroschini, 2017; Shukan, 2017). In 2021, during tensions and orchestrated migratory influx from Belarus to Poland and Lithuania, the Ukrainian state strengthened its controls on the Ukrainian side of the border with Belarus. However, the visa-free regime shared by most CIS countries has continued to facilitate the mobility of CIS citizens who can live and work in Ukraine for 90 days without a visa.

With the new phase of the Russian-Ukrainian war in 2022, Russian travel to Ukraine became more restricted. In July 2022, Ukraine introduced a visa regime for Russian citizens. By that time, visa-freedom has been maintained for Belarusian citizens but the Ukrainian authorities recommend travellers from Belarus to bring documentary evidence of the purpose of their trip to Ukraine. Moreover, all checkpoints between Russia and Ukraine as well as Belarus and Ukraine being closed, residents of these two countries need to travel via a third country.

While mobility within most of the CIS has been encouraged, the Ukrainian state gradually tried to regulate unwanted migration flows into, through and out of Ukraine—insisting increasingly on the importance of the legality of migration, especially since 2001. The state defined which groups of immigrants were desirable and which were not, following categories of socio-economic status (e.g. introduction of a yearly quota system in 2001) and of the country of origin (e.g. since 2005, facilitation of immigration for citizens from the CIS, Europe and North America vs. restrictions for citizens of other countries). The Ukrainian state has passed laws and undertaken measures to fight irregular immigration since 1996 (e.g. liabilities for transport companies, stricter procedures for student visas, stronger border control, detention and to a lesser extent deportation of migrants without a regular visa or residence permit). Since 1998, it has also sought to reduce human trafficking by increasingly criminalising it. The rhetoric employed in legal and executive documents has constructed irregular immigration as a security threat. For instance, the Decrees on Improvements of the State Migration Policy of Ukraine of 2007 and on the Concept of the State Migration Policy of 2011 stated that irregular migration represented a serious threat to national security of Ukraine and therefore called for measures to fight such migration, including by harmonising the Ukrainian legislation with European and international standards. Even though the Ukrainian state treated unwanted immigrants increasingly harshly, in practice the state was unable to fully control the borders and often failed to deport irregularised migrants.

This growing attention to the control of unwanted migration accompanied a general process of state building in the course of which Ukrainian politicians and authorities tried to gain control over the national territory and the people living on it. It is related, as well, to the inclusion of Ukraine into international migratory movements and control attempts. The Ukrainian state thus developed legislation and participated in international agreements regulating the mobility of its own citizens abroad (e.g. on labour migration, border traffic, and irregular migration) and in the fight against irregular migration across its territory. Indeed, since 1993 Ukraine has signed various readmission agreements, including the EU-Ukraine agreement, which became effective for Ukrainian nationals in 2008 and for third-country nationals in 2010 (European Union & Ukraine, 2007). The circulation of international norms and Ukraine's inclusion in international migration regimes thus contributed to the development of restrictive migration policies in the Ukrainian state. While the development of restrictive migration policies thus benefited from the political context and widespread social norms, the development of asylum policies faced a lack of idealistic value attributed to asylum.

The Low Domestic Prioritisation of Asylum: From Weak Soviet Heritage to Competing Political Priorities in Contemporary Ukraine

Sparse International Asylum Norms Under Soviet Rule

In the USSR, political asylum was very different from the Western understanding of asylum. The Soviet Union did not take part in the international asylum regime and did not accede to the 1951 Refugee Convention nor the 1976 Protocol. Nevertheless, the Constitution of the USSR (article 38) referred to asylum. Yet, in the absence of asylum laws or administration, it was the Presidium of the Supreme Soviet itself that individually attributed the asylum status to a few pro-communist activists from states of the Western block (Shevel, 2011, p. 3; Vollmer & Malynovska, 2016, p. 24). Asylum was only very occasionally used for political purposes in the context of the Cold War, namely to demonstrate the Soviet ideological superiority vis-à-vis the Western block. The contemporary international principle of asylum has therefore little historical foundations in Ukraine.

Nevertheless, in the late 1980s, facing fleeing people from other Soviet Republics, the Ukrainian Soviet Socialist Republic undertook measures to coordinate employment, accommodations, and material assistance for these Soviet citizens (Frejka et al., 1999, p. 4). In 1988–1989, people from Azerbaijan as well as Meskhetian-Turks from Uzbekistan fled to Ukraine. In its first years of existence, the newly independent Ukrainian state continued to host and to care for further groups of fugitives from former Soviet Republics. Ukraine faced the arrival of more than 60,000 people fleeing the conflict in Transnistria in 1992 (Malynovska, 2006). Out of the 15,000 people arriving in Ukraine as a consequence of the conflict in Abkhazia, 3000 obtained "war refugee status" (Söderköping/Cross-Border Cooperation Process, 2008, p. 56). In 1994 and 1995, about 5000 people entered Ukraine annually as they fled the violence in their countries of origin (Armenia, Azerbaijan, Georgia, Tajikistan, and Russia) and requested help from authorities in Ukraine. First the Ukrainian Soviet Socialist Republic, then the newly independent Ukrainian state adapted to the new challenges of arriving war fugitives. However, in the first years, these challenges continued to correspond to the logic of proximity, consisting of supporting "traditional" immigrants from (former) Soviet Republics. Indeed, these measures, instead of legislative and general, were procedures of temporary and executive nature, directed explicitly and exclusively at specific national groups.

No Public Interest in Asylum

Even though the Ukrainian authorities have implemented general asylum laws since 1996, asylum has remained in the Ukrainian context of the last decades a minor issue by comparison to domestically more prominent and prioritised migratory phenomena. Between 1000 and 3000 asylum applications have been handed in every year. By comparison to Western

European states, the number of asylum seekers in Ukraine has been very low.[1]

Probably due to the small size of this population and the limited Soviet tradition of asylum, asylum seekers and refugees did not have a public group image or reputation of their own in the first three decades of independent Ukraine. The level of knowledge and awareness of asylum was very low in the Ukrainian population, and as a result asylum seekers and refugees were often assimilated with other groups of migrants. The usual terms to designate refugees "беженец" (biezheniets) in Russian and "біженець" (bizhenets) in Ukrainian stem from the verbs meaning "run", "run away" or "avoid somebody or something". According to an interview conducted for this research with a local employee of UNHCR (2013), this term may account for some Ukrainians' image of refugees as avoiding prosecution (rather than persecution) for crimes they have committed. Immigration in general was not a major issue in election campaigns and was rarely debated in the Ukrainian public. More generally, in the states of the Eastern Partnership, few political debates took place around migration issues (Makaryan, 2015). Occasionally, however, politicians warned about Ukraine being swamped by foreigners, or underlined the link between immigration and security threats (European Commission Against Racism and Intolerance—Council of Europe, 2012, p. 20; Ghosh, 2010, p. 31; Zhyznomirska, 2006). The media contributed to the proliferation of the negative perception of immigrants in Ukrainian society through its claims that immigrants lead to the dumping of salaries, harm the Ukrainian economy because they transfer the major part of their salary abroad, carry exotic and infectious diseases, do not want to integrate, and are sources of terrorism, crime, and drug abuse.

The negative Ukrainian media coverage of immigration and the increased influx of asylum seekers in Europe since 2015 have generated more hostile attitudes towards asylum in Ukraine. While Ukraine was barely touched by the increased migration of asylum seekers into Europe, local anti-refugee initiatives and protests occasionally arose. For example, right-wing activists and inhabitants of Yahotyn, in the region of Kyiv, demonstrated their opposition to the opening of an accommodation centre for recognised refugees in their neighbourhood—and managed to prevent it from opening (Kozak, 2016; Prozorova, 2016;

[1] For instance, according to UNHCR, in Spain, a country of similar population size, about 120,000 people applied for asylum in 2019, 65,000 in 2021.

'Siriytsy pod Kiyevom. Ukraintsy protiv migrantov (Syrians are near Kyiv. Ukrainians are against the migrants)', 2016). Right-wing movements such as Svoboda, Right Sector, and Azov, inspired by their contacts with European colleagues, benefited from the media coverage of the European "refugee crisis" and contributed to the "outburst of long-distance racism" (Gorbach & Budraitskis, 2017). This right-wing mobilisation of the coverage of the influx of refugees into Europe has deepened the cleavage between pro-European liberals calling for the respect of the principle of asylum and nationalists who proclaimed "the decline of the west". Nevertheless, asylum in Ukraine has overall not been a salient political issue.

Ukrainians Seeking Protection Abroad from the 2022 War
Reading about asylum in Ukraine may seem inappropriate at a time when millions of people have been displaced within and out of Ukraine due to the Russian invasion. Yet, this book can help understand the situation of Ukrainians who are abroad now, their relations to other foreigners and to their own situation as "refugees". In the last thirty years, xenophobia has been widespread and non-Western and non-Slavic migrants have had a difficult stance in Ukraine. Many Ukrainians have been convinced that Western Europe made a mistake in accepting too many foreigners but many were also aware of the fact that being a refugee in Europe meant low social status and bad treatment. Most Ukrainians had very little knowledge about asylum and were unaware of the existence of asylum policies, asylum seekers and recognised refugees in Ukraine. Ukrainians who left their country since February 2022, many of whom obtained a temporary protection status in the host country, deal in different ways with the label "refugee". Part of them refer to themselves as "refugees", while others reject the term as it has a negative connotation in their ears or as it suggests that they would stay in the host country for a prolonged period while they expect to return to Ukraine soon.

Even before Russia's full-scale invasion in 2022, Ukrainians saw their country primarily as a country of emigration, instead of immigration. Between the country's independence in 1991 and early 2022, several million Ukrainians have emigrated to the EU, North America, Israel and Russia. In 2022, several million more (by July 2022 around 6 million according to UNHCR) left Ukraine for an uncertain duration to escape the war. While Ukrainian emigration was considered a major problem for the country already prior to 2022, immigration to Ukraine was ignored or considered irrelevant. It was thought unlikely that foreigners would want to live in Ukraine while Ukrainians wished to emigrate. Moreover, many Ukrainians have suspected asylum seekers in Ukraine of wishing to move on to the EU. As a country perceived by its own inhabitants and by external observers as a transit country, many Ukrainians, including politicians, deemed Ukraine not responsible for asylum seekers' rights and well-being.

After the emergence of internally displaced persons (IDPs) in Ukraine in 2014, the care for foreign asylum seekers and refugees was seen as even less important. The annexation of Crimea, the war, the creation of two Russia-backed republics, and the economic difficulties in the Donbas led to a large number of Ukrainian IDPs for whom the Ukrainian state struggled to provide. The term refugee ("беженец"/"біженець") was then used to refer to Ukrainian IDPs, which caused confusion between the two groups. That IDPs were greater in number than "foreign refugees" and that that they were Ukrainian citizens (they were commonly referred to as "*our* refugees") turned IDPs into a more prominent public policy problem than "foreign refugees". In addition to the IDPs, many Ukrainians were destitute and received little support from the state. Many of my Ukrainian interviewees, even the more pro-asylum ones, pointed out the socio-economic difficulties of Ukrainians that the state did not manage to address. Consequently they raised doubts about the legitimacy of prioritising asylum policies, which would mean using state funds on foreigners rather than destitute Ukrainian citizens. The problems faced by the Ukrainian state and its citizens have become a lot more fundamental and pressing since the new phase of the Russian invasion in 2022. The situation of foreign asylum seekers and refugees, if they have remained in Ukraine, has become even more marginal. In the first half of 2022, only about a hundred people applied for asylum in Ukraine.

Even before 2022, apart from economic considerations opposing the spending of parts of the limited Ukrainian state budget on foreigners, asylum encountered further political obstacles. Attributing refugee status to nationals of another country always means undermining state sovereignty to control its citizens and questioning its image as a democracy governed by the rule of law (Schuster, 2004). It presupposes that the refugee-hosting state has the willingness and the power to defend this critical position and is able to protect its territory (and thus the refugee) against the intervention of the state of origin. Until the early

2010s, both the willingness to prioritise asylum over interstate relations and the capacity to defend this position were missing in Ukraine. In the case of citizens from CIS countries, namely from Russia, Uzbekistan, and Tajikistan, international organisations documented series of cases of refoulement, that is, the forcible transfer of persons to a place where they face a risk of serious human rights violations or abuses (Amnesty International, 2013; ECRE, 2007). According to these reports, these CIS states prosecuted some of their citizens under criminal charges, while actually criminalising them for political reasons. Ukrainian authorities blocked access to the asylum procedure or to the refugee status for these CIS citizens and also extradited some of them to their country of origin. Between 2008 and 2012, the number of documented cases of refoulement per year ranged from 3 to 17. International organisations explain this practice by referring to the Ukrainian politicians' wish to avoid endangering harmonious relations with other CIS states. In some cases, documentation suggests that CIS protection seekers were abducted from the Ukrainian territory and reappeared in prison in their home country. It is usually unclear to what extent the Ukrainian authorities were actively or passively involved in this informal forced return (Amnesty International, 2013, p. 32; 'Razvozzhayev Rozpoviv Povnu Versiyu Yoho Vykradennya (Razvozzhayev Told the Full Version of His Abduction)', 2012; Shpigov, 2012). In any case it meant that the Ukrainian state was not able or not willing to protect certain CIS protection seekers from their state's authorities.

Conclusion

The Ukrainian domestic context to which international actors tried to transfer asylum norms was unfavourable. Society and lawmakers firstly viewed asylum as a migration issue. It was therefore affected by the perceptions and policies in the field of migration. The lack of encounters with non-CIS ("non-traditional") immigrants, the ensuing xenophobia, and the development of restrictive immigration policies towards non-CIS and socio-economically unattractive immigrants placed "non-traditional" asylum seekers into a hostile setting. Moreover, asylum in Ukraine had not been valued highly in the past, given that it was used only occasionally for political purposes in the Soviet Union. In contemporary Ukraine, asylum has been an issue without public interest. It was undermined by competing political considerations such as migration and flight of

Ukrainians, difficulties of ensuring the public social support of destitute Ukrainians, and the protection of cooperative political relations with CIS countries whose political elites might be upset by the recognition of their political opponents as refugees. These obstacles cut across various scales, obstructing the establishment of asylum in Ukraine.

Neither preferential nor normative fit, the two factors that, according to scholars, shape the adoption of foreign norms and policies, smoothed the way for the transfer of international asylum norms to Ukraine (Dimitrova & Dragneva, 2013; Tulmets, 2014). The following chapter explores how and why—despite the clear lack of a favourable domestic context—Ukrainian legislators nevertheless integrated international asylum norms into Ukrainian law in the three decades following the independence of the state.

References

Aleksynska, M. (2011). Relative deprivation, relative satisfaction, and attitudes towards immigrants: Evidence from Ukraine. *Economic Systems, 35*(2), 189–207. https://doi.org/10.1016/j.ecosys.2010.06.002

Amnesty International. (2013). *Return to torture: Extradition, forcible returns and removals to Central Asia* (EUR 04/001/2013). https://www.amnesty.org/en/documents/eur04/001/2013/en/

Braichevska, O., Volosiuk, H., Malynovska, O., Pylynskyi, Y., Popson, N., & Ruble, B. A. (2004). *Nontraditional Immigrants in Kyiv*. Woodrow Wilson Center for International Scholars.

Brubaker, R. (1994). Nationhood and the national question in the Soviet Union and post-Soviet Eurasia: An institutionalist account. *Theory and Society, 23*(1), 47–78. https://doi.org/10.1007/BF00993673

Brubaker, W. R. (1992). Citizenship struggles in Soviet Successor States. *International Migration Review, 26*(2), 269–291.

Chindea, A., Majkowska-Tomkin, M., Mattila, H., & Pastor, I. (2008). *Migration in Ukraine: A country profile 2008*. IOM International Organization for Migration. http://publications.iom.int/system/files/pdf/ukraine_profile 2008.pdf

Dimitrova, A., & Dragneva, R. (2013). Shaping convergence with the EU in foreign policy and state aid in post-orange Ukraine: Weak external incentives, powerful veto players. *Europe-Asia Studies, 65*(4), 658–681.

Düvell, F. (2008). On the fringes of Europe: Refugees in Ukraine. *Research Resources Report: Country Profile, 2*, 1–9.

Düvell, F., & Vollmer, B. (2009). Irregular migration in and from the neighbourhood of the EU. A comparison of Morocco, Turkey and Ukraine. *Clandestino*, 1–44.

Eckert, D. (2017). L'Ukraine ou les contours incertains d'un Etat européen. *L'Espace Politique, 3*(33). https://doi.org/10.4000/espacepolitique.4411

Eckert, D., & Lambroschini, S. (2017). La ligne de démarcation entre séparatistes du Donbass et reste de l'Ukraine. *M@ppemonde, 119*. http://mappemonde.mgm.fr/119lieu1/

ECRE. (2007). *Belarus, Moldova, Russian Federation and Ukraine—Situation for refugees, asylum-seekers and internally displaced persons (IDPs)* (Country Report). http://www.refworld.org/docid/48e4a7c32.html

European Commission Against Racism and Intolerance—Council of Europe. (2012). *Fourth report on Ukraine* (CRI(2012)6). ECRI. https://rm.coe.int/fourth-report-on-ukraine/16808b5ca5

European Union, & Ukraine. (2007). *Agreement between the European Community and Ukraine on the readmission of persons*. http://ec.europa.eu/world/agreements/downloadFile.do?fullText=yes&treatyTransId=11681

Frejka, T., Okólski, M., & Sword, K. (1999). *In-depth studies on migration in central and eastern Europe: The case of Ukraine* (Economic Studies No. 12). United Nations Economic Commission for Europe, United Nations Population Fund.

Ghosh, M. (2010). Ukraine: Migration, diversity and transformation. In N. Popson (Ed.), *Demography, migration and tolerance: Comparing the Russian, Ukrainian, and U.S. Experience* (pp. 18–36). Woodrow Wilson International Center for Scholars & Kennan Institute.

Gorbach, D., & Budraitskis, I. (2017, February 9). Dreams of Europe: Refugees and xenophobia in Russia and Ukraine. *OpenDemocracy*. https://www.opendemocracy.net/od-russia/denys-gorbach-ilya-budraitskis/dreams-of-europe-refugees-and-xenophobia-in-russia-and-ukra

Katsakioris, C. (2016). Les étudiants de pays arabes formés en Union soviétique pendant la Guerre froide (1956–1991). *Revue européenne des migrations internationales, 32*(2), 13–38. https://doi.org/10.4000/remi.7758

Kazmierkiewicz, P. (2011). *Non-paper integration of migrants in Ukraine—Situation and needs assessment*. OSCE Office for Democratic Institutions and Human Rights (ODIHR).

Kozak, T. (2016, March 29). Pochemu v Yagotine ne khotyat bezhentsev (Why in Yagotine they don't want refugees). *BBC Ukraine*. http://www.bbc.com/ukrainian/ukraine_in_russian/2016/03/160329_ru_s_yahotyn_migrants

Law, I. (2012). *Red racisms—Racism in communist and post-communist contexts*. Palgrave Macmillan.

Light, M. A. (2012). What does it mean to control migration? Soviet mobility policies in comparative perspective. *Law & Social Inquiry, 37*(2), 395–429.

Makaryan, S. (2015). Construction of migration policies in the eastern neighbourhood of the European Union. *Journal of Contemporary European Studies, 23*(2), 222–237. https://doi.org/10.1080/14782804.2015.1029241

Malynovska, O. (2006, January). *Caught between east and west, Ukraine struggles with its migration policy.*

Matusevich, M. (2009). Probing the limits of internationalism: African students confront soviet ritual. *Anthropology of East Europe Review, 27*(2), 19–39.

Mellakh, K. (2016). La formation des étudiants marocains dans les pays de l'Est de l'Europe (1960–2015). *Revue européenne des migrations internationales, 32*(2), 39–56. https://doi.org/10.4000/remi.7777

OSCE. (2007). *High-level conference on combating discrimination and promoting mutual respect and understanding—Adaptation and integration of the Crimean Tatars and other repatriates in Ukraine* (PC.DEL/546/07). http://www.osce.org/cio/25604?download=true

Popson, N. E. (2000). Kyiv's nontraditional immigrants. *Post-Soviet Geography and Economics, 41*(5), 365–378.

Pribytkova, I. (2011). Post-Soviet migration transition in Ukraine: From the passport regime to the freedom of movement. In V. Iontsev (Ed.), *International migration of population in the post-Soviet territory: Two decades of successes, mistakes and expectances* (pp. 45–62).

Pribytkova, N. O. (2015). racism and xenophobia as phenomena of criminality: current state and separate issues of counteraction. *Journal of Eastern European Law, 2015*, 162.

Prozorova, M. (2016, July 6). V Yagotin tak i ne zaselili bezhentsev s Blizhnego Vostoka (Refugees from the Middle East have not settled in in Iahotyn). *Komsomolskaia Pravda.* https://kp.ua/life/544360-v-yahotyn-tak-y-ne-zaselyly-bezhentsev-s-blyzhneho-vostoka

Razvozzhayev rozpoviv povnu versiyu yoho vykradennya (Razvozzhayev told the full version of his abduction). (2012, October 25). *Ukrainska Pravda.* http://www.pravda.com.ua/news/2012/10/25/6975364/

Rechitsky, R. (2016). Global migration and extraterritorial controls: The case of international refugee policy in Ukraine. *International Journal of Sociology, 46*(3), 169–188. https://doi.org/10.1080/00207659.2016.1163990

Schuster, L. (2004). Chapter 2: The origins and development of asylum. In *The use and abuse of political asylum in Britain and Germany* (pp. 61–87). Routledge.

Shevel, O. (2011). *Migration, refugee policy, and state building in postcommunist Europe.* Cambridge University Press.

Shpigov, D. (2012, October 25). The Ministry of Interior of Ukraine said that the intelligence agencies of the Russian Federation did not have to share with them the plans about Razvozzhaev. *UNN—Ukrainian National News.*

http://www.unn.com.ua/en/news/989911-u-mvs-ukrayini-kageut,-scho-spetsslugebi-rf-ne-mali-dilitis-z-nimi-svoyimi-planami-schodo-rozvazgeaeva

Shukan, I. (2017). La Biélorussie après la crise ukrainienne. *Étude de l'IRSEM, 50*. http://institut-crises.org/la-bielorussie-apres-la-crise-ukrainienne-etude-de-lirsem-n50

Siriytsy pod Kiyevom. Ukraintsy protiv migrantov (Syrians are near Kyiv. Ukrainians are against the migrants). (2016, March 1). *Korrespondent.net*. https://korrespondent.net/ukraine/3636998-syryitsy-pod-kyevom-ukrayntsy-protyv-myhrantov

Söderköping/Cross-Border Cooperation Process. (2008). *The local integration of refugees in the Republic of Belarus, the Republic of Moldova and Ukraine "A strategy for action"*. http://www.refworld.org/docid/47ce77f72.html

The "Social Action" Centre—"No Borders" Project, & Minority Rights Group International. (2011). *Shadow Report to Ukraine's 19th to 21th periodic report under the ICERD—Submission to the 79th session of the Committee on the Elimination of Racial Discrimination*. https://tbinternet.ohchr.org/Treaties/CERD/Shared%20Documents/UKR/INT_CERD_NGO_UKR_79_10238_E.pdf

Tolstokorova, A. (2011). The Ukrainian Migratory Corridor. *EU–US Immigration Systems 2011/2012*.

Tulmets, E. (2014). Analyser l'exportation des normes au-delà de l'Union européenne—Pour une approche éclectique. *Politique Européenne, 46*, 8–32.

Vollmer, B., Bilan, Y., Lapshyna, I., & Vdovtsova, S. (2010). Ukraine country and research areas report. *EUMAGINE Imagining Europe from the Outside, 3*.

Vollmer, B., & Malynovska, O. (2016). Ukrainian migration research before and since 1991. In O. Fedyuk & M. Kindler (Eds.), *Ukrainian migration to the European Union: Lessons from migration studies* (pp. 17–33). Springer International Publishing.

Zakharov, N. (2015). Race and racism in the Russian past. In *Race and racism in Russia* (pp. 21–45). Palgrave Macmillan.

Zhyznomirska, L. (2006). Externalities of the EU immigration and asylum policy: The case of Ukraine. *Review of European and Russian Affairs, 2*.

CHAPTER 3

Norm Transfer into Law: Delaying, Selecting, Translating

> What kind of 'filter' do we have? Article 2 states that the refugee status is not granted only when a person has committed a crime. But where is medical control? Recently newspapers reported that in Kyiv dozens of illegal families suffering from malaria were discovered. Spring will show us what this will cost. With illegal refugees, drug addiction, AIDS, and increase in crime are coming to us. A. I. Bondarchuk, MP of the People's Council (Verkhovna Rada of Ukraine, 1993)

This Member of Parliament contested the introduction of international asylum norms into the Ukrainian legislation during the parliamentary debate on the first Law on Refugees in 1993. This quote reflects a normative and a preferential clash: asylum norms conflict with xenophobia and politicians expect asylum to entail political costs such as financial expenses and political problems. Beyond discursive contestation, how do domestic political actors involved in lawmaking shape transfer processes and outcomes?

Adopting a macro perspective, this chapter analyses the developments of the national Ukrainian asylum legislation between 1993 and 2015. This perspective and focus on the domestic political arena make it possible to compare legislative adoption processes of very different asylum norms so as to grasp the differences in adoption processes.

I. Mützelburg, *Transferring Asylum Norms to EU Neighbours*, The European Union in International Affairs, https://doi.org/10.1007/978-3-031-04528-8_3

Asylum norms differ in strength. The strength of an international norm depends, first, on its codification, also called the legal specification of the norm, that is to what extent it is codified clearly, precisely, and with a strong formulation in legitimate normative documents to which the state has formally adhered (Freyburg et al., 2011). In the present case, those documents are the 1951 Convention and the 1967 Protocol. Second, the strength of the norm depends on its generalised inclusion into the legislation of other states, namely those which are considered legitimate in this field, in the present case EU member states (Finnemore & Sikkink, 1998). The norm is even stronger if its violation triggers an international outcry, in particular by foreign media, politicians, and diplomats. A norm is weakened when different internationally legitimate actors disagree on it, for instance if EU member states fail to respect a refugee-friendly norm that is promoted by UNHCR.

Norms also fit more or less the domestic context—in terms of identity and normative structure (Avdeyeva, 2015, p. 5; Björkdahl et al., 2015, p. 2; Checkel, 1999, p. 87; Schimmelfennig, 2009, p. 20) or in terms of political interests (Ademmer & Börzel, 2013; Hagemann, 2013; Lavenex & Uçarer, 2004, p. 421). Based on this literature, one can expect normative or preferential clashes to cause resistance or translation of the international norm into domestic law that would stray significantly from the model.

I have selected specific norms of five very different thematic areas of the asylum legislation which are commonly considered crucial by promoters of asylum norms: the non-refoulement principle, the avoidance of detention of asylum seekers, asylum seekers' and refugees' socio-economic rights (social benefits and labour rights), criteria restricting access to the substantive evaluation of the asylum claim, and additional protection statuses (complementary / subsidiary and temporary protection). The first three areas are enshrined in the 1951 Convention whereas the following two are not. Subsidiary protection is defined in the EU Qualification Directive (2004). I have analysed these norms' legislative adoption in terms of timing, depth, completeness, and congruence.

The analysis of the legislative changes that have taken place over time shows how the law-makers taken together shaped the outcomes of norm transfer. Yet, because lawmaking is a collective process involving diverse actors, certain outcomes can originate from various underlying processes, for instance compromises, specific actors who managed to impose their position, institutional deadlock, and lack of consensus on certain points.

Instead of a sociological study of legislative practices, this chapter offers a study of the ways in which international norms can be transferred into domestic law.

Studying legislative adoption of international norms as a process has allowed me to go beyond the existing dichotomy of adoption vs. non-adoption. Scholars have come a long way going beyond the dichotomy of practical norm application vs. non-application (insisting for instance on processes of translation in policy implementation), but they have paid little attention to the nuances of legislative adoption. Though legislators could, in principle, translate international norms freely or produce new principles or formulations in their law, I will demonstrate that they shaped the adoption process in a narrower way, and mainly in four respects:

1) Selection:
    a. Legislators can choose not to adopt a certain norm. Yet, external pressure can make this a difficult option.
    b. Legislators can choose among alternative international norms: When different (and potentially contradictory) international norms exist, legislators can choose more freely. For instance, when UNHCR promotes one norm and EU member states follow another, contradictory one, this allows domestic legislators to pick the one that suits them best.
    c. Legislators can select foreign models or instruments that do not have the status of a compulsory international norm according to international law, but that fit domestic law-makers' interests or beliefs. Without pressure by international norm promoters, domestic legislators adopt these models by imitation or lesson drawing.
2) Translation: Legislators translate an international norm to adapt it to the domestic context and their own beliefs or preferences. In the present case, they mostly choose to import the model selectively, for instance by interpreting it narrowly, by leaving out part of a norm, or by adding a restricting clause or condition that limits the scope of the norm.
3) Shallow adoption: In parallel to the existing concept of "shallow application", this means that the norm is integrated into a very "visible" (i.e. monitored) law (here mostly the Law on Refugees), often in a vague way, but is not or not coherently integrated into related

laws, nor into secondary legislation necessary for implementation. Legal contradictions or obstacles to the application of the apparently adopted norm remain. Scholars have overlooked the phenomenon of shallow legislative adoption, which can hinder rule application or which can be a preliminary step in the process of rule adoption.

4) Timing: Legislators may adopt norms more or less quickly (in comparison with the first Law on Refugees, if the norm has existed abroad before, or in comparison with the emergence and the establishment of the norm in international and European law; also in comparison with international norm promoters' requests for changes).

Overview of the Developments of the Ukrainian Asylum Policies

The Law on Refugees from 1993 introduced the concept of "refugee" for the first time into the legislation of the independent state of Ukraine. Its formulation closely mirrored that of the Refugee Convention, but its implementation began only in 1996. The Ukrainian Parliament introduced several amendments to the Law in 2001, 2003, and 2005. With the new Law on Refugees and Persons in Need of Complementary and Temporary Protection in Ukraine from 2011, the legal grounds under which a person may obtain protection in Ukraine have been significantly enlarged. In particular, based on the new law, individuals who cannot obtain the conventional refugee status but who cannot return to their country of origin because they fear torture, the death penalty, or inhuman or degrading treatment can obtain this status of complementary protection. However, UNHCR and the European Commission criticised the Ukrainian definition of the grounds for obtaining this protection status as being narrower than the European Union Council Directive's definition in that it excluded people fleeing indiscriminate violence. In 2014, the Ukrainian law was harmonised with the EU directive. The new law from 2011 also established the status of persons in need of temporary protection. Such a status foresees protection of a maximum of one year on the grounds of "external aggression, foreign occupation, civil war, clashes on an ethnic basis, natural or man-made disasters, or other events that violate public order in part or in the whole territory of the country of origin". This status was limited to residents of a neighbouring country of Ukraine until the amendment of 2014 lifted this limitation. So far, this status has not been attributed in practice. In 2012 an Action Plan on the Integration of Refugees and Persons in Need of Complementary Protection into the Ukrainian Society until 2020 was adopted, slowly followed by Action Plans at the regional scale. Until 2011, the Ukrainian state bodies in charge of asylum procedures were reorganised numerous times, strongly affecting the implementation of Ukrainian asylum policies.

Resistance to Norms that Limit the State's Control Over Its Territory

Certain international asylum norms clash with prerogatives of traditional state sovereignty and established practices, supported by some actors from the political elite. Law-makers resisted the transfer of such norms by failing to adopt them, by delaying their adoption, or by adopting them in a shallow or selective way.

Prohibition of Refoulement: Shallow and Selective Adoption of a Strong International Norm

Protection against refoulement is a major international asylum norm stated explicitly and clearly in the Convention Relating to the Status of Refugees from 1951 (Article 33), but also in other, more general human rights treaties, and in EU member states' national legislation. Its violation often triggers a major outcry in international media, and by other states and international organisations (Lang, 2002; Wouters, 2009). However, the principle that prohibits forcibly sending foreigners to a country where they may be subject to human rights violations may clash with political objectives of migration control and harmonious relations with other states. CIS states sometimes request an extradition, claiming that their citizen, who is seeking asylum in Ukraine, is prosecuted under criminal charges back home.

Since 1993, Ukraine has prohibited the forcible repatriation of refugees according to the Law on Refugees (article 14). However, this refugee-specific prohibition was not mentioned in the Criminal Procedural Code until 2010. Hence, until 2010 the prohibition of refoulement of refugees was only adopted in a shallow way. As far as refoulement was concerned, national laws were contradictory, in the same way that political positions where the aim to conform to Western standards clashed with the aim to maintain cooperative relations with other CIS states.

Following the amendment from 17 June 2010, the Criminal Procedural Code indicated that an extradition request would be denied if the extradition of the person conflicted with Ukraine's obligations under international treaties and, more specifically: "The person who was granted refugee status cannot be extradited to a foreign country where her health, life or freedom would be threatened on grounds of race, belief (religion), ethnicity, citizenship (nationality), membership of a particular social group or political opinion, except as provided by an international treaty of Ukraine" (Article 466). However, the exception at the end entailed the possibility of refoulement via international treaties, such as the Minsk Convention on Legal Assistance and Legal Relations in Civil, Family, and Criminal Matters from 1993 that regulates extraditions among several CIS countries and that lacks non-refoulement provisions. In 2010, Ukrainian law-makers hence translated the international norm of the prohibition of non-refoulement in a way that left open the possibility of refoulement to fellow CIS-states.

This exception to the prohibition of non-refoulement was removed by a 2012 amendment to the Law on Refugees and Persons in Need of Additional or Temporary Protection. With this amendment, Ukrainian law-makers harmonised the law with the international norm on non-refoulement as it concerned recognised refugees.

In contrast to the refoulement of recognised refugees, the refoulement of asylum seekers was not mentioned at all in Ukrainian law until 2012, when the new Criminal Procedural Code (articles 589 and 590) was introduced. In other words, until 2012, Ukrainian law-makers translated the non-refoulement norm so as to leave open the possibility of extraditing asylum seekers during the asylum procedure.

In brief, the principle of non-refoulement was adopted early (1993) but in a shallow and selective way in Ukraine. Until 2012, this translation into Ukrainian legislation allowed for a compromise between an apparent adoption of this clear and strong international norm and the effective upholding of established extradition practices among CIS states.

The Right to Breach Immigration Laws to Seek Asylum: No Adoption of a Weak International Norm

Asylum norms often clash with restrictive migration control. For instance, the UN Convention relating to the status of refugees (Article 3) foresees that the "seeking of asylum can require [not yet legally recognised] refugees to breach immigration rules" so that "subject to specific exceptions, refugees [i.e. protection seekers] should not be penalized for their illegal entry or stay". Yet, asylum seekers' right to liberty and freedom of movement and the non-penalisation of infringements of immigration legislation is a weak norm. The Convention weakens the principle as being "subject to specific exceptions" and stipulates that migrants seeking protection should not be penalised for their illegal entry or presence "provided they present themselves without delay to the authorities and show good cause for their illegal entry or presence" (Article 31–1). In its publications, UNHCR criticises the detention of asylum seekers. However, it also mentions exceptions justifying this practice, for example, "if there are grounds for believing that the specific asylum seeker has lodged an appeal or introduced an asylum claim merely in order to delay or frustrate an expulsion or deportation decision which would result in his or her removal, the authorities may consider detention" (UNHCR, 2012a, p. 20).

The European Union has also contributed to legitimising the detention of asylum seekers. In 2002, the Council of the European Union proposed that member states have the right to restrict asylum seekers' freedom of movement to a particular place (Proposal for a Council Directive Laying down Minimum Standards for the Reception of Applicants for Asylum in Member States, 2002). More recent normative publications of the European Union, binding for most EU member states, enumerate six reasons why an asylum seeker may be detained (Directive on Standards for the Qualification of Third-Country Nationals or Stateless Persons as Beneficiaries of International Protection, for a Uniform Status for Refugees or for Persons Eligible for Subsidiary Protection, and for the Content of the Protection Granted (Recast), 2011), Article 8–3). Since the mid-2000s the practice of detaining asylum seekers has become widely accepted among the EU institutions and widely practised by EU member states (Servent & Trauner, 2014). The principle of not penalising migrants for violating immigration laws is subject to many exceptions in the normative texts and is frequently violated by European states. It is a weak norm.

This norm has not been introduced into Ukrainian legislation. As mentioned in the previous chapter, since 1996 and especially since 2001, the Ukrainian state has increasingly focused on the fight against irregular immigration. Foreign citizens and stateless people may be detained and deported on the grounds of immigration-related infractions. For instance, the Law on the Legal Status of Foreigners and Stateless Persons (2011, Articles 26 and 30) penalises the attempt to enter Ukrainian territory without proper documentation and the irregular presence on Ukrainian territory. This may also concern protection seekers who either have not managed to hand in their asylum application before their arrest or who have tried to move on to a third country—usually in the EU—to apply for asylum there. Migrants who apply for asylum in detention are usually kept in detention until the end of the maximum detention period. This practice has been repeatedly criticised by international actors (European Commission, 2013; European Commission to the European Parliament and the Council, 2015; UNHCR, 2013, pp. 13–17; Working Group on Arbitrary Detention, 2009, p. 18). At the same time, the EU exerts pressure on Ukraine to keep unwanted migrants from transiting to the EU—which includes detention as a means of discouraging migrants from irregular migration. In Ukraine, in 2016, the Law on the Legal Status of Foreigners and Stateless Persons (Article 30–4) explicitly stated that persons who have been arrested and detained for violation of immigration laws and then applied for asylum are to be kept in detention until the final decision of their asylum claim. While this can be read as resistance to the transfer of international norms (the migrant-friendly non-detention norm), it can also be read as norm adoption (that is, adoption of the restrictive widespread practice of detaining asylum seekers). The parallel existence of two contradictory norms allows domestic law-makers to choose the norm that best suits their beliefs or political objectives.

Narrow, Shallow, and Slow Adoption of Norms Entailing Budgetary Costs

Law-makers resist the transfer of norms whose adoption and application entail budgetary costs. This is facilitated if the international norm is formulated vaguely. Given that the Convention does not distinguish between the legal categories of asylum seekers and recognised refugees, calling all of them "refugees" if they correspond to the substantial criteria, the norm can be interpreted widely. It can apply to asylum seekers during the procedure, or can be applied more narrowly as to cover only recognised refugees. Ukrainian law-makers translated the term "refugee" from the Convention in the narrow fashion, that is, as "recognised refugees", when seeking to limit the right to social benefits, but broadly as "recognised refugees and asylum seekers" when granting the right to work.

The Right to Social Benefits: Narrow, Shallow, and Slow Adoption

According to the 1951 Convention Relating to the Status of Refugees, states should "accord to refugees lawfully staying in their territory the same treatment [...] as is accorded to their nationals" with respect to several areas including public relief and assistance (Article 23) and social security (Article 24–1-b). Most EU member states have translated this norm into their legislation treating recognised refugees and asylum seekers in different ways. Yet, most grant asylum seekers a minimum amount of social support.

While in 1993, the Ukrainian law foresaw social benefits for asylum seekers, since 2001, Ukrainian law-makers have used the vague formulation of the norm on social benefits to exclude asylum seekers. They have interpreted this international norm in a narrow way. Furthermore, this process shows that legislative transfer should not be analysed in a linear or teleological way: Over time, domestic law-makers can intensify the differences between national law and international norm.

The legislative process on the social benefits for recognised refugees was long and contradictory (Table 3.1). Since 1993, the Law on Refugees has foreseen a right to social benefits for recognised refugees, but it has not provided for the same right to social benefits for refugees as for nationals; the international norm was only selectively adopted. Furthermore, the law has left the concrete implications of this right to social benefits vague, referring to other rules or decisions (from the Cabinet of Ministers or "the Ukrainian legislation"). Most importantly, until 2012, Ukrainian law-makers had not harmonised the legislation on social protection with the Law on Refugees. Refugees' rights were not specified in the social protection legislation or in the rules for the respective authorities. Thus, refugees were usually unable to access social benefits. I qualify this as shallow adoption: The international norm was translated only into one law, but not in all the laws that would be required for the norm to be implemented.

Table 3.1 Evolution of the laws on asylum seekers' rights to employment and social benefits (1993–2016)

Law on Refugees	*Asylum seekers have the right to…*	*Refugees have the right to…*
1993–2001	• temporary employment or education • social benefits	• employment and education as other aliens • social benefits as decided by the Cabinet of Ministers
Since 2001	• temporary employment or education	• employment and education as nationals • social benefits as foreseen by the Ukrainian legislation

Source Author's production

In 2012, Ukrainian legislators amended the legislation, legally entitling refugees to the same social support as Ukrainian citizens and introducing this into the law on social services (Law on the Introduction of Changes to Several Legal Acts of Ukraine on Questions of Refugees and Persons in Need of Complementary or Temporary Protection, 2012, and Law on Social Services, Article 6, 2012). They enlarged and deepened this norm with regard to refugees, while continuing to interpret it narrowly with regard to asylum seekers.

The Right to Work: Early Adoption

The 1951 Convention relating to the status of refugees foresees that with respect to wage-earning employment, refugees should be treated at least as favourably as other aliens, and recommends the same treatment as for nationals (Article 17). Most EU member states offer asylum seekers limited right to work.

The right to work for asylum seekers and refugees does not entail direct costs for the state budget and the Ukrainian law-makers introduced it quickly. Since 1993, asylum seekers have had the right to work temporarily during the examination of their asylum application. Recognised refugees were granted the right to work—but only like other foreign citizens (Law on Refugees from 1993). This right was extended by the Law on Refugees from 2001, which stipulated that recognised refugees have the same rights to employment as Ukrainian citizens. In this realm, Ukrainian legislators took up the norms of the 1951 Convention before Ukraine's accession in 2002 and even went beyond a narrow interpretation.

Yet, the access to the above-mentioned rights to social benefits and to legal employment has been restricted by legal obstacles. In order to benefit from these rights, everyone—Ukrainian nationals and migrants—needs valid identification documents and up-to-date registration. Given that Ukrainian citizens themselves often struggle to obtain these documents—registration in particular—foreigners encounter even more obstacles. Registration obligations and other documentation hurdles frequently block asylum seekers' and refugees' access to social services. Migrants also struggle to obtain a tax number, the precondition for legal employment.

Moreover, asylum seekers only obtain a work permit once they are admitted to the substantive phase of the asylum procedure and only for the period of validity of their asylum seeker certificate (i.e. a few months). Until 2014 an employer wanting to hire an asylum seeker had to pay a fee which represented four times the minimum monthly salary. The legislators have therefore added legal obstacles or failed to remove them, effectively adopting certain international norms in a shallow way.

Imitation and Translation of Foreign Norms that Fit Domestic Political Interests

The Ukrainian legislators have adopted technical rules, instruments, and concepts from abroad that were not strong international and binding norms—but which fit restrictive migration policies. International norm producers, namely UNHCR, repeatedly denounced this adoption, requesting that Ukrainian law be adapted to their own version of the norm. This concerned, for instance, the grounds on which an asylum application could be rejected even before its substantive examination. International organisations criticised the fact that a series of legal provisions can block access to the asylum procedure in Ukraine.

The Broad Safe Third Country Provision: Early Imitation

In 1993, Ukrainian legislators imported the concept of safe third country into the first Ukrainian Law on Refugees. The safe third country concept has been widespread in international and national normative asylum documents after having appeared in the mid-1980s in Scandinavian countries as "country of first asylum" and having spread to other European states (Moreno-Lax, 2015, p. 666). The Ukrainian Law on Refugees from 1993 foresaw that a person could not be granted refugee status if the person had "stayed" (перебувала) in a state where he or she could have obtained the protection in due course. The law from 1993 neither defined a "safe third country" nor "stayed". Consequently all 133 countries taking part in the UN Refugee Convention, the Protocol, or countries that had adopted laws on refugee protection were considered to be safe third countries. For this reason, asylum seekers who had crossed such a supposedly safe country were automatically refused access to asylum without examination of their individual case (United States Committee for Refugees and Immigrants, US, 1998).

International organisations criticised this stipulation until 2001, when a definition of a safe third country was added to the Law on Refugees (Article 1). The definition clarified that a safe third country is not merely a transit country but a country where the applicant had remained for a longer period of time. Moreover, a safe third country must not only formally adhere to international principles such as the Geneva Convention but also must have asylum legislation, with institutions to implement it, and it must provide protection to applicants. Furthermore, the transit country needs to accept to process the asylum seeker's application. Only if these criteria are fulfilled can the Ukrainian state reject asylum applications. This corresponds to the criteria developed by UNHCR in the 1990s, which were added to the EU Procedures Directive in 2005. At the time of the article's amendment by the Ukrainian Parliament, the EU Procedures Directive had not yet had its harmonising effect onto EU national legislation. As a result, national laws in the EU were heterogeneous and many did not yet comprise the concept. Ukrainian legislators very early imitated an instrument from abroad that fit the objective of restrictive migration control. They later aligned it with UNHCR norms that limited the possibilities to use this restrictive instrument.

Filing Deadlines: Imitation of Restrictive Instruments from Abroad

Another instrument which travelled across some European countries and also to Ukraine was the filing deadline. For instance, since 1980, Belgian asylum legislation has foreseen precise time limitations indicating within how many days a person must apply for asylum after having entered Belgian territory, depending on the legal status of the entry. In the same way, in Ukraine, the Law on Refugees from 1993 indicated within how many days after entering Ukrainian territory a migrant had to apply for asylum. Similarly to the Belgian law, the Ukrainian law has not specified the consequences of handing in the asylum application too late. The adoption of this rule by the Ukrainian Parliament cannot be explained by the normative domination of this instrument in Europe given that only a minority of European states foresaw these deadlines at the time of their adoption in Ukraine. It also was not actively promoted by international organisations. It rather appears as the result of circulation of instruments and Ukrainian legislators' search for instruments from abroad which fit restrictive migration policies. This can be considered a case of imitation or lesson drawing.

International organisations strongly criticised this rule, stating that Ukrainian state officials often interpreted it as a reason to deny access to the asylum procedure (UNHCR, 2013, pp. 10–11). They argued that the vagueness of the Ukrainian law allowed for an application which was in contradiction with international normative documents. For example, the 2005 EU Procedures Directive (Article 8–1) states that an asylum application should not be rejected or excluded from examination on the unique ground that they were not made as soon as possible. However, the EU Procedures Directive (23–4-l) itself suggests that states could impose an accelerated or prioritised procedure if the applicant violates immigration legislation and, "without good reason", fails to apply "for asylum as soon as possible, given the circumstances of his/her entry". Accelerated procedures reduce the asylum seekers' possibilities to prepare their application, for instance with the help of a lawyer, and de facto reduce their chances of being granted refugee status. The directive thus promotes the perception of undermined legitimacy of asylum applications which are submitted too late, weakening the above-mentioned protection principle.

Instead of indicating the consequences of belated applications, the Ukrainian legislators repeatedly modified the time frame for asylum procedures. Some laws specified that migrants must apply for asylum within one or five days after entering Ukrainian territory, but sometimes those numbers were replaced by "promptly", or there was no indication at all. Legislators thereby imitated an instrument from abroad that allowed for restrictive practices as far as asylum requests were concerned. They translated the instrument into Ukrainian law in a vague way that allowed for more leeway at the asylum authorities. Contradictory international norms were weak and did not limit this instrument.

The Prohibition of "Impersonation": Import and Restrictive Interpretation of a European Instrument

Punishment of asylum seekers who provide false information during their application was also imported into the Ukrainian legislation. Laws in EU states and the 2005 EU Procedures Directive foresee that the provision of false information can justify the prioritisation or acceleration of the procedure, de facto reducing asylum seekers' chances of obtaining the refugee status without openly excluding them from an examination of their claim.

Ukrainian legislators adopted this instrument in a more restrictive way. In Ukraine, since the Law on Refugees from 2003, individuals could be refused access to the asylum procedure due to impersonation. Impersonation is defined as persons giving false information about themselves, or having already applied for asylum under another identity. UNHCR criticised Ukraine's willingness to reject an asylum application based on 'impersonation' alone because, on those grounds, "[t]he substance of the individual's application for asylum is not given due consideration" (UNHCR, 2013, p. 11). Despite this criticism, the possibility of rejecting an asylum application due to impersonation has been maintained throughout all the versions of the law until the one from 2016 (still valid in 2022).

Ukrainian legislators imported concepts and rules from abroad, even when they were not strong widespread norms in Europe. They adopted these concepts and rules either by adapting them in the sense of restrictive migration policies or by leaving them vague so as to apply them in a restrictive way. This triggered the criticism of international organisations seeking to promote a more migrant-friendly version of these instruments. However, the strength of the migrant-friendly interpretation of these instruments was weakened both by the absence of codification in the 1951 Convention and by the laws and normative documents in the EU and its member states. Indeed, even if the EU directives state that a certain instrument should not fully block access to the asylum procedure, they have spread the idea that the curtailment of the right to asylum due to these factors is legitimate. The parallel existence of restrictive instruments and refugee-friendly principles in the EU allowed Ukrainian legislators to pick what fit them best.

Late but Full Adoption of EU Protection Statuses

The EU formalised two new protection statuses, which were later integrated into Ukrainian legislation. International organisations repeatedly criticised the absence of subsidiary forms of protection in the Ukrainian legislation (UNHCR, 2007, p. 10). However, refugee status remained the only protection status until 2011.

In 2011, Ukrainian law-makers introduced a protection status called complementary protection (Law on Refugees and Persons in Need of Complementary and Temporary Protection in Ukraine from July 2011). They followed closely the definition of a subsidiary protection status laid down by the EU Qualification Directive (2004). In the law, they explicitly referred to the 1951 Convention and the 1967 Protocol, indicating that the new status concerned individuals who cannot obtain conventional refugee status but who cannot return to their country of origin due to threats to their life, safety, or freedom based on the fear of death penalty or execution, torture, or inhuman or degrading treatment or punishment. The Ukrainian and the EU definitions overlapped on "death penalty", "torture", "inhuman or degrading treatment"—even in the wording—but contrary to the EU directive, the Ukrainian law did not include "indiscriminate violence" as grounds for obtaining complementary protection.

International organisations welcomed the introduction of the complementary protection status but also requested it to be expanded. The yearly evaluation reports of the European Commission for the visa-liberalisation process demanded an expansion of the grounds for the complementary protection status (European Commission, 2013, p. 10; European Commission & High Representative of the European Union for Foreign Affairs and Security Policy, 2012, p. 9). UNHCR also criticised that the introduced status excluded persons fleeing "serious and indiscriminate threats to life, physical integrity or freedom resulting from generalized violence or events seriously disturbing public order" (UNHCR, 2012b, p. 3). UNHCR legitimised the criticism by pointing out that the notion was narrower than the one in the EU.

In 2014, the Ukrainian Law on Refugees and Persons in Need of Complementary or Temporary Protection (Article 1) was indeed amended, adding, "widespread violence in situations of international or internal armed conflict or systematic human rights violations". Ukrainian legislators thus adopted the EU formulation of "widespread violence in situations of international or internal armed conflict", adding another reason not found in the EU definition. The introduction of the status of a person in need of complementary protection and its expansion were a clear case of harmonisation of the Ukrainian asylum legislation with UNHCR and EU norms.

The Law on Refugees and Persons in Need of Complementary and Temporary Protection in Ukraine from 2011 also introduced the status of persons in need of temporary protection. The Ukrainian law thus included a protection status which existed in other parts of the world but was codified in 2001 by the Council Directive on Minimum Standards for Giving Temporary Protection in the Event of a Mass Influx of Displaced Persons. The status of temporary protection concerns people who are "massively forced to seek protection in Ukraine as a result of external aggression, foreign occupation, civil war, clashes on an ethnic basis, natural or man-made disasters or other events that violate public order in part or in the whole territory of the country of origin".

Initially, the law-makers translated the EU norm into a more restrictive version, limiting the status to people who resided in a country sharing a border with Ukraine. This translation corresponded to political objectives and social norms. It limited the people who could possibly obtain this status in terms of numbers and countries of origin, restricting it to those perceived as culturally similar and more welcome in Ukrainian society. The EU criticised this limiting clause, stating that it "seems too limited by comparison with European standards" (European Commission & High Representative of the European Union for Foreign Affairs and Security Policy, 2012, p. 9). Ukrainian law-makers followed this criticism in 2014 and took out the condition of the neighbourhood of the state.

Since 2014, the Ukrainian legal provisions on the two additional protection statuses have been very similar—including in wording—to the ones in the EU directives. Even though these norms do not appear in the 1951 Convention and are therefore not a formal obligation for the Ukrainian state, they are part of EU directives and have become the norm in the EU member states.

Conclusion

This chapter has scrutinised how Ukrainian legislators adopted international norms, going beyond the common dichotomy of adoption vs. non-adoption. I have shown that domestic legislators shape the import of international norms, selecting certain norms instead of others, failing to adopt certain norms, translating norms, in particular by adopting them selectively (by interpreting them narrowly, by leaving out parts, or by adding a restricting clause or condition that limits the scope of the norm), adopting norms superficially or deeply, and delaying or speeding up the adoption.

This chapter has deconstructed a policy area into the norms that compose it. It has shown that within a policy area, norms differ and are therefore adopted in a heterogeneous way. This illustrates that comparing different policy areas as unitary blocks is problematic as it obscures the major differences within one sector (Langbein & Wolczuk, 2012, p. 867).

Internationally strong norms were adopted early but at first, until 2010, in a shallow way. This finding is in line with the argument put forward by Tom Casier according to which Ukrainian state actors undertook mostly visible reforms in a formal (as opposed to substantive) way in order to gain recognition and a potential membership perspective from the EU, without threatening domestic elites' interests (Casier, 2011). These internationally strong norms were adopted in a deep way between 2010 and 2014. The timing of full adoption hints to the role of the political context and certain actors' interventions, which will be explored in the next chapter. The analysis qualifies the argument from the literature according to which a norm's codification strongly matters for its adoption (Freyburg et al., 2011). Indeed, the norms' strength of codification alone was not sufficient for their full and deep adoption.

The Ukrainian legislators also adopted instruments, concepts, and rules from abroad which were not strong and compulsory international norms. These were adopted if they fit restrictive migration policies, for instance the safe third country notion. Conversely, weakly codified norms that would have entailed budgetary spending by the state—social benefits for asylum seekers, for example—were not adopted or only in a narrow and superficial way.

Overall, this chapter has found that norms that diverged from major political objectives were only fully and deeply adopted during a certain period—between 2010 and 2014. The following chapter explores this political context and the role of international norm promoters in the transfer.

References

Ademmer, E., & Börzel, T. A. (2013). Migration, energy and good governance in the EU's Eastern neighbourhood. *Europe-Asia Studies, 65*(4), 581–608.

Avdeyeva, O. A. (2015). *Defending women's rights in Europe: Gender equality and EU enlargement*. SUNY Press.

Björkdahl, A., Chaban, N., Leslie, J., & Masselot, A. (Eds.). (2015). *Importing EU Norms—Conceptual framework and empirical findings*, (Vol. 8). Springer International Publishing. https://doi.org/10.1007/978-3-319-13740-7

Casier, T. (2011). The EU's two-track approach to democracy promotion: The case of Ukraine. *Democratization, 18*(4), 956–977. https://doi.org/10.1080/13510347.2011.584734

Checkel, J. T. (1999). Norms, institutions, and national identity in contemporary Europe. *International Studies Quarterly, 43*, 83–114.

European Commission. (2013). *Third report on the implementation by Ukraine of the action plan on visa Liberalisation—Report from the commission to the European parliament and the council* (COM (2013) 809 final). https://ec.europa.eu/transparency/regdoc/rep/1/2013/EN/1-2013-809-EN-F1-1.Pdf

Directive on standards for the qualification of third-country nationals or stateless persons as beneficiaries of international protection, for a uniform status for refugees or for persons eligible for subsidiary protection, and for the content of the protection granted (recast), Pub. L. No. 2011/95/EU (2011). http://doi.org/eur-lex.europa.eu/LexUriServ/LexUriServ.do?uri=OJ:L:2011:337:0009:0026:en:PDF

European commission, & High representative of the European union for foreign affairs and security policy. (2012). *Second progress report on the implementation by Ukraine of the Action Plan on Visa Liberalisation* (SWD (2012) 10 final).

European Commission to the European Parliament and the Council. (2015). *Fifth progress report on the implementation by Ukraine of the action plan on Visa Liberalisation* (COM (2015) 200 final). https://ec.europa.eu/home-affairs/sites/homeaffairs/files/e-library/documents/policies/international-affairs/general/docs/fifth_progress_report_on_the_implementation_by_ukraine_of_the_action_plan_on_visa_liberalisation_en.pdf

Finnemore, M., & Sikkink, K. (1998). International norm dynamics and political change. *International Organization, 52*(04), 887–917.

Freyburg, T., Lavenex, S., Schimmelfennig, F., Skripka, T., & Wetzel, A. (2011). Democracy promotion through functional cooperation? The case of the European Neighbourhood Policy. *Democratization, 18*(4), 1026–1054. https://doi.org/10.1080/13510347.2011.584738

Hagemann, C. (2013). External governance on the terms of the partner? The EU, Russia and the republic of moldova in the European Neighbourhood Policy. *Journal of European Integration, 35*(7), 767–783. https://doi.org/10.1080/07036337.2012.732073

Lang, H. J. (2002). *Fear and sanctuary: Burmese refugees in Thailand*. SEAP Publications.

Langbein, J., & Wolczuk, K. (2012). Convergence without membership? The impact of the European Union in the neighbourhood: Evidence from Ukraine. *Journal of European Public Policy, 19*(6), 863–881.

Lavenex, S., & Uçarer, E. M. (2004). The external dimension of Europeanization: The case of immigration policies. *Cooperation and Conflict, 39*(4), 417–443.

Moreno-Lax, V. (2015). The legality of the "Safe Third Country" notion contested: Insights from the law of treaties. In G. S. Goodwin-Gill & P. Weckel (Eds.), *Migration & Refugee Protection in the 21st Century: Legal Aspects* (pp. 665–721). The Hague Academy of International Law Centre for Research (Martinus Nijhoff).

Proposal for a council directive laying down minimum standards for the reception of applicants for asylum in Member States, 7802/02 (2002). https://data.consilium.europa.eu/doc/document/ST-7802-2002-INIT/en/pdf

Schimmelfennig, F. (2009). Europeanization beyond Europe. *Living Rev. Euro. Gov., 4*(3). http://europeangovernance.livingreviews.org/Articles/lreg-2009-3/

Servent, A. R., & Trauner, F. (2014). Do supranational EU institutions make a difference? EU asylum law before and after 'communitarization. *Journal of European Public Policy, 21*(8), 1142–1162. https://doi.org/10.1080/13501763.2014.906905

UNHCR. (2007). *UNHCR Position on the situation of asylum in Ukraine in the context of return of Asylum-Seekers*. http://www.refworld.org/docid/472f43162.html

UNHCR. (2012a). *Guidelines on the applicable criteria and standards relating to the detention of Asylum-Seekers and alternatives to detention*. http://www.refworld.org/docid/503489533b8.html

UNHCR. (2012b). *Aide Memoire. Ukraine's Asylum System*. http://doi.org/unhcr.org.ua/attachments/article/226/Briefing%20Note%20on%20asylum%20system%20JUNE%202012b.pdf

UNHCR. (2013). *Ukraine as a country of asylum. Observations on the situation of asylum-seekers and refugees in Ukraine*.

United States Committee for Refugees and Immigrants, US. (1998). *World Refugee Survey 1998—Ukraine*. http://www.refworld.org/country,COI,USCRI,ANNUALREPORT,UKR,,3ae6a8bb10,0.html

Verkhovna Rada of Ukraine. (1993). *Protocol of the 29th plenary session of the Verkhovna Rada*. http://iportal.rada.gov.ua/meeting/stenogr/show/4843.html

Working Group on Arbitrary Detention. (2009). *Report of the mission to Ukraine* (A/HRC/10/21/Add.4; 10th Session). Human Rights Council of the United Nations. http://daccess-ods.un.org/TMP/4743135.86950302.html

Wouters, K. (2009). *International legal standards for the protection from refoulement*. Intersentia.

CHAPTER 4

Why Adopt International Norms? Legislators Between Contestation and Submission to International Organisations

> In any case, the presence of a Law on Refugees is a sign of a civilised state; it is one of the necessary conditions for joining the Council of Europe. MP Stefan Vasylovych Batyushko. (Verkhovna Rada of Ukraine, 1993a)

The justification for the need of a Law on Refugees in Ukraine by this member of the Parliament was a common argument for the introduction of international asylum norms into Ukrainian legislation in the 1990s. In this phase, parliamentarians justified the introduction of these norms not by what they did, but by what they symbolised, and not by the domestic asylum policies they entailed but by the message they conveyed, in particular to international organisations.

Scholars frequently distinguish among different types of transfer mechanisms such as lesson drawing, imitation, socialisation, persuasion, and conditionality (Dolowitz & Marsh, 1996; Tulmets, 2014). Yet, these mechanisms often lack operationalisation because their identification relies on an assessment of processes occurring within actors' minds. Instead, to understand varying reasons why Ukrainian decision makers introduced international asylum norms into the Ukrainian legislation, I have chosen to rely on a combination of the analysis of norm promoters' resources and practices as well as norm addressees' discourse.

I. Mützelburg, *Transferring Asylum Norms to EU Neighbours*, The European Union in International Affairs, https://doi.org/10.1007/978-3-031-04528-8_4

In this chapter,[1] I study how the norm addressees reacted discursively to the norm promotion activities. MPs' and leading civil servants' discourse in parliamentary debates (1993–2021) and in interviews reflects to what extent the domestic actors presented the promoted norms and the norm promotion activities as legitimate and which reasons they considered legitimate to justify the legislative adoption of the norms. This approach is compatible with rationalist and constructivist theoretical approaches, because the discursive acceptance of norm promoters' transfer activities can originate from domestic actors' beliefs as well as from their interest in the IOs' conditionality.

This chapter elaborates a typology of norm addressees' discursive reactions to norms and norm promoters. Domestic actors can…

- …talk about the **norm's content**: Domestic actors refer to specific ideas contained in the norms to justify the adoption either
  - without further justification, as a **moral norm** (e.g. it is the duty of a state not to send back protection seekers whose life would be threatened in their home country) or
  - with reference to its **instrumental value**: the norm, when adopted and applied, would solve a public policy problem.
- …talk about the **norm's symbolic value** (Burg, 2001): Domestic actors justify a norm's adoption by suggesting that it represents something, thus creating an image that the domestic actors want to convey (e.g. the adoption of international human rights norms conveys the image of a democratic state).
- …talk about the **norm's exchange value**: Domestic actors refer to the advantage they will obtain in exchange for the adoption of the norm.
- …**not mention** the norm promoters' requests.
- …**contest** the interference, question the norm promoters' legitimacy.

This typology of operational categories can be applied to empirical material such as public political discourse and interviews. It can be used to analyse the evolution of the norm addressees' discourse about transfer

[1] Some content from this chapter has been published here (Mützelburg, 2019).

over time, their perceptions of what was legitimate to voice, and power relations between norm promoters and norm addressees.

Norm Promotion by International Organisations in a Context of Lack of Domestic Political Interest in Asylum (1993–2010)

Introducing International Asylum Norms for Their Symbolic Value

International asylum norms were introduced into Ukrainian legislation at a few key moments. The major moment of change took place in 1993, under President Leonid Kravchuk, with the elaboration of a first Law on Refugees, which came into force in 1996 under President Leonid Kuchma. A major amendment was carried out in 2001, whereas in 2003 (still under Kuchma) and 2005 (Victor Yushchenko), Ukrainian legislators amended minor aspects of asylum legislation. It can be seen that the major changes in the period between 1991 and 2010 cannot be linked to the political orientation of the President. Despite the fact that Yushchenko is considered to have been the most pro-Western President of the 1990s and 2000s, adoption of international asylum norms slowed down during his presidency (Shevel, 2011, p. 192). This can be partly explained by chaos and political power struggles in the executive in the aftermath of the Orange Revolution, which took place under Yushchenko's presidency. Representatives of migration authorities within the executive, which at that time came largely from the liberal and pro-Western intelligentsia, usually drafted and proposed the asylum-related bills to the Parliament, itself dominated by communists until 2002 (Shevel, 2011, pp. 186–193).

However, the parliamentarians' interventions on asylum did not follow clear patterns according to their political party or the party's overall ideological orientation. This was first due to political parties' low level of interest in the topic of asylum. Ukrainian political parties did not develop a uniform position on asylum which the members of the party would represent in Parliament. Instead, Ukrainian politicians primarily discussed asylum as a means to discuss Europe. This is why, depending on the political context and timing, political parties mattered due to their position concerning Europe or concerning their political rivals' positions concerning Europe. Second, the weak explanatory role of the political parties was related to the general state of Ukrainian party politics. Ukrainian parties represented clear ideological differences and positions only concerning some topics and were frequently restructured and renamed around their leaders, rather than around topics and positions (Kuzio, 2011, p. 98).

Elaborating a First Law on Refugees as a Response to a Public Policy Problem?

Despite the unfavourable Ukrainian context for the development of asylum policies, in 1993, the Ukrainian Parliament introduced the concept of "refugee" into the national legislation, following closely the formulation of the International Refugee Convention. Did this move correspond to a logic of lesson drawing, that is, did MPs seek to solve a domestic public policy problem, resorting to the solutions elaborated abroad (Rose, 1991)? Was the influx of fleeing people presented as a public policy problem which needed to be addressed with asylum laws?

While the Ukrainian Soviet Socialist Republic received Soviet fugitives already before its independence and set up, in 1989, departments on Refugees and Migration Affairs in the Ministry of Labour of the Ukrainian SSR for the regulation of their social and economic assistance, legal status was of no concern because those arriving were Soviet citizens (Shevel, 2011, p. 157). Since 1991, Ukraine has had to tackle foreign citizens' immigration as a sovereign state. According to estimations, from 1991 until 1993, Ukraine received between 70,000 and 130,000 fleeing people from former Soviet Republics (Frejka et al., 1999, p. 4; Malynovska, 2006; Shevel, 2011, p. 158). As a response to this new flow of immigration, in June 1992 a Commission on Refugee Affairs was put in place within the Cabinet of Ministers.

A reason named for the necessity of introducing the first Law on Refugees during the debate in the Verkhovna Rada of 21 April 1993 was the influx of fleeing persons, especially from Transnistria. The First Deputy Minister of Interior of Ukraine, V. M. Nedryhaylo[2] stated when presenting the bill:

[2] Valentyn Mykhaylovych Nedryhaylo (1936–2005) had a career of high positions in the field of internal affairs in the Soviet Union (beginning in 1976) and in the independent Ukraine. He was elected MP (1994–1998), was a member of the committee on legislation and law enforcement and of the committee on foreign affairs. In 2002 he was on the second position of the list of the block "ZUBR" ("for Ukraine, Belarus, and Russia"—an electoral block formed by the political parties "Light from the East" and "Union of Labor" for the parliamentary elections of 2002, in favour of closer ties between Ukraine, Belarus, and Russia) (Official Ukraine Today, n.d.-d).

> As you know, due to the events that took place there, more than 60 000 people came from the Republic of Moldova to the territory of Ukraine last year, of which 60% were women and children. Because of the acts of war in Abkhazia and Georgia about 2000 people came to Ukraine. (Verkhovna Rada of Ukraine, 1993a)

To stress the importance of the bill on refugees, the Deputy Minister of Interior referred both to the high number of fleeing people and to the percentage of women and children, who are common figures of vulnerability and innocence and are therefore seen as being in need of assistance (Ticktin, 2015). Bondarchuk,[3] the chairman of the subcommittee of the Verkhovna Rada of Ukraine on publicity and media and MP of the Horokhivskiy electoral district in the Volyn region, pointed to the multiplication of fleeing immigrants and the diversification of their countries of origin. This conveyed an impression of urgency to tackle the problem. MPs and high civil servants legitimised the adoption of the first Law on Refugees with the norms' content, in particular their instrumental value in regard to an existing and anticipated migratory influx. It therefore seems like the first Law on Refugees was adopted in order to respond to the influx of fugitives in the first half of the 1990s—a situation construed as a public policy problem.

However, during the parliamentary debate, three MPs criticised the bill as not addressing this problem. M. V. Kosiv,[4] member of the Commission of the Verkhovna Rada on questions of state sovereignty, inter-republican and international relations, MP from the Lviv region, argued:

[3] Andriy Ivanovych Bondarchuk (1936–) was a journalist and member of the Communist Party in the USSR. He left the party in 1990 and was elected into the Parliament between 1990 and 1994 for the "Народна Рада", the "People's Council", a parliamentary opposition block, opposing the conservative-communist majority (Verkhovna Rada of Ukraine, 2004b).

[4] Mykhaylo Vasylovych Kosiv (1934–), a philologist and historian, worked as a teacher in the USSR and was arrested and detained for anti-Soviet agitation and propaganda. He participated in illegal dissident cultural activities and promoted the revival of the Greek-Catholic Church in Western Ukraine. He joined "Rukh" (People's Movement of Ukraine) as early as 1989 and remained in the centre-right party until 2002, when he joined the liberal, centre-right party "Реформи і порядок" (Reforms and Order) participating in the block of Yuliya Timoshenko (Official Ukraine Today, n.d.-c) (Ovsiyenko & Kharkiv Human Rights Group, 2013).

> In article 1 you define the term 'refugee' and list the grounds on which a person can be qualified as a refugee, 'based on race, nationality, religion, citizenship, membership of a particular social group, or political opinion'. But in fact in our case none of these characteristics is the cause for flight. In our country quite different circumstances are the reason for flight, including the stay in an area of hostilities which threaten the life and health of citizens. This is in our situation the main reason for flight. I know you are looking to apply the standards of international norms, but they do not fit our situation. (Verkhovna Rada of Ukraine, 1993a)

A. V. Kornyeyev,[5] deputy chairman of the Commission of the Verkhovna Rada of Ukraine on State Sovereignty, inter-republican and interethnic relations, from the Donetsk region, supported Kosiv's position (Verkhovna Rada of Ukraine, 1993a). He pointed out that military action and mass riots were the major reasons for the influx of asylum seekers from Central Asia to Ukraine—but were not included in the definition of a refugee in the law. This criticism did not affect the formulation of the law. Even though the adopted law did not correspond to the Ukrainian refugee situation at that time, some politicians legitimised the import of international asylum norms referring to their instrumental function. This type of legitimisation disappeared from the debates in the following years.

The Lack of Legitimacy of the Asylum Norms' Content in the Verkhovna Rada

The debates about refugee laws increasingly reflected the parliamentarians' overall lack of interest in asylum norms. Until 2001, MPs and high civil servants occasionally discussed the laws' content, in particular concerning the number of migrants, the risks they entailed for Ukraine, and the expected costs—but very little the migrants' situation and the impact the amendment might have on them. From 2001 onwards, even these limited debates about the instrumental function of the law largely disappeared.

[5] Albert Vasylovych Kornyeyev (1937–) was a member of the Communist Party until 1991 and worked as a lawyer and at universities in the USSR. He was elected MP in 1990 for one term. In the 1990s he worked at the Secretariat of the Parliament, at the Presidential Administration, as a consultant of the President of Ukraine, at the Constitutional Commission, and at the Constitutional Court of Ukraine (Official Ukraine Today, n.d.-b).

Until 2010, debates about refugee bills were dominated by the representation of migrants as a threat to Ukraine and Ukrainians. The necessity for asylum legislation was often explained by the need for migration control. This dimension was already present in 1993 but increased over time as migration in Ukraine has been constructed as a security threat (Zhyznomirska, 2006, p. 48). In fact, parliamentarians from the entire political spectrum depicted the "developing world migrants in Ukraine [as] illegal immigrants rather than refugees" (Shevel, 2011, p. 162).

MPs regularly conflated different groups of foreigners while debating a Law on Refugees, namely people fleeing political persecution, victims of armed conflict, illegal migrants, drug traffickers, mafia-businessmen, and other criminals of foreign origin. S. V. Kivalov, chairman of the subcommittee on Legal Policy of the Verkhovna Rada of Ukraine and former official of the Soviet Ministry of Interior, explained the necessity for the bill on refugees by stating:

> If someone believes that the processes of illegal migration are not such a big problem in our country, he is deeply mistaken, since the bulk of illegal immigrants who come to Ukraine are from those countries where there are large active drug-mafia clans and various terrorist organisations. Because of this, our country automatically enters the sphere of influence of international organised crime, which controls the flow of illegal immigrants. As a consequence of the transit channels of migrants across the territory of Ukraine, delivery channels of weapons, drugs, insurgents, and terrorists will inevitably expand here as well. *(*Verkhovna Rada of Ukraine, 2000*)*

Discussions in the Verkhovna Rada around asylum laws reflected the fears associated with migration, especially that migrants would lead to an increase in diseases, crime rate, terrorism, and drug abuse (Verkhovna Rada of Ukraine, 1993b). MPs often highly exaggerated the current and expected number and sometimes presented Ukraine as being flooded and soon dominated by immigrants (Verkhovna Rada of Ukraine, 1996). Paradoxically, MPs mobilised the migratory threat to justify the need for a bill which increased the asylum seekers' rights (the above-cited Kivalov, for example, proposed to extend the definition of a refugee to victims of war and man-made disasters). This shows that the argument of migration control was considered legitimate in Parliament—and was often mobilised without an obvious link to the content of the amendment.

Apart from the supposed number of immigrants and the crimes they might commit, the situation of refugees and asylum seekers in Ukraine and the concrete changes that the legal amendment would entail were barely discussed in the Verkhovna Rada. MPs redirected the debate to adjacent topics such as irregular immigration, supposed threats related to migration, or the misery of Ukrainians and their emigration.

Parliamentary debates on asylum legislation reveal most MPs' lack of interest in the situation of asylum seekers and refugees as well as the competing political priorities (such as migration control and the use of the state budget for other purposes) and xenophobia. However, in most cases, instead of blocking the adoption of international asylum norms, these competing political interests were rhetorically reconciled with the adoption of international asylum norms, which the MPs rarely contested. In particular from 2001 onwards, debates about the laws' content and practical implications largely disappeared as debates became shorter. Interest in the more practical concerns was replaced by interest in the symbolic value of the asylum laws.

The Symbolic Value of International Asylum Norms in the Parliamentary Debates

The overall unquestioned adoption of international asylum norms was based on their symbolic value, virtually unrelated to the norms' content. The symbolic value of the adoption of these international norms was already obvious in the debate on the first Law on Refugees in 1993. Indeed, facing the above-mentioned criticism concerning the fact that the first Law on Refugees did not solve the situation of people fleeing indiscriminate violence, the MP S. V. Batyushko,[6] chairman of the Committee on Human Rights of the Verkhovna Rada, replied:

> For us, the concept of a refugee is often associated with a person who is forced to leave his place in connection with the ongoing fighting there or riots. But they are not refugees. They do not fit the definition of a refugee determined by the United Nations. Because of this, they may not be covered by this law. (Verkhovna Rada of Ukraine, 1993a)

[6] Stefan Vasylovych Batyushko (1949–) was a member of the Communist Party and worked for the military in the USSR. He was a member of the Verkhovna Rada between 1990 and 1994. In 1994 he worked for the ministry of defence. He later supported President Yushchenko (Verkhovna Rada of Ukraine, 2004a).

This representative of the Parliamentary Committee on Human Rights argued that complying with legitimate international standards and definitions was more important than tackling a domestic public policy problem. He dismissed the criticism that the proposed bill did not tackle the current problems in Ukraine by suggesting another bill, decrees, or resolutions to be written on this issue. However, a law foreseeing a protection status for persons fleeing indiscriminate violence was not adopted until 2011. Addressing the public policy problem of fugitives in Ukraine was therefore not a priority for the legislators in the 1990s and 2000s. In the ensuing debate, both defenders of the bill, Nedryhaylo and Batyushko, legitimised it by referring to international standards. The defenders listed these sources of legitimacy as if the accumulation of international documents and organisations with which the bill complied justified its necessity.

In the following years, MPs systematically legitimised the amendments of Ukrainian asylum legislation and the elaboration of new laws in this sphere by reference to international norms. This reference to the international norm often stood alone—without further explanation of the ensuing advantage of compliance. The MPs presented the alignment to the norm as a goal in itself. It was commonly reinforced with the argument of the objective to formally accede to the 1951 Refugee Convention.

The need to accede to the Convention was rarely explained. H. P. Sereda, the head of the Department of the Affairs of Nationalities and Migration argued in 2002 that 142 countries had already joined the Convention and that Ukraine was the only country in Europe that was not yet part of it (Verkhovna Rada of Ukraine, 2002). Ukraine elaborated its asylum legislation at a time when most other post-communist states adopted first laws on refugees and / or acceded to the 1951 Convention (UNHCR, 2015). Consequently, in the 1990s, the adoption of a Law on Refugees and the ratification of the Convention were a norm among post-communist states. This generalised spread of international asylum norms explains why Ukrainian politicians did not justify the adoption further. This corresponds to Finnemore and Sikkink's finding according to which once a large number of states, in particular "critical states", have adhered to a norm, a "norm cascade" takes place in the course of which more states adopt the norm more rapidly (Finnemore & Sikkink, 1998, pp. 901–902).

The adoption of international asylum norms and the accession to the Refugee Convention in 2002 led to a circular justification of the following amendments. MPs also justified the amendments with the necessity of coherence with previous decisions or legal texts which were higher up in the hierarchy of legal norms. Furthermore, since the ratification of the Convention, legal change was systematically explained by Ukraine's obligations under the 1951 Refugee Convention (Verkhovna Rada of Ukraine, 2004c).

Beyond this circular logic, the alignment to the international norm was legitimised by the need to join the international community of democratic states. For instance, H. I. Udovenko, who had repeatedly worked for the United Nations,[7] defended a draft law in the name of the State Committee for Nationalities and Migration as:

> an important bill which indicates that despite all the problems in our state, the state still heads towards at least developing democratic legislation which meets modern requirements, the requirements of the Council of Europe, the United Nations, and other international organisations. (Verkhovna Rada of Ukraine, 2001)

The speakers associated the norms with positive characteristics such as modern and democratic. In another debate, Udovenko referred to the "European path"which Ukraine followed and which necessitated the passing of the respective law (Verkhovna Rada of Ukraine, 2000). V. Ia. Shybko[8] from the socialist party underlined:

> A document that indicates that today we still progress towards European standards. When we ratify this or another convention, or some kind of

[7] Hennadiy Yosypovych Udovenko (1931–2013) entered diplomatic service at the Department of International Economic organisations of the Ministry of Foreign Affairs of the UkrSSR in 1959. He repeatedly worked for the United Nations (including in Geneva and in New York) and as Ambassador and Minister of Foreign Affairs of Ukraine. 1998–2007 he was MP and chairman of the Parliamentary Committee on Human Rights, National Minorities and Interethnic Relations. He was a member of the centre-right party "People's Movement of Ukraine" ("Народний Рух України"), and then joined "Our Ukraine" Bloc (Блок Наша Україна), associated with Victor Yushchenko (Smolij & Boriak, 2013, pp. 209–210).

[8] Vitaliy Iakovych Shybko (1948–2021) worked both at university and at higher positions of committees of the city of Dnipropetrovsk during the USSR. 1995–1997 he worked as an advisor to the President of Ukraine on Science and Education and as a Ukrainian diplomat in Lebanon. He joined the Socialist Party of Ukraine in 1991 and was an MP between 1994 and 1998 and between 2002 and 2007, chairman of the Committee on Foreign Affairs (Verkhovna Rada of Ukraine, 2012).

> agreement, it already shows that today the legislator works so that the country, from the territorial features becomes a European state. (Verkhovna Rada of Ukraine, 2004c)

Ukrainian politicians legitimised the introduction of international asylum norms into Ukrainian law with reference to its symbolic function: It showed that Ukraine was becoming democratic and European. This confirms Shushanik Makaryan's argument according to whom states of the Eastern Partnership conformed to international models of legitimate states, adopting migration policies even though the measures clashed with the states' interests, because they sought to gain international legitimacy and integration (Makaryan, 2015).

International Organisations' Transfer Attempts Between Persuasion, Exchange of Favours, and Monitoring Without Incentives

In the 1990s, Ukrainian political elites, especially in the executive, were rather pro-Western and were eager to decrease Ukraine's dependence vis-à-vis Russia and to intensify the relations with Western organisations (Shevel, 2011, p. 192). Decision makers of the newly independent Ukrainian state pursued international praise and inclusion in international organisations. While so far, the adoption of asylum norms resembles a process of imitation, I will in the following show that this transfer was actively promoted by international organisations, primarily the Council of Europe, UNHCR, and the EU. Their legitimacy among Ukrainian law-makers differed over time depending on their transfer practices and resources.

Between 1993 and 2010, Ukrainian politicians mentioned several international organisations in the debates on asylum legislation in the Verkhovna Rada: sporadically the International Organization for Migration and the Organization for Security and Co-operation in Europe and predominantly UNHCR and the Council of Europe. While UNHCR opted for a field office in Kyiv, the Council of Europe interacted with Ukrainian politicians and officials via meetings in Strasbourg and occasional visits to Kyiv. Even though it is difficult to reconstruct the concrete interactions between Ukrainian decision makers and representatives of these two international organisations that took place in the 1990s and 2000s, some comments from the parliamentary debates shed light on moments and channels of influence.

The Council of Europe Pre-Accession Conditionality and Interactions: Legitimacy Despite Limited Official Focus on Asylum

In the early 1990s, MPs and high state officials mentioned the Council of Europe (CoE) and its requests for asylum reforms as legitimate arguments in Parliament. They referred to their interactions with representatives of the CoE concerning asylum norms to justify the need for their adoption. For instance, during the debate on the Law on Refugees in 1993, S. V. Batyushko, head of the Commission of the Verkhovna Rada on Human Rights, stressed the conditionality of the CoE as well as their interactions, namely during a "recently held seminar on human rights organised by the Department of Human Rights of the Council of Europe [that] emphasised the need for our Parliament for such a law" (Verkhovna Rada of Ukraine, 1993a). When discussing the amendment to the Criminal Code concerning the depenalisation of asylum seekers' irregular border crossing in 1995, Serhiy Petrovych Brychenko, First Deputy Minister of Ukraine for Migration, Nationality and Religions explained:

> This issue is very important for us. I will explain why: you know that now is discussed the question of the acceptance of Ukraine to the Council of Europe. And those experts who come to Ukraine, almost every day, well, not every day, every week to our ministry, raise that issue. (Verkhovna Rada of Ukraine, 1995)

In the context of the 1990s, when the politicians of the newly independent Ukrainian state tried to convey the impression of contributing to the democratisation process of Ukraine, MPs and officials considered that it was legitimate in the Verkhovna Rada to justify a legislative amendment with the request of the CoE.

During this time, the Ukrainian state tried to accede to the Council of Europe. In 1992, Ukraine applied to join the CoE, which was seen as a way to integrate into Europe and the international community (Anders Nordström, 2008, p. 6). The application was strongly supported across the political spectrum in Ukraine. Beginning in 1992, the CoE repeatedly met with Ukrainian officials. A few months after the application, the Ukrainian Parliament obtained special guest status with the Parliamentary Assembly of the Council of Europe. Ukraine then took part in intergovernmental cooperation and assistance programmes on legal reform and human rights (Parliamentary Assembly of the Council of Europe,

1995). The CoE commented little on asylum in its official communication concerning Ukraine's accession. Nevertheless, as the parliamentary debates show, Ukrainian decision makers paid attention to the CoE's comments, while it was considering the acceptance of Ukraine. The CoE's role in the elaboration of the Law on Refugees in Ukraine in first half of the 1990s was shaped both by the incentive of the accession and, related to it, by interactions with the CoE rapporteurs. In 1994 and 1995, the CoE Assembly's rapporteurs travelled to Ukraine noticed "fast progress" in the harmonisation of Ukraine's Constitution and legislation with the CoE's principles. Further deep reforms would be necessary but could be carried out after joining the CoE. Consequently, Ukraine acceded to the Council of Europe in 1995.

However, since the accession in 1995, the Council of Europe's criticism and demands disappeared from the parliamentary debates. At the rare occasions when the CoE appeared in the debates, the politicians mentioned it very shortly together with other international organisations as having reviewed a legislative amendment (Verkhovna Rada of Ukraine, 2004c). It still appeared as legitimate but not as a major argument to support the amendment. As a difference to the EU, the CoE has low accession conditions. However, after formally joining the CoE, the country is subject to a temporary open-ended monitoring period to supervise the respect of the new member states' commitments. For Ukraine this monitoring process was still unfinished in 2021.

Since the accession, the bodies of the CoE commented on asylum in Ukraine (Parliamentary Assembly of the Council of Europe, 2000; Parliamentary Assembly of the Council of Europe & Rapporteur Filimonov, 1997). Like all other member states, Ukraine was also monitored by specialised bodies of the CoE such as the European Commission against Racism and Intolerance which has regularly written reports, approximately one every four years since 1999, about the situation of migrants and ethnic minorities in Ukraine. In addition to using information from publications by UNHCR and the Organization for Migration, the CoE reports were based on visits to Ukraine during which the rapporteurs met with government officials and representatives of NGOs. Several reports criticised the asylum laws and practices in detail, formulating recommendations for the Ukrainian authorities (European Commission Against Racism & Intolerance - Council of Europe, 2002, 2008, 2012, 2017).

Despite the CoE's increased attention and criticism of asylum in Ukraine after the accession in 1995, Ukrainian politicians did not report on the CoE's comments in Parliament. This may be explained by the lack of accession conditionality, the overall tense relations between Ukraine and the CoE in the monitoring process, as well as the Ukrainian government's resistance to the CoE's requests of compliance (Anders Nordström, 2008, p. 68).

The Importance of UNHCR Lobbying and Exchange of Favours on the Ground

In the 1990s and 2000s, without any major incentives to propose, UNHCR enjoyed strong legitimacy in the parliamentary debates on asylum in Ukraine thanks to its office in the capital, its lobbying, and its exchange of favours with domestic decision makers.

In the parliamentary debates on asylum laws, UNHCR was the major and most frequent reference. MPs cited it as legitimate in its standards and experience and used its position as a crucial argument in the debate. For instance, the MP Nedryhaylo claimed to have elaborated the bills "based on the recommendations of the United Nations" (Verkhovna Rada of Ukraine, 1993a). MPs and representatives of the administration regularly underlined that the bill had been submitted to the expertise of UNHCR or even received its praise, which they presented as a guarantee of the bill's quality. These comments reflect not only UNHCR's legitimacy in the Parliament but also hint to the meetings which took place between Ukrainian officials and UNHCR during which the UN agency tried to spread the knowledge and legitimacy of its norms and influence draft laws.

UNHCR's role in the transfer of asylum norms in Ukraine can be explained by its long-lasting presence on the ground, its lobbying activities, and its exchange of favours with the domestic migration authorities. Indeed, in the second half of the 1990s, UNHCR built up harmonious relations with the Ukrainian authorities. In the mid-1990s, the office in Kyiv was composed only of one international and one local employee who built up contacts with some decision makers (Shevel, 2011, p. 167). UNHCR undertook an important citizenship campaign for returning Crimean Tatars. The Ukrainian asylum policies in the second half of the 1990s consisted largely in a "reciprocal act by the Ukrainian authorities for the UNHCR's assistance with FDPs [formerly deported persons] in Crimea", which were a major political problem for the Ukrainian government at the time (Shevel, 2011, p. 173). UNHCR's projects with respect to Crimean Tatars were perceived as successful and established

UNHCR's good reputation in the eyes of Ukrainian officials. This led to reciprocated "good will" from the government concerning asylum seekers. In addition, UNHCR materially supported Ukrainian migration authorities and thus maintained the good relations and influential position of UNHCR. UNHCR also generously praised Ukraine's refugee policies as "an example for the CIS region" (Shevel, 2011, p. 176). This enabled UNHCR to lobby when the executive prepared a bill as well as when the bill was submitted to the Verkhovna Rada and debated in parliamentary committees. The Ukrainian administration shared draft laws with UNHCR. The harmonious relations in the 1990s and early 2000s between UNHCR and Ukrainian authorities allowed UNHCR to obtain liberalised asylum policies several times, for instance concerning the safe third country provision in the Law on Refugees in 2001.

According to Shevel, UNHCR's influence decreased around 2001. She explains this by the growing securitisation of migration issues in Ukraine and changes in UNHCR's strategy. Indeed, the Crimean Tatars campaigns ended as most Tatars obtained Ukrainian citizenship. The UNHCR budget in Ukraine decreased at that time (Shevel, 2011, p. 184). The UN agency could therefore offer less assistance to Ukrainian authorities—and especially less assistance to groups that were of interest to the authorities such as formerly deported persons. This reduced the organisation's bargaining power to get Ukrainian authorities to care for refugees for whom no domestic lobby existed in Ukraine. This can partly explain the slowing down of the adoption process of international asylum norms after 2001. Nevertheless, thanks to its long-lasting presence on the ground and the developed ties and reputation, UNHCR remained a legitimate reference in the parliamentary debates and the most influential international actor at that time, by comparison to the other, even less influential organisations, such as the European Union.

UNHCR has also tried to exert influence on the Ukrainian asylum legislation by shaping the action of the EU. Already in the early 2000s, based on its experience, UNHCR advised EU officials concerning the reforms to be undertaken in Ukraine on asylum (Interview, former representative of the EU delegation in Kyiv and former representative of the EU Commission, 2015). In addition, UNHCR informed EU officials from the Commission and the Delegation about the situation of asylum in Ukraine and played the role of an alternative source of information to the one delivered by the Ukrainian authorities. However, in the 2000s this indirect channel of influence of UNHCR was of limited impact, as the EU had only weak influence on asylum in Ukraine.

The Weak Legitimacy of EU Monitoring and Criticism

In the early 2000s, after the signature of the Treaty of Amsterdam, the EU began to become involved in asylum in Ukraine. However, in the 1990s and 2000s, Ukrainian politicians did not mention the EU requests for reforms in their debates and questioned the EU's legitimacy in the area of asylum.

The few times the EU and its member states appeared in parliamentary debates they did so in an ambiguous way. Ukrainian politicians did not present Europe as a model of refugees' rights which Ukraine should follow. They presented some EU member states (often without naming them precisely) as counter-examples of excessively liberal migration policies, pointing out migration-related problems in these countries (e.g. "social tension" and a "criminal environment" [Verkhovna Rada of Ukraine, 1993b]), which Ukraine should avoid. From time to time, they spoke of EU member states as models during debates about asylum laws—in a sense of restrictive approaches to asylum and migration. In the 2000s, they cited European countries, such as Germany, France, and Italy, as examples of migration control to justify that Ukraine should follow a similar—restrictive—approach. Indeed, a recurring statement was that Ukraine should not be more liberal than European countries (Verkhovna Rada of Ukraine, 2010). These references to Europe as a model of restrictive immigration policies can be seen as the results of circulation or diffusion—though not of international asylum norms but of restrictive migration policies. They also show that Ukrainian politicians constructed Europe as a space distinct from Ukraine, following different policies and values.

Moreover, domestic decision makers contested the EU's attempts to transfer asylum norms to Ukraine. They formulated the fear that Ukraine had become or might become an involuntary host country for large numbers of asylum seekers instead of the EU. The EU restricted its immigration legislation and might try to keep migrants in Ukraine. Ukraine, so the fear expressed, would become a "buffer zone", a "sink" or "reservoir" ("vidstiynyk") for migrants instead of the EU (Verkhovna Rada of Ukraine, 2000, 2004c). Ukrainian MPs presented the EU as hypocritical, granting refugee status only to a small part of its own applicants but requesting generous asylum policies from Ukraine (Shevel, 2011, pp. 182–183). Until 2010, concerning asylum, the EU enjoyed little legitimacy and visibility in the Ukrainian Parliament.

This weak role of the EU in asylum matters can be explained firstly by the overall weak influence of the EU on Ukrainian domestic policy making at that time. Until the Orange Revolution in 2004, Ukrainian politicians declared pursuing EU integration but undertook little rapprochement. As early as 1993, the Verkhovna Rada expressed the objective of European integration. At the Helsinki European Council in 1999, Ukrainian politicians expected a clear political signal from the European elites whereas the EU attributed the candidate status to Turkey and not to Ukraine—which many scholars see as the beginning of Ukrainian elites' frustration with regards to the EU (Svyetlov, 2007, p. 535). Ukrainian elites viewed the Partnership and Cooperation Agreement (1994) and the EU Common Strategy towards Ukraine (CSU—1999) as a "consolation prize" instead of the candidate status (Ferreira-Pereira & Vieira, 2015, p. 148). Moreover, during the presidency of Leonid Kuchma, Ukrainian political elites were convinced that Ukraine was too important to be left aside by the EU and cared little about the fulfilment of contractual obligations with the EU such as those contained in the Partnership and Cooperation Agreement (Wolczuk, 2008, pp. 91–92).

After the Orange Revolution, European integration was framed as a domestic policy area but the domestic effects remained limited. The years 2004–2005 are often considered to be a fundamental shift in the EU-Ukraine relations due to both the accession to power of the new "Orange" elites and the launch of the European Neighbourhood Policy (ENP) and the EU-Ukraine Action Plan. Though initially reluctant about the ENP, Ukrainian elites accepted it, hoping for a closer relationship that might eventually lead to a membership perspective (Balfour, 2013, p. 58). The "Orange" elites promised the practical implementation of the changes required by the EU instead of declarations. Ukrainian political parties largely agreed over the question of European integration, but reforms failed to take place due to other domestic factors, for example due to the competition between the Cabinet and the Presidential Secretariat over EU matters. The government set up a series of institutional structures to coordinate the EU integration—but with limited effect (Stegniy, 2011, pp. 52–53).

Yanukovych's government, elected in 2006, did not radically change the attitude towards the EU but the approach became more pragmatic and business oriented. The government sought access to the European market thanks to the Free Trade Area while some reforms were rejected. Wolczuk (2008) observed that the Yanukovych government showed less eagerness to implement reforms demanded by the EU. In fact, the Action Plan necessitated extensive and costly domestic changes which concerned most areas of the state and all scales of state authorities and would have required a coordinating framework and organ which was not formed. Nevertheless, the ENP and the three-year action plan (2005–2008) were the first EU instruments which had some effect on domestic policy making in Ukraine (Wolczuk, 2008, p. 102).

Secondly, the EU's weak power on asylum in Ukraine can be explained by the EU's limited resources to promote asylum norms. In the 2000s, the EU mostly provided project funding, regularly met with Ukrainian officials, and wrote evaluation reports. The Ukrainian officials' lack of interest and ensuing hidden resistance by passivity and circumvention (Saurugger & Terpan, 2013, p. 25) are evident in the recurring complaints of EU officials about the lack of initiative by the Ukrainian officials (European Commission, 2002).

Since the 2000s, the European Union sought more and more to shape asylum policies in Ukraine by evaluating them in its reports. While the EU did not discuss asylum in Ukraine in the 2005 ENP Action Plan, it discussed it in the Action Plan on Justice and Home Affairs (2001). Until 2007, ENP country reports only briefly commented on the evaluation of the Ukrainian asylum system (European Commission, 2004, pp. 8–9, 2006, p. 13). But since 2007, the EU focused more on asylum in Ukraine in its ENP progress reports (European Commission, 2008, pp. 13–14) and included it in the 2007 Revised EU-Ukraine Action Plan on Freedom, Justice and Security. The reports frequently demanded the harmonisation of the legislation with the 1951 Refugee Convention and EU standards. However, there was little domestic political interest in asylum and the EU only relied on reports to advise and shame Ukraine without having any incentives to offer.

In short, between 1993 and 2010, the phase of mostly shallow legislative adoption of international asylum norms, domestic lawmakers primarily legitimised this adoption by referring to norms' symbolic value. The adoption functioned as a sign of democratisation of the Ukrainian state, that is, of becoming part of a democratic international community.

Lawmakers also cited the exchange value of the adoption of the norms, which allowed them to access the Council of Europe. While the CoE's role in the norm transfer decreased with the end of its accession conditionality, UNHCR enjoyed more stable legitimacy, most likely thanks to its direct lobbying among decision makers. The EU's legitimacy was weak, which correlated with the EU's lack of incentives for Ukrainian politicians.

Deep Adoption of International Asylum Norms: EU Sector-Specific Conditionality (2010–2016)

Which factors, between 2010 and 2016, enabled international actors to cause deeper legislative adoption? The EU suddenly managed to strengthen its role after 2010.

The Power of EU Sector-Specific Conditionality from 2010 Onwards

Researchers have repeatedly demonstrated the importance of EU conditionality for norm transfer (Schimmelfennig & Sedelmeier, 2004, p. 671). They have usually done this by comparing different countries or policy fields. The present research traces the EU's influence in the same country in the same policy field over 30 years—including before and after the introduction of sector-specific conditionality.

The Introduction of an Attractive Incentive into EU-Ukraine Relations

When examining EU-Ukraine relations from a macro perspective, weak EU influence on Ukrainian laws can be expected between 2010 and 2014. The momentum following the Orange Revolution had disappeared by 2009–2010 (Delcour & Wolczuk, 2015, p. 462). Ukrainian foreign policy objectives remained unclear and their implementation was often declarative (Stegniy, 2011, pp. 61–62). Despite the launching of the Eastern Partnership Initiative in 2009, supposed to prepare the Association Agreement, relations between the EU and Ukraine deteriorated under the increasingly authoritarian presidency of Yanukovych (2010–2014). The EU hesitantly insisted on democratisation and postponed the signature of the Association Agreement as a conditionality measure. However, the political costs for democratisation were too high for Yanukovych, threatening his power. Ukrainian politicians criticised the EU interference in

Ukrainian internal affairs, prioritised the aspiration to EU membership less, and focused more on relations with Russia (Wetzel, 2016). During this phase, scholars therefore evaluated the impact of the EU on domestic policy making as minor (Delcour & Wolczuk, 2015, pp. 465–466; Dragneva-Lewers & Wolczuk, 2015).

However, in the area of asylum, the EU managed to drastically increase its influence in 2010 by introducing its sector-specific conditionality (Wetzel, 2016). Since 2001, the EU incorporated in its agreements and action plans objectives, criticism, and recommendations to reform Ukrainian migration and asylum policies—but initially without any explicit sector-specific conditionality. The EU Action Plan from 2001, which listed the changes Ukraine should undertake in terms of asylum and migration policies (including the harmonisation of asylum legislation with EU standards), foresaw very vaguely the "continuation of a dialogue on visa issues". It did so without explicitly establishing the realisation of these changes as the condition for visa liberalisation.

The conditionality, linking reforms of Ukrainian migration policies to the incentive of visa facilitation, became increasingly obvious in the second half of the 2000s. In October 2008, the visa dialogue was opened with the long-term perspective of establishing a visa-free regime between the EU and Ukraine. While the EU introduced limited visa liberalisation together with the agreement on readmission, it held back the carrot of visa-free travel for Ukrainians so as to be able to request further changes in the Ukrainian migration policies (Council of the European Union, 2009). In 2010 the EU set up explicit conditionality for various migration reforms: the long-term goal of a visa-free regime in exchange for a range of measures namely in the area of migration, including on asylum (General Secretariat of the Council of the European Union, 2010, p. 3). In the first phase, the Visa Liberalisation Action Plan (VLAP) foresaw the "adoption of legislation in the area of asylum in line with international standards (1951 Geneva Convention with New York Protocol) and EU standards" and in the second phase its implementation (General Secretariat of the Council of the European Union, 2010, pp. 6–7). The EU documents consistently presented the objective of a visa-free regime in a vague way and as a long-term perspective that was conditional upon a large number of changes to be undertaken by the Ukrainian state (General Secretariat of the Council of the European Union, 2010, p. 3).

Ukrainian politicians were extremely interested in a visa-free regime for Ukrainian tourists in the EU. The issue became more pressing for

Ukrainian politicians when in 2004 visas became necessary for Ukrainians to travel to the neighbouring countries Poland, Slovakia, and Hungary. In February 2011, the government of Ukraine established the Centre on the Implementation of the VLAP and adopted the national plan on the implementation of the VLAP (Nizhnikau, 2015). It designed this national plan as a roadmap for reforms and included a detailed list of the necessary measures, time frames, and responsible agencies. Two years later, in 2013, the Vice Premier Kostiantyn Gryshchenko underlined that the President of Ukraine "personally oversees the implementation by Ukraine of the action plan for visa liberalization with the EU" and considered the visa-free regime "a key task for the authorities" ('Gryshchenko', 2013). Having pointed out the importance attributed to the VLAP by the Ukrainian president, Gryshchenko encouraged the agencies to accelerate their work on laws foreseen in the EU action plan and focus on them in Parliament.

EU officials as well as a representative of the Mission of Ukraine to the EU stressed the importance of the VLAP in my interviews. Representatives of the European External Action Service (EEAS), the European Commission, and the EU Delegation in Kyiv explicitly recognised the power of the incentive, the visa-free regime, for the Ukrainian officials they met. For instance, a member of the EU Delegation in Kyiv commented, "The Prime Minister and the President are obsessed with visa liberalisation" (Interview, representative of the EU delegation in Kyiv, 2015). Another representative of the EU Delegation stressed, "The visa liberalisation action plan is the biggest carrot we have. It's better than giving them lots of money. They are very keen on having that." (Interview, representative of the EU delegation in Kyiv, 2014). The visa-free regime was a strong incentive and replaced, at least temporarily, the membership perspective which many scholars present as the major incentive for EU neighbours.

Nevertheless, until the Maidan protests, MPs occasionally criticised the adoption of international asylum norms. Similarly to the previous period, between 2010 and 2013, the MPs sometimes exaggerated the number of refugees and raised the threats associated with irregular immigration. Otherwise, the MPs continued to show little interest in the content of the asylum norms and instead regularly drew attention to the situation of Ukrainians when discussing an asylum law. This Ukrainians-centred perspective also took the shape of criticism of Western Europe. During a debate on the bill on refugees and persons in need of complementary or temporary protection in 2011, Iu. V. Hnatkevych, despite being the head of the Subcommittee on Victims of Political Repressions, Ethnic Policy, Prevention of National Conflicts, Refugees, Migration and Relations with Ukrainians Living Abroad and of the Committee on Human Rights, National Minorities and International Relations[9] criticised the bill, saying:

> Firstly, it is a European tendency to liberalise immigration laws. Europe loves liberalisation based on human rights. Yet we have been watching some realities and some practices, and we also see what is happening now in the world, especially in North Africa, and we understand the large influx of refugees who will seek asylum here. Well, this position is seen ambiguously and we do not very much want to liberalise it. (Verkhovna Rada of Ukraine, 2011)

MPs presented Europe as excessively liberal concerning immigration regulation. They distanced themselves from this liberal policy, underlining the necessity for another, more restrictive approach in Ukraine. Moreover, several politicians stated that migrants tried to transit via Ukraine to the EU (Verkhovna Rada of Ukraine, 2014). They continued to stress that the EU restricted its immigration legislation and might try to keep unwanted migrants in Ukraine (Verkhovna Rada of Ukraine, 2011). Until early 2014, MPs considered it legitimate to voice their mistrust and dissatisfaction with the power relations between the EU and the Ukrainian state.

Although the Ukrainian politicians officially agreed on the commitments to reforms, they did so in a context of limited options and power relations with the EU. Ukrainian politicians formally accepted the EU-funded asylum projects in Ukraine, agreements including commitments

[9] Iuriy Vasylovych Hnatkevych (1940–) was sentenced in 1958 for anti-Soviet agitation and afterwards worked as a worker at a brick factory. Later he studied foreign languages, worked as a teacher and then as head of a German language department at a university. He began his political career with the People's Council and was an MP from 1990 to 1994. He was a member of the Central Council of the People's Self-government Platform "Sobor" (1999–2005), which in 2002 became part of the Yulia Timoshenko Electoral Block. From 2006 to 2012, Hnatkevych was MP for the party "Batkivshchyna", head of the Subcommittee on Victims of Political Repressions, Ethnic Policy, Prevention of National Conflicts, Refugees, Migration and Relations with Ukrainians Living Abroad and of the Committee on Human Rights, National Minorities and International Relations (Official Ukraine Today, n.d.-a; Verkhovna Rada of Ukraine, n.d.).

on asylum and EU action plans. However, the EU decided unilaterally on the action plan on visa liberalisation. As shown by scholars underlining the structural asymmetry between the EU and neighbouring states, the conditions and orientations of the rapprochement had been defined by the EU actors (Jeandesboz, 2015, p. 443). Ukrainian politicians did not have any means of influence, facing the choice between taking or leaving the VLAP (Interview, Representative of the European Commission, DG Home, 2015). Moreover, Ukraine had already abolished visa requirements for EU citizens in 2005, which meant that negotiations for visa-free travel for Ukrainians could not be undertaken on the basis of an exchange of mutual visa liberalisation. Ukrainian politicians made the choice of sacrificing some of their autonomy in policy making in exchange for an expected gain in popularity among the Ukrainian people thanks to the visa liberalisation. However, only very few MPs criticised the adoption of asylum norms due to EU conditionality. The incentive of the visa-free regime largely outweighed the limitation of the Ukrainian state's sovereignty.

The Increase of the Power of the EU Sector-Specific Conditionality After the Maidan Protests

Between 2014 and 2015, the parliamentary debates about asylum laws reflected an increase in the EU's power. Leading national scale civil servants and MPs focused on the EU demands in exchange for visa liberalisation. For example, in 2014 the head of the State Migration Service of Ukraine, S. I. Radutnyy, explained that his service developed the draft law amending the Law on Refugees and Persons in Need of Complementary or Temporary Protection in order to "implement the leading and first phase of the action plan for liberalisation of the EU visa regime for Ukraine defined in the third report of the European Commission and the implementation plan of 15 November 2013" (Verkhovna Rada of Ukraine, 2014). In 2014 MPs also justified the need for a legislative amendment by the need to improve the image of Ukraine vis-à-vis the European Union and the international community.

In 2014 and 2015, politicians in the Verkhovna Rada sought to fulfil EU demands as fast as possible to obtain visa liberalisation. In the debates, asylum law reforms were presented as inevitable and urgent. Members of Parliament quickly approved of various legislative packages that the EU had demanded. For instance, in November 2015 I. V. Herashchenko, head of the Committee on Issues of European integration[10] from the party UDAR, stressed the importance of a bill on amendments to the Law of Ukraine on Refugees and Persons in Need of Complementary or Temporary Protection to improve the procedure of documenting people, saying that it was one of the bills "related to commitments of Ukraine on the implementation of the action plan for visa liberalisation" (Verkhovna Rada of Ukraine, 2015). Later the same day concerning a bill on judicial protection of foreigners and stateless persons and the fight against illegal migration, she said, "Let's vote together in order to get the visa-free regime." (Verkhovna Rada of Ukraine, 2015).

The Ukrainian politicians presented the requests of the EU as compulsory and did not question or discuss them. The content of the legislative amendments became irrelevant in the presence of the argument of the visa-free regime. The MPs continued to show no interest in asylum as such and if they intervened on the content of the amendments, they tended to conflate refugees with Ukrainian internally displaced persons (IDPs). Given that IDPs were commonly called refugees, discussions about laws on refugees (foreign citizens) occasionally drifted to the topic of IDPs. MPs stopped criticising the asylum reforms in 2014 and 2015—as they had occasionally done before. During the peak of the EU visa conditionality, the incentive was so legitimate that it became illegitimate in the Parliament to raise criticism of the reforms demanded by the EU.

The post-Maidan Ukrainian governments showed a stronger interest in European integration. Russian aggression has made the Ukrainian elites more determined to join Western organisations. Given the tensions with Russia, the Ukrainian leadership lacked a geopolitical alternative to the EU and accepted to undertake changes due to the pro-EU government and pro-European social movements requesting change. This strengthened pro-EU stance of the Ukrainian government lasted despite frustration about the EU's responses to the Maidan protests and to Russian

[10] Iryna Volodymyrivna Herashchenko (1971–) studied journalism in the newly independent Ukraine. After working as a journalist, she worked as a presidential press secretary for Victor Yushchenko and became president of the Ukrainian information agency UNIAN. She was an MP since 2007, consecutively for Our Ukraine—People's Self-Defense Bloc, for the Ukrainian Democratic Alliance for Reform of Vitalij Klitshko, for the Petro Poroshenko Bloc (head of the Committee on issues of European integration), and finally for European Solidarity (*Herashchenko Iryna Volodymyrivna*, n.d.; Official Ukraine Today, 2016).

aggression as well as the about the lack of a membership perspective until 2022.

After the Maidan protests, the change of government, and the war with Russia, the incentive of a visa-free regime became an even stronger factor for asylum reforms. Interviewees, especially at the EU Delegation in Kyiv, underlined the difference in the interest of Ukrainian officials. In interviews conducted in 2013, representatives of the EU Delegation complained that they struggled to organise meetings with Ukrainian officials because the latter showed no interest in such events. In contrast, in interviews conducted in 2014 and 2015, officials from the Delegation stressed that since 2014 the Ukrainian officials agreed easily on monthly meetings. The Ukrainian law making also reacted more rapidly to EU requests. For instance, in its second and third progress reports, from February 2012 and from November 2013 respectively, the EU criticised Ukraine for still not having amended the two definitions of the alternative protection statuses "despite earlier recommendations by the Commission" (European Commission, 2013, p. 9). Yet, in May 2014, the fourth progress report highlighted that on 13 May 2014, a few weeks after the Maidan, the Ukrainian Parliament amended the definitions as demanded by the EU (European Commission to the European Parliament and the Council, 2014, p. 3).

In short, between 2010 and 2015, thanks to its visa conditionality and the change in the post-Maidan Ukrainian political leadership, the EU suddenly enjoyed major legitimacy in imposing asylum reforms. While the norms' symbolic value and, more, their exchange value dominated the parliamentary debates, the EU did not manage to create asylum as a public policy problem in Ukraine or to establish international asylum norms' content as a legitimate or even known reference among the Ukrainian MPs.

Power in Practice: Interactions Between EU and Ukrainian Officials

The power relations between EU and Ukrainian officials were an interactive process, negotiated during encounters at different scales and shaped by the actors' changing resources and interests. To grasp these processes it is necessary to adopt multiple perspectives.

As far as the PCA Action Plan is concerned, scholars have demonstrated that a few pro-EU ministerial officials in key positions—and who had interacted with EU actors—managed to cause piecemeal convergence with EU rules without political backing (Langbein & Wolczuk, 2012). Wolczuk and Langbein observed a situation of lack of high-level political interest in convergence with EU rules combined with resistance on the part of powerful actors, especially economically powerful ones. But the asylum situation in Ukraine, notably from 2014 to 2015, was shaped by politicians' pressure on the bureaucratic apparatus to obtain positive evaluations in EU monitoring. Following representations of international and national political scales dominating national administrative and regional scales, the positions of senior and intermediary administrative agents depended on top-down pressure from domestic politicians and the monitoring mechanism set up by the EU. Rationalist scholars have argued that monitoring crucially affects the effectiveness of the transfer attempts via conditionality (Grabbe, 1999; Schimmelfennig & Sedelmeier, 2004, 2005, pp. 13–15; Vachudová, 2005). As the politicians of the targeted state agree on reforms in exchange for certain incentives, the reforms are carried out only if the EU is able to control them. However, it remains unclear in the literature how monitoring practically affects the EU's position and the transfer process.

Monitoring to Counter Suspected Resistance

Several EU officials claimed that Ukrainian politicians and bureaucrats were reluctant to carry out the requested reforms. They voiced mistrust towards Ukrainian politicians and officials, referring to the lack of political will to undertake "real reforms". Officials of the European Commission expressed annoyance about Ukrainian officials' attempts to resist the EU influence while still obtaining the benefits from the EU. They often discussed the efficiency of certain measures by evaluating the "leverage" of the measure. For instance, they said that they were critical about "sectoral budget support because the leverage is not so big" and does not allow to "build up pressure" (2015). Using vocabulary of force such as "shocked" and "hurt" (for the Ukrainians), "pressure" and "leverage" (for the EU action), EU officials' rhetoric reflects that the EU was forcefully pushing Ukrainian decision makers to change policies and laws according to EU demands against domestic resistance, consisting of passivity.

Under the VLAP, in order to counter this suspected resistance, the EU set up a large control and communication framework. With its monitoring practices, the EU actors constructed the EU as hierarchically dominant. In other words, the European scale was placed above the Ukrainian national scale. At the same time, they constructed equivalences of hierarchies by defining which officials of the EU and Ukraine appropriately met. Interactions ranged from political encounters[11] to meetings between high civil servants[12] and intermediary state officials. These meetings and interactions between EU and Ukrainian state officials of various hierarchical positions enabled EU officials to gather information about the state of the reforms and to build up and maintain pressure so that Ukrainian civil servants would carry out the requested reforms. A first way of pressuring consisted in the EU's collection of information for the writing of the progress reports, which were then sent to the Council, which would make the decision to grant the visa-free regime. Officials of the EU Commission and experts from member states went on monitoring missions to Ukraine, before writing "progress reports" on the changes in the policy areas relevant for the visa-liberalisation process. According to the EU Commission officials, the visits (including of certain sites such as accommodation centres for asylum seekers and detention centres for irregular migrants) would make it possible to evaluate the changes undertaken in Ukraine. The next progress report could then be prepared and, more largely, the Commission could decide whether or not to recommend abolishing the visa obligation for Ukrainian citizens (Interview, European Commission, 2015).

In addition to collecting information, the EU organised the monitoring mechanism in such a way as to increase pressure on the Ukrainian civil servants to comply with the EU requests. Indeed, the EU's monitoring went beyond the short missions in Ukraine, before which, as EU officials claimed, the reform process in Ukraine accelerated. Instead, it was continuous. Members of the European Commission were in "constant

[11] Annual bilateral summit meetings between the President of Ukraine and the EU Presidency, the President of the Commission, and the EU's High Representative. Below this level were annual Cooperation Councils, namely the Association Council, where the Prime Minister of Ukraine and members of the Government met with the High Representative for Foreign Affairs and Security Policy and members of the Council of the EU and of the European Commission.

[12] Namely the Association Committee where Ukrainian deputy ministers and heads of departments met with the Managing Director for Europe and Central Asia of the EEAS, heads of departments of EU institutions such as of the EEAS and the European Commission, and the head of the Ukraine Support Group; but also the slightly lower-level thematic Subcommittees such as "Justice, Freedom, and Security" at expert level where Ukrainian deputy ministers, heads of departments, and deputy heads of units met officials from the EEAS, the European Commission, and the EU Delegation.

contact" with the Ukrainian officials who informed them "immediately" of changes (Interview, representative of the European Commission, DG Home, 2015). After the visit, the Ukrainian officials were repeatedly instructed of the results of the evaluation. The EU "experts" who travelled to Ukraine informed the Ukrainians directly of their judgements and recommendations at the end of their trip—that is before the official publication of the progress report.[13] The EU used the time between the monitoring mission and the publication of the report as an instrument to increase its influence. An official of the European Commission stressed the "efficiency" of this approach: The threat of the criticism in the report encouraged Ukrainian state officials to undertake quick reforms to avoid being blamed internally for delays in the visa abolition. An interviewee from the Commission added that in Moldova they used this "pressure function of the reporting" only on issues on which there was strong opposition in the society, namely on LGBTI rights, whereas in Ukraine they used it more systematically to "get the administration moving" (Interview, European Commission, 2015).

The monitoring missions reflected at the level of interpersonal relations the asymmetric international relations (Jeandesboz, 2015; Kurowska, 2014). The controlled Ukrainian officials had access to limited means of resistance: They could remain passive and present reforms inaccurately when questioned by EU monitoring delegations. The civil servants' access to these already limited means of resistance became even more restricted in 2014 and 2015 given the EU control mechanism and the top-down pressure exerted on civil servants within the state apparatus to fulfil all EU demands. For example, according to interviewees from the European Commission and the EU Delegation in Kyiv, the Ukrainian authorities never refused and diligently organised all EU requests, for example for site visits during monitoring missions. Moreover, during the meetings at the monitoring missions, the representatives of the EU questioned the attending Ukrainian civil servants in a technical and detailed way concerning the progress they expected them to have made. EU officials sometimes opposed the technicality of their questions to the presentation of the Ukrainians who "present things in the most positive light" and "try to impress" the monitoring delegation (Interviews, European Commission SGUA and DG Home, 2015 and EU Delegation in Kyiv,

[13] Between 2011 and the end of 2015, the Commission produced six VLAP progress reports which indicated a list of measures, which the Ukrainian state should undertake.

2017). During the monitoring missions, the Ukrainian officials tried to convey the impression that they fulfilled the EU demands and could be mentioned positively in the next report. When EU officials from Brussels came, all relevant Ukrainian officials attended the meetings and seemed to take the meeting very seriously. A representative of the EU Delegation in Kyiv (2017) compared the behaviour of the Ukrainian officials during the monitoring missions and the monthly meetings he held with them. During regular meetings that took place every month, Ukrainian officials did not have time to "rehearse" their speeches before the meeting and some were be busy elsewhere so that not all relevant officials attended. In contrast, during meetings of monitoring missions, Ukrainian officials "cancel everything else. This is the most important." The suspected rehearsals of the officials' speeches reflect the thin line between diligence to fulfil EU demands and resistance by setting up a façade.

The EU thus managed to increase its power through its monitoring set-up and most importantly, through domestic political interest in the EU's positive evaluation and incentive. Indeed, the Ukrainian politicians accepted the construction of the EU as a superior scale and participated in this transfer across scales, by transmitting the pressure top-down across the state apparatus.

Transmitting the Pressure to Fulfil EU Demands

The Ukrainian civil servants sought to follow precisely the EU requests. Indeed, EU and Ukrainian officials related how Ukrainian officials sought to clarify EU demands to align their reforms with them. For instance, a representative of the Mission of Ukraine to the EU[14] explained:

> Sometimes there are questions from the Ukrainian side: how to implement some benchmarks. Then we should organise a meeting to get the

[14] The Mission of Ukraine to the European Union was a mediator in this communication. On the one hand, the Mission of Ukraine transmitted information about reforms from Ukraine, namely the Ministry for Foreign Affairs, to the EU, mostly the Commission. On the other hand, it transmitted the European Commission's expectations to Ukrainian ministries (Interview, representative of the Mission of Ukraine to the EU, 2015). Several representatives of DG Home of the European Commission referred to the requests from the Ukrainian side for clarification of EU demands and advice concerning reforms. During monitoring missions and everyday communication, Ukrainian officials enquired how to implement a reform so that it would conform to EU expectations (Interview, representative of the European Commission, DG Home, 2015).

> information. [...] So we asked the Commission if we could do such a reorganisation. [...] It is important for us to receive the position from the European Commission on this issue because it is related to the VLAP. [...] In Ukraine, I'm in contact with our Ministry for Foreign Affairs. It's mostly written communication. The European Commission's response depends on the EU legislation. We don't know all the EU legislation. European Commission experts could clarify any issues. (Interview, representative of the Mission of Ukraine to the EU, 2015)

This quote reflects the asymmetric relations between the Ukrainian state and the EU, but also the active submission by the Ukrainian officials to this asymmetry. Moreover, the Ukrainian officials urged the European Commission to translate vague demands in official documents into precise legal texts. Representatives of DG Home of the Commission explained in several interviews that the Ukrainian authorities sent them the draft laws and asked them to comment on them. In fact, the domestic actors' lack of interest in the policy area affected the norm promoters' capacity to transfer the norms. Indeed, given that the Ukrainian actors had little interest in the content of the asylum reforms, it was convenient for them to ask the Commission to take over the work of translation (Interviews, representatives of the European Commission, DG Home, 2014 and 2015). In a way, the Ukrainian officials thus put themselves into a dominated position, asking the EU officials what they should do to satisfy EU demands. The lack of strong domestic interests and positions concerning asylum policies meant that the EU could define more precisely the changes to be undertaken in Ukraine.

Ukrainian civil servants presented the EU demands as compulsory and therefore unquestionable. In an interview, a senior official from the State Migration Service, involved in the draft writing process, stated: "We understand that to pass this step [the visa-free regime] we have to do this, whether we want it or not." (Interview, senior state official at the State Migration Service, 2014). In interviews in summer 2015, mid-level state officials of the State Migration Service, involved in the monitoring missions, presented the EU observers' "recommendations" as compulsory to obtain the desired benefit of the visa-free regime (Interview, senior state official at the State Migration Service, 2015). While the Ukrainian officials' presentation of the monitoring visits conveyed the impression of asymmetric power relations, they did not voice any open criticism (for similar observations see Kratochvíl, 2008). Instead, they declared that they were doing their best to fulfil the VLAP requirements. In the interviews between 2013 and 2015, civil servants expressed their duty to fulfil EU demands. This duty might be hindered by material limitations but its sense and legitimacy were not openly questioned. Similarly to the debates in the Ukrainian Parliament in those years, the interviewed civil servants did not question the necessity of the visa-free regime and referred to the VLAP as a justification on its own. A leading representative of the refugee Department of the State Migration Service presented the "obligations" of the administration:

> In the plan for the implementation of the visa-free regime between Ukraine and EU there was a huge chapter about refugees and asylum. Ukraine was obliged to implement the plan as part of its commitments to EU standards. [...] Everything that's written in the plan has to be implemented as a new legal norm. The first norm was the creation of the Migration Service by uniting two organs. This led to the change of structure. The legislation also changed in all spheres: for foreigners, refugees. This was all written in the plan for visa liberalisation. It is also written that we should provide all the necessary conditions for the refugees and asylum seekers. Some have been provided already, the others are under development. We follow the plan strictly. This is discussed on the level of the Cabinet of Ministers, President's Administration. They set the goals. (Interview, High-level official of the State Migration Service, 2015)

This senior official presented the administration as precisely implementing the demands of the EU without adaptation or questioning of the demanded modifications; they were an obligation. In their discourse, officials confirmed the scalar organisation of themselves following the orders from the national political scale, itself following the orders from the EU scale.

The Interrelatedness of UNHCR and EU Power

Some scholars have pointed out how the EU benefits from other international organisations to increase its capacity to transfer norms (Franke et al., 2010). Yet, the other international organisations' strategies and interests in their alliance with the EU have remained under-researched. Sandra Lavenex argued that UNHCR, while being able to maintain a certain role of counterweight vis-à-vis the EU, has at the same time increasingly acted as a subcontractor for the EU (Lavenex, 2016).

Nevertheless, Michal Natorski explained that other international actors also normatively influence the action of the EU in its neighbourhood (Natorski, 2016). This section complements this research, investigating not only the reasons why the EU seeks other international actors' support, as analysed by Natorski, but also why other international actors deliver it. Moreover, it will be discussed how this interdependence between the different international actors affects their power and their role in the transfer process. Interdependence means mutual relations of dependence (in particular, reliance on each other's resources, for example information, staff, money, legitimacy, and conditionality) and interrelated activities (Natorski, 2016).

The EU's Reliance on UNHCR Knowledge Production

The EU Delegation, itself a source of information for the European Commission in Brussels, struggled to collect information on its own. Employees of the Delegation acknowledged in interviews in 2013 and 2014 that they had difficulties communicating with Ukrainian officials, referring to language barriers and lack of interest from the Ukrainian side. All interviewees from the EU Delegation voiced mistrust towards Ukrainian officials. They preferred to obtain information and evaluation from international organisations in Ukraine.

The EU Delegation was guided by the norms and interests of UNHCR. Employees of the Delegation acknowledged in interviews in 2013 and 2014 that they received most of their information on asylum from the office of UNHCR in Kyiv. They based their evaluation of Ukrainian asylum laws and practices on the evaluation made by UNHCR. UNHCR, as the major knowledge producer on asylum in Ukraine, spread its evaluation via reports and press releases and shaped the EU officials' vision of the asylum policies in Ukraine. For instance, the critical UNHCR report from 2013 remained in the memories of EU officials and was often mentioned in interviews, namely the conclusion "Ukraine is not a safe country for asylum seekers". UNHCR was able to encourage EU officials to act according to the international organisations' norms and demands, for example to contact and criticise the State Migration Service. Given that the European Commission in Brussels requested information from the EU Delegation in Kyiv, UNHCR indirectly shaped the European Commission's knowledge and positions.

UNHCR also actively spread its positions among EU institutions in Brussels, such as the EEAS and DG Home (Interview, employee of UNHCR in Brussels, Brussels, 2015). The Commission sometimes referred to the reports of UNHCR in its reports, for instance, criticising the Ukrainian authorities for not undertaking certain changes despite them being recommended in a UNHCR report (European Commission, 2013, pp. 9–10). Interviewees of DG Home mentioned UNHCR as the "main interlocutor" and the main source of information.

UNHCR also influenced the EU monitoring missions in Ukraine (Interview, representative of the European Commission, DG Home, 2014). EU officials who travelled to Ukraine and had to evaluate the Ukrainian reforms in only a few days, mistrusted the Ukrainian officials' accounts. They first asked employees of the EU Delegation, UNHCR, and UNHCR-funded NGOs about their observations and judgement of the measures carried out by the Ukrainian authorities. However, despite UNHCR's capacity to shape the EU's knowledge and evaluation of asylum in Ukraine, its own power in regard to the Ukrainian authorities was limited.

UNHCR's Limited Power on Its Own

Since the beginning of its work in Ukraine, UNHCR tried to influence the national asylum laws. Its offices in Ukraine and in Geneva evaluated existing and draft laws and issued recommendations for new laws and policies. UNHCR also directly contacted domestic officials and politicians to lobby for reforms. UNHCR was part of working groups elaborating asylum laws. A representative of the State Migration Service, who had a favourable attitude towards UNHCR, described the involvement of UNHCR in the legislative drafting process at the State Migration Service, explaining that UNHCR Kyiv "helped to draft" different laws related to refugees given that it was a member of the working group on social integration. A senior representative of UNHCR pointed out the need for "allies in the Parliamentary Committees". He explained that UNHCR was in contact with the chairman of the Parliament speaker and with chairmen and some members of the Parliamentary Committees that worked on refugee law amendments (the Committees on Human Rights, Foreign Affairs, and Finance) in order to convince them of the importance of the amendments and to make sure they were put on the agenda. Having the right to intervene in the Parliamentary Committees, UNHCR showed them documents and texts of international law, arguing that the domestic refugee legislation did not comply with certain international norms.

UNHCR struggled to raise awareness on asylum matters among politicians and high-level officials. MPs showed little interest in UNHCR attempts to attract their attention. Senior UNHCR employees resorted primarily to behind-the-scenes lobbying among leading officials, especially the heads of the State Migration Service. A senior employee of UNHCR Kyiv explained that the heads of the State Migration Service changed on average once per year:

> You are starting from scratch! First it took weeks if not months to see the new head. When you got to see him, you start developing some sort of relationship of trust and explaining you are not in this country to make his life difficult but to actually help him and his department function in a proper way. […] It [asylum] was always a marginal issue for the head. […] Never was someone appointed who actually understood the issue so you were starting from scratch. […] Explaining even the basics and when there were a lot of gaps it took months of effort and I am not even mentioning that I would invite those people sometimes for dinner, that I would meet them at receptions and try to raise issues informally. Usually it took up to a year to get to solid working relationship and then, bingo, the head was changed. (Interview, former foreign senior employee of UNHCR in Ukraine, 2015)

This interview shows how UNHCR lobbying balanced between criticism and reassurance, presenting itself as an ally and avoiding being perceived as a threat. Moreover, UNHCR primarily tried to influence the heads of the SMS through personal networking and the establishment of individual ties, including through informal interactions. Yet, the turnover among the heads of the State Migration Service undermined these efforts. In addition, this UNHCR employee contrasted his own perception of the importance of the necessity of reforms on asylum with the state officials' view of asylum as a minor issue. On its own, UNHCR struggled to attract officials' and politicians' attention to asylum matters.

UNHCR's Increase in Power through the Alliance with Other International Organisations

UNHCR managed to increase its power vis-à-vis the Ukrainian authorities thanks to the introduction of EU conditionality in 2010 and then further thanks to the heightened political interest in the conditionality in 2014.

A senior representative of UNHCR explained that in summer 2013 UNHCR published its very critical report which strongly upset the

Ukrainian officials—especially in the VLAP context. For this reason, relations between UNHCR and Ukrainian authorities deteriorated. When they met again in March 2014, after the Maidan protests, to discuss the controversial points of the report, the situation had changed and the relations improved again. Ukrainian officials had instructions to progress in the VLAP and were more collaborative with UNHCR. UNHCR explained this change both by the political will to fulfil VLAP conditions and by the changes in staff, for instance the head of the State Migration Service. Following these changes and "using the VLAP", UNHCR managed to get through some changes against the initial will of the State Migration Service. An example of such a change was Order no. 649, which increased the validity of the asylum seeker certificate to six months (Interview, former foreign senior employee of UNHCR in Ukraine, 2015).

The EU supported the influence of UNHCR in Ukraine. It is debatable whether the EU supported UNHCR due to the latter's lobbying or whether the EU used the neutral and value-driven reputation of UNHCR in order to strengthen the legitimacy of the EU action. In any case, the EU regularly mentioned UNHCR in the Action Plan and in reports, demanding that Ukrainian authorities cooperate with UNHCR and follow its advice. EU documents conveyed the impression that UNHCR and the EU pursued the same goals and norms.

Conversely, UNHCR sought to encourage the EU to pay more attention toon asylum in their conditionality. During the VLAP, and especially the peak from 2014 to 2015, UNHCR intensified its lobbying activities at the EU Delegation (Interview, representative of the EU delegation in Kyiv, 2015) and the participants of the monitoring missions to persuade them "to make more critical comments on asylum that we could use. We managed to get some critical comments." (Interview, former foreign senior employee of UNHCR in Ukraine, 2015).

UNHCR also intensified its lobbying activities in regard to the Ukrainian authorities when the VLAP process gained momentum (Interview, former foreign senior employee of UNHCR in Ukraine, 2015). When interacting with Ukrainian officials and politicians, UNHCR tried to convey the image of an ally, supporting Ukraine's desire to fulfil the EU demands and obtain visa freedom. However, as my interviews in 2014 and 2015 showed, representatives of the Ukrainian administration were aware of the fact that the EU obtained most of its information on asylum from UNHCR. While this capacity of denunciation conferred more influence on UNHCR during the VLAP process, it also undercut the image of assistance to Ukrainian authorities.

As the state authorities were more interested in EU directives and EU national legislation than in UNHCR norms, UNHCR followed this interest. In press releases and meetings with state authorities, UNHCR stressed how the changes it recommended were also required by the VLAP (Interview, mid-level Ukrainian employee of UNHCR in Ukraine, 2014). For instance, UNHCR organised a seminar on European asylum standards for MPs, their assistants, employees of the SMS, ministries, and the judiciary. The "seminar reviewed the main EU directives in the area of asylum, and then Ukrainian counterparts analysed the current state of national legislation, indicating where it complies with and where it falls short of EU standards" (UNHCR, 2013). UNHCR framed the topic of its seminar as "European standards" and EU directives instead of UNHCR norms. This labelling of the norms as "EU norms" shows that UNHCR sought to benefit from the Ukrainian officials' attempts to follow EU demands. This way, UNHCR also legitimised the EU requests (Lavenex, 2016, pp. 12–13). The activities of the EU and UNHCR in Ukraine were interrelated. Occasionally, UNHCR also managed to obtain the support of the Council of Europe to push through certain legislative changes (Mützelburg, 2019).

In short, transfer of norms and representations did not only occur from the EU to Ukraine but also from international organisations to EU bodies via knowledge production and dissemination, namely through publications and lobbying. While the EU compensated for its own limited resources, in terms of information, network, staff, and language skills, by relying on knowledge produced by UNHCR, UNHCR was able to shape the EU's perception of and action on asylum in Ukraine. Furthermore, UNHCR was able to transfer its norms indirectly to Ukraine by using EU conditionality.

However, this channel of influence stopped when in December 2015 the EU Commission announced that Ukraine had fulfilled all benchmarks and in November 2016 the Council of the EU agreed to introduce the visa-free regime.[15] In at least the following four years, the Ukrainian parliament did not substantially modify asylum legislation.[16]

Conclusion

This chapter has analysed transfer as an interactive process between domestic political and high-level administrative decision makers and employees of international organisations. Seeking to understand the reasons why domestic legislators adopted international asylum norms, I have examined their public political discourse. This has revealed little interest in the norms' content. Instead, it has made clear the strong legitimacy of the norms' symbolic value: In the first years after the state's independence, asylum laws were valued as a sign of a democratic and European state, crucial for the Ukrainian state's reputation in the eyes of international organisations. Indeed, after a state's independence or change of political regime, that state's politicians tend to seek the recognition of international organisations and may even seek integration into the same organisations in order to strengthen the state's domestic legitimacy, that is, the state's citizens' belief that the state's institutions ought to be obeyed (Finnemore & Sikkink, 1998, p. 903).

In addition to the norms' symbolic value, their exchange value mattered. Both the Council of Europe's preaccession conditionality and the European Union's visa conditionality strengthened the international organisations' power and place in the parliamentary debates. In particular, EU conditionality allowed the IOs to push for deep adoption of asylum norms, as observed in the previous chapter.

Drawing on written sources such as protocols of parliamentary debates and international organisations' reports, I have been able to examine transfer over nearly three decades. As a result, I've taken stock of the

[15] I discuss the end of EU conditionality more in detail here (Mützelburg, 2019).

[16] However, in April 2020, MPs submitted a draft law on Granting Protection to Foreigners and Stateless Persons (n°3387), which as of July 2021 had not been adopted. Minor legislative changes concerned the material support provided to asylum seekers and refugees staying at temporary accommodation centres (Про Затвердження Вимог До Матеріально-Побутового Забезпечення Біженців Та Осіб, Які Потребують Додаткового Захисту, Що Проживають у Пунктах Тимчасового Розміщення Біженців (Order on the Approval of Requirements for the Material Supply of Refugees and Persons in Need of Additional Protection Residing at Temporary Refugee Accommodation Centres), 2016; Про затвердження Положення про пункти тимчасового розміщення біженців (Order on the approval of the regulations on temporary accommodation centres for refugees), 2018).

changing weight of the different actors based on their changing resources and practices and the domestic and international political context. This macro perspective has allowed me to go beyond the common EU-focused accounts on transfer in the EU neighbourhood and to show the role of other international organisations that were involved in this process long before the EU.

Complementing this macro perspective with occasional micro and meso ones has made it possible to open the black box of EU conditionality. This chapter contributes to research on conditionality by specifying how domestic political interest in EU conditionality practically affects domestic policy making. All actors involved produced and performed scales that set the EU above the national political scale, which was set above the national and regional administrative agents. Due to the EU's monitoring practices, administrative agents were under hierarchical pressure to obtain a positive evaluation by the EU. The lack of domestic interest in asylum policies paradoxically furthered the EU's power because domestic actors asked the EU to prescribe in detail the reforms to be undertaken. Moreover, the different international actors benefited from each other's resources to increase their power (Tables 4.1 and 4.2).

Table 4.1 The IOs' role in the legal norm adoption (1993–2010)

	CoE	*UNHCR*	*EU*
Domestic politicians' justification of norm adoption	Until 1995: norms' exchange and symbolic value	Norms' symbolic value	Not mentioned
Domestic politicians' comments regarding the IOs	Legitimate reference. But since 1995 requests not mentioned anymore	Legitimate and frequent reference	Rare reference. Legitimacy contested
IOs' resources, practices, and overall relations with state actors	Until 1995: pre-accession conditionality & persuasion	Until early 2000s: exchange of favours, public praise, lobbying	Criticism, shaming
	Since 1995: monitoring, criticism	Then: lobbying	
	Overall contentious relations	Overall harmonious relations	Ukr. aspiration of accession, but disappointing EU offers

Source Author's production

Table 4.2 The IOs' role in the legal norm adoption (2010–2015)

	CoE	*UNHCR*	*EU*
Domestic politicians' justification of norm adoption	Rarely mentioned	Norms' symbolic value	Norms' exchange value (+ symbolic value)
Domestic politicians' comments regarding the IOs	Legitimate but rare reference. Mentioned together with EU	Legitimate reference; rather mentioned together with EU	Very frequent reference 2010–'13 legitimacy occasionally contested 2014–'15: Legitimacy uncontested
IOs' resources and practices	Monitoring, criticism	Lobbying, personal contacts, benefiting from EU conditionality (knowledge production, monitoring)	VLAP conditionality, monitoring, criticism. Benefiting from UNHCR knowledge production

Source Author's production

Conclusion to the First Part

Ukrainian legislators adopted international asylum norms since the independence of the state. In contrast to most research on transfer, the first part of this book has analysed legislative adoption not only as a result, but as a process. Highlighting the role of power asymmetries, different actors' practices and resources as well their agency in shaping the transfer process, it has shown that transfer takes place in a gradual, uncertain, and heterogeneous way.

Fabrizio Gilardi and Fabio Wasserfallen have argued that "policy-makers signal adherence to international best practice, while local adaptations allow them to either water down the effectiveness of a policy or even pursue goals that are not consistent with the original version of a policy. This way, policy-makers can serve, at the same time, an international and domestic constituency" (Gilardi & Wasserfallen, 2019, p. 1251). In line with this argument, this first part has shown that, in a first phase after the independence, Ukrainian politicians adopted asylum norms in a partial and shallow way, focusing discursively on the symbolic value of the norm adoption as a way to show that they were democratising and Europeanising their country—in particular in the eyes of international organisations. Yet, later, especially from 2014 to 2015, when EU sector-specific conditionality became attractive in the eyes of domestic legislators, they adopted the norms in a deeper way. In line with recent studies on transfer, I stress the importance of sector-specific attractive conditionality, which can cause change despite the absence of an EU membership perspective. I contribute to the research on conditionality by analysing more specifically how the set-up of the monitoring process participates in transfer processes.

This first part of the book complements existing research on transfer in several ways. First, transfer research has pointed to lacking or façade norm adoption, but has paid little attention to the underlying legislative processes. This book identifies four modes of domestic agency in legislative adoption of international norms: Domestic legislators select the norms, translate them, adopt them in a shallow or deep way, and delay or speed up the adoption process. Some of these practices can be seen as subtle resistance to imposed norm transfer. This first part has demonstrated that different norms within the same policy area can be adopted differently depending on their fit with domestic beliefs and political objectives, their strength (of codification and legitimacy among legitimate actors in the field), and the extent to which norm promoters push for their adoption.

Second, while macro perspective research often categorises transfer mechanisms as lesson drawing, imitation, socialisation, persuasion, and conditionality, it fails to offer methods to apply them operationally to empirical material. This first part has proposed a typology of norm addressees' discursive reactions to norms and norm promoters, corresponding to different perceptions of legitimacy, interests, knowledge, and power relations. Norm addressees can refer to the need for the norms mentioning their content (either based on their moral or on their instrumental value), their symbolic value, or their exchange value. In addition, they can fail to mention the norm promoters' requests or contest the interference.

Third, this part contributes to the emerging research (Natorski, 2016) on the interrelatedness between different international actors in norm promotion, by showing that the increase in the EU's power also enhanced UNHCR's power. While the EU benefited from UNHCR resources—particularly for monitoring—through its knowledge production and lobbying, UNHCR shaped the EU's representation of asylum in Ukraine and encouraged it to insist more on asylum reforms in its conditionality. The alliance between different international actors with different practices and resources strengthened their influence and allowed them to counter Ukrainian attempts to resist the transfer via façade change.

In short, Ukrainian decision makers only reluctantly introduced international asylum norms into the national legislation, trying to limit themselves to façade change. This raises the question of the practical implementation of these formally adopted norms.

References

Balfour, R. (2013). *Human rights and democracy in EU foreign policy: The cases of Ukraine and Egypt*. Routledge.

Council of the European Union. (2009). *Joint Declaration of the Prague Eastern Partnership Summit* (8435/09 (Presse 78)). http://europa.eu/rapid/press-release_PRES-09-78_en.htm

Delcour, L., & Wolczuk, K. (2015). Spoiler or facilitator of democratization? Russia's role in Georgia and Ukraine. *Democratization, 22*(3), 459–478. https://doi.org/10.1080/13510347.2014.996135

Dolowitz, D., & Marsh, D. (1996). Who learns what from whom: A review of the policy transfer literature. *Political Studies, 44*(2), 343–357. https://doi.org/10.1111/j.1467-9248.1996.tb00334.x

Dragneva-Lewers, R., & Wolczuk, K. (2015). The EU and the Yanukovych regime: The widening gap. In *Ukraine between the EU and Russia: The integration challenge* (pp. 51–62). Palgrave Macmillan. http://www.palgrave.com/us/book/9781137516251

European Commission. (2002). *JHA Scoreboard elaborated on the basis of the EU Action Plan on Justice and Home Affairs in Ukraine (June 2002).*

European Commission. (2004). *Country Report: European Neighbourhood Policy—Ukraine (until 2004) Commission staff working paper* (SEC(2004) 566). http://aei.pitt.edu/38135/

European Commission. (2006). *ENP Progress Report Ukraine 2005/2006* (SEC(2006) 1505/2). http://ec.europa.eu/smart-regulation/impact/ia_carried_out/docs/ia_2006/sec_2006_1505_en.pdf

European Commission. (2008). *Implementation of the European Neighbourhood Policy in 2007—Progress Report Ukraine* (SEC(2008) 402). https://eur-lex.europa.eu/legal-content/EN/ALL/?uri=CELEX%3A52008SC0402

European Commission. (2013). *Third report on the implementation by Ukraine of the Action Plan on Visa Liberalisation—Report from the Commission to the European Parliament and the Council* (COM(2013) 809 final). https://ec.europa.eu/transparency/regdoc/rep/1/2013/EN/1-2013-809-EN-F1-1.Pdf

European Commission Against Racism and Intolerance - Council of Europe. (2002). *Second report on Ukraine* (CRI (2002) 23). http://hudoc.ecri.coe.int/XMLEcri/ENGLISH/Cycle_02/02_CbC_eng/02-cbc-ukraine-eng.pdf

European Commission Against Racism and Intolerance - Council of Europe. (2008). *Third report on Ukraine*. ECRI. https://rm.coe.int/third-report-on-ukraine/16808b5ca2

European Commission Against Racism and Intolerance - Council of Europe. (2012). *Fourth report on Ukraine* (CRI(2012)6). ECRI. https://rm.coe.int/fourth-report-on-ukraine/16808b5ca5

European Commission Against Racism and Intolerance - Council of Europe. (2017). *Fifth report on Ukraine* (CRI(2017)38). ECRI. http://rm.coe.int/fifth-report-on-ukraine/16808b5ca8

European Commission to the European Parliament and the Council. (2014). *Fourth report on the implementation by Ukraine of the Action Plan on Visa Liberalisation* (COM(2014) 336 final). https://ec.europa.eu/home-affairs/sites/homeaffairs/files/e-library/documents/policies/international-affairs/general/docs/fourth_report_on_the_implementation_by_ukraine_of_the_action_plan_on_visa_liberalisation_en.pdf

Ferreira-Pereira, L. C., & Vieira, A. V. G. (2015). Ukraine in the European Union's partnership policy: A case of institutionalized ambiguity. *European Politics and Society, 16*(2), 143–158. https://doi.org/10.1080/23745118.2014.981949

Finnemore, M., & Sikkink, K. (1998). International norm dynamics and political change. *International Organization, 52*(04), 887–917.

Franke, A., Gawrich, A., Melnykovska, I., & Schweickert, R. (2010). The European Union's relations with Ukraine and Azerbaijan. *Post-Soviet Affairs, 26*(2), 149–183.

Frejka, T., Okólski, M., & Sword, K. (1999). *In-depth studies on migration in Central and Eastern Europe: The case of Ukraine* (Economic Studies No. 12). United Nations Economic Commission for Europe, United Nations Population Fund.

General Secretariat of the Council of the European Union. (2010). *EU-Ukraine Visa Dialogue—Action Plan on Visa Liberalisation* (No. 17883/10).

Gilardi, F., & Wasserfallen, F. (2019). The politics of policy diffusion. *European Journal of Political Research, 58*(4), 1245–1256. https://doi.org/10.1111/1475-6765.12326

Grabbe, H. (1999). A partnership for accession? The implications of EU conditionality for the Central and East European applicants. *Robert Schuman Centre Working Paper, 12*(99), 35.

Gryshchenko: Kyiv Successfully Fulfilling Action Plan on Visa Liberalization with EU. (2013, January 16). *KyivPost/European Space*. http://euprostir.org.ua/news/ukraine_lost_to_moldova_and_georgia_in_the_pace_of_european_integration_/

Herashchenko Iryna Volodymyrivna. (n.d.). Єдність.Інфо. Retrieved 11 September 2017, from https://www.ednist.info/dossier/45

Jeandesboz, J. (2015). Intervention and subversion: The EU border assistance mission to Moldova and Ukraine. *Journal of Intervention and Statebuilding, 9*(4), 442–470.

Kratochvíl, P. (2008). Constructing the EU's external roles: Friend in the south, teacher in the East? In L. Delcour & E. Tulmets (Eds.), *Pioneer Europe?* (pp. 217–228). Nomos Verlagsgesellschaft mbH & Co KG. https://doi.org/10.5771/9783845212272-217

Kurowska, X. (2014). Practicality by judgement: Transnational interpreters of local ownership in the Polish-Ukrainian border reform encounter. *Journal of International Relations and Development, 17*(4), 545–565. https://doi.org/10.1057/jird.2013.15

Kuzio, T. (2011). Political culture and democracy: Ukraine as an immobile state. *East European Politics and Societies, 25*(1), 88–113. https://doi.org/10.1177/0888325410388410

Langbein, J., & Wolczuk, K. (2012). Convergence without membership? The impact of the European Union in the neighbourhood: Evidence from Ukraine. *Journal of European Public Policy, 19*(6), 863–881.

Lavenex, S. (2016). Multileveling EU external governance: The role of international organizations in the diffusion of EU migration policies. *Journal of Ethnic and Migration Studies, 42*(2), 554–570.

Makaryan, S. (2015). Construction of migration policies in the Eastern neighbourhood of the European Union. *Journal of Contemporary European Studies, 23*(2), 222–237. https://doi.org/10.1080/14782804.2015.1029241

Malynovska, O. (2006, January). *Caught between East and West, Ukraine struggles with its migration policy*.

Про затвердження Вимог до матеріально-побутового забезпечення біженців та осіб, які потребують додаткового захисту, що проживають у пунктах тимчасового розміщення біженців (Order on the Approval of Requirements for the Material Supply of Refugees and Persons in Need of Additional Protection Residing at Temporary Refugee Accommodation Centres), Pub. L. No. 833/28963 (2016). http://zakon3.rada.gov.ua/laws/show/z0833-16

Про затвердження Положення про пункти тимчасового розміщення біженців (Order on the approval of the regulations on temporary accommodation centres for refugees), Pub. L. No. 503, 788/32240 (2018). https://zakon.rada.gov.ua/go/z0788-18

Mützelburg, I. (2019). The role of EU and international organizations' strategies and interdependencies in the transfer of international norms: The case of Ukrainian Asylum Law. In L. Delcour & E. Tulmets (Eds.), *Policy transfer and norm circulation: Towards an interdisciplinary and comparative approach* (pp. 162–181). Routledge.

Natorski, M. (2016). Power relations in practice of the EU inter-organizational relations in the neighbourhood—Imperator or primus inter pares? In S. Gstöhl & S. Schunz (Eds.), *Theorizing the European neighbourhood policy* (pp. 164–184). Taylor & Francis Ltd.

Nizhnikau, R. (2015). Institutional change in the eastern neighbourhood: Environmental protection and migration policy in Ukraine. *Southeast European and Black Sea Studies*, 1–23. https://doi.org/10.1080/14683857.2015.1050274

Nordström, A. (2008). *The interactive dynamics of regulation: Exploring the Council of Europe's monitoring of Ukraine*. Stockholm University.

Official Ukraine Today. (n.d.-a). *Information: Hnatkevych Yuriy Vasylovych*. Retrieved 11 September 2017, from http://dovidka.com.ua/user/?code=40289

Official Ukraine Today. (n.d.-b). *Information: Kornyeyev Albert Vasylovych*. Retrieved 11 August 2017, from http://dovidka.com.ua/user/?code=43585

Official Ukraine Today. (n.d.-c). *Information: Kosiv Mykhaylo Vasylovych*. Retrieved 11 August 2017, from http://dovidka.com.ua/user/?code=43751

Official Ukraine Today. (n.d.-d). *Information: Nedryhaylo Valentyn Mykhaylovych*. Retrieved 11 August 2017, from http://dovidka.com.ua/user/?code=93522

Official Ukraine Today. (2016, April 15). *Information: Herashchenko Iryna Volodymyrivna*. https://web.archive.org/web/20160415031218/http://dovidka.com.ua/user/?code=240818

Ovsiyenko, V. V., & Kharkiv Human Rights Group. (2013, February 14). *Kosiv Mykhaylo Vasylovych—Ukrainian national movement*. Virtual Museum—Dissident Movement in Ukraine. http://museum.khpg.org/index.php?id=1360876996

Parliamentary Assembly of the Council of Europe. (1995). *Application by Ukraine for membership of the Council of Europe* (Assembly Debate No. 190). http://assembly.coe.int/nw/xml/XRef/Xref-XML2HTML-en.asp?fileid=13929&lang=en

Parliamentary Assembly of the Council of Europe. (2000, January 25). *Restrictions on asylum in the member states of the Council of Europe and the European Union*. Recommendation 1440 (2000). http://assembly.coe.int/nw/xml/XRef/Xref-XML2HTML-en.asp?fileid=16768&lang=en

Parliamentary Assembly of the Council of Europe, & Rapporteur Filimonov, V. (1997). *Refugees, asylum-seekers and displaced persons in the Commonwealth of Independent States (CIS)* (No. 7829). https://assembly.coe.int/nw/xml/XRef/X2H-Xref-ViewHTML.asp?FileID=7747&lang=EN

Rose, R. (1991). What is lesson-drawing? *Journal of Public Policy, 11*(01), 3–30. https://doi.org/10.1017/S0143814X00004918

Saurugger, S., & Terpan, F. (2013). Resisting EU norms. A framework for analysis. *Sciences Po Grenoble Working Paper, n°2.*

Schimmelfennig, F., & Sedelmeier, U. (2004). Governance by conditionality: EU rule transfer to the candidate countries of Central and Eastern Europe. *Journal of European Public Policy, 11*(4), 661–679. https://doi.org/10.1080/1350176042000248089

Schimmelfennig, F., & Sedelmeier, U. (2005). Conceptualizing the Europeanization of Central and Eastern Europe. In *The Europeanization of Central and Eastern Europe* (pp. 1–28). Cornell University Press.

Shevel, O. (2011). *Migration, refugee policy, and state building in Postcommunist Europe*. Cambridge University Press.

Smolij, V. A., & Boriak, H. V. (2013). Udovenko Hennadiy Yosypovych. In V. M. Lytvyn, V. M. Heiets, & L. V. Huberskyj (Eds.), *Encyclopedia of the history of Ukraine*. Institute of the history of Ukraine.

Stegniy, O. (2011). Ukraine and the Eastern partnership: 'Lost in translation'? *Journal of Communist Studies and Transition Politics, 27*(1), 50–72. https://doi.org/10.1080/13523279.2011.544383

Svyetlov, O. (2007). Ukraine's 'return to Europe': Path dependence as a source of mutual elite misunderstanding. *Perspectives on European Politics and Society*, *8*(4), 528–543. https://doi.org/10.1080/15705850701641072

Ticktin, M. (2015, June 10). *Innocence: Understanding a political concept*. https://soundcloud.com/refugeestudiescentre/innocence-understanding-a-political-concept-annual-elizabeth-colson-lecture-2015

Tulmets, E. (2014). Analyser l'exportation des normes au-delà de l'Union européenne—Pour une approche éclectique. *Politique Européenne*, *46*, 8–32.

UNHCR. (2013, April 5). *Website: Advocacy on improving asylum legislation takes step forward in Ukraine*. http://unhcr.org.ua/en/2011-08-26-06-58-56/news-archive/1025-advocacy-on-improving-asylum-legislation-takes-step-forward-in-ukraine

UNHCR. (2015, April 17). *States parties to the 1951 convention and its 1967 protocol*. http://www.unhcr.org/protection/basic/3b73b0d63/states-parties-1951-convention-its-1967-protocol.html

Vachudová, M. A. (2005). *Europe undivided: Democracy, leverage, and integration after communism*. Oxford University Press.

van der Burg, W. (2001). The expressive and communicative functions of law, especially with regard to moral issues. *Law and Philosophy*, *20*(1), 31–59. https://doi.org/10.1023/A:1006492921790

Verkhovna Rada of Ukraine. (n.d.). *MP of Ukraine Hnatkevych Yuriy Vasylovych*. Retrieved 11 September 2017, from http://static.rada.gov.ua/zakon/new/DEPUTAT1/8.htm

Verkhovna Rada of Ukraine. (1993a). *Protocol of the 28th plenary session of the Verkhovna Rada*. http://iportal.rada.gov.ua/meeting/stenogr/show/4842.html

Verkhovna Rada of Ukraine. (1993b). *Protocol of the 29th plenary session of the Verkhovna Rada*. http://iportal.rada.gov.ua/meeting/stenogr/show/4843.html

Verkhovna Rada of Ukraine. (1995). *Protocol of the 94th plenary session of the Verkhovna Rada*. http://iportal.rada.gov.ua/meeting/stenogr/show/3704.html

Verkhovna Rada of Ukraine. (1996). *Protocol of the 43rd plenary session of the Verkhovna Rada*. http://iportal.rada.gov.ua/meeting/stenogr/show/3949.html

Verkhovna Rada of Ukraine. (2000). *Protocol of the 55th plenary session of the Verkhovna Rada*. http://iportal.rada.gov.ua/meeting/stenogr/show/2507.html

Verkhovna Rada of Ukraine. (2001). *Protocol of the 33rd plenary session of the Verkhovna Rada*. http://iportal.rada.gov.ua/meeting/stenogr/show/3424.html

Verkhovna Rada of Ukraine. (2002). *Protocol of the 58th plenary session of the Verkhovna Rada*. http://iportal.rada.gov.ua/meeting/stenogr/show/3449.html

Verkhovna Rada of Ukraine. (2004a, April 27). *MP of Ukraine Batyushko Stefan Vasylovych*. http://web.archive.org/web/2004a0427040550/http://www.rada.gov.ua/zakon/new/DEPUTAT1/374.htm

Verkhovna Rada of Ukraine. (2004b, May 5). *Bondarchuk Andriy Ivanovych*. http://web.archive.org/web/2004b0505154923/http://www.rada.gov.ua/zakon/new/DEPUTAT1/44.htm

Verkhovna Rada of Ukraine. (2004c). *Protocol of the 17th plenary session of the Verkhovna Rada*. http://iportal.rada.gov.ua/meeting/stenogr/show/1795.html

Verkhovna Rada of Ukraine. (2010). *Protocol of the 22nd plenary session of the Verkhovna Rada*. http://iportal.rada.gov.ua/meeting/stenogr/show/1000.html

Verkhovna Rada of Ukraine. (2011). *Protocol of the 47th plenary session of the Verkhovna Rada*. http://iportal.rada.gov.ua/meeting/stenogr/show/1149.html

Verkhovna Rada of Ukraine. (2012, November 29). *Shybko Vitaliy Yakovych*. http://web.archive.org/web/20121129003234/http://w1.c1.rada.gov.ua/pls/site/p_exdeputat?d_id=943&skl=6

Verkhovna Rada of Ukraine. (2014). *Protocol of the 33rd plenary session of the Verkhovna Rada*. http://iportal.rada.gov.ua/meeting/stenogr/show/5255.html

Verkhovna Rada of Ukraine. (2015). *Protocol of the 21st plenary session of the Verkhovna Rada*. http://iportal.rada.gov.ua/meeting/stenogr/show/6024.html

Wetzel, A. (2016). From halt to hurry: External and domestic influences on Ukrainian asylum policy. *Eurasian Geography and Economics, 57*(1), 66–88.

Wolczuk, K. (2008). Ukraine and its relations with the EU in the context of the European neighbourhood policy. In S. Fischer (Ed.), *Ukraine: Quo Vadis?* (pp. 87–118). Institute for Security Studies. www.iss.europa.eu/uploads/media/cp108.pdf

Zhyznomirska, L. (2006). Externalities of the EU immigration and asylum policy: The case of Ukraine. *Review of European and Russian Affairs, 2*.

PART II

Transforming State Practices: Norm Promoters' Multi-Scalar Adaptation to Obstacles

The dominant approaches of transfer studies neither grasp nor explain the empirical heterogeneity of the practical effects of transfer attempts. Indeed, mainstream policy transfer studies usually classify practical change (rule application) according to its strength, along a linear continuum from complete to absent, which implicitly assumes homogeneity across the analysed country. Studies explain the level of implementation either by the political elites' willingness to enforce implementation (Ademmer & Börzel, 2013), thus framing the target state as hierarchically structured so that political elites' decisions directly shape the degree of implementation, or by a clash of norms (Lenschow et al., 2005) presented as homogeneous across the state. However, alternative approaches focusing actors' agency, for instance on translation, have shown a more complex picture of transfer outcomes (Kluczewska, 2019).

This research addresses the underlying causes for the heterogeneous effects of transfer attempts on state practices. In addition to the dimensions of transfer identified in the existing literature, which are formal change, practical change, and discursive change (Schimmelfennig & Sedelmeier, 2005), the second part of this book proposes operationalised sub-dimensions, such as resources made available for the implementation, top-down control of local state practices, and local officials' knowledge of the norms. This makes it possible to go beyond the binary view, opposing absent and full implementation. Focusing on the actors involved in the transfer process (Jacquot & Woll, 2004), this study analyses the role of norm promoters and norm addressees as well as of their interactions and relationships. Framing the transfer attempts as a "transfer chain", I seek to uncover the transfer, translations of, and resistance to the international norms. In the context of unstable and overall weak domestic political interest in the implementation of international asylum norms, I scrutinise the role of domestic and international non-state actors as well as domestic subordinate and mid-level state officials (Lipsky, 1980). At the same time, I take into consideration the impact of the larger political context, namely of the temporary sector-specific EU conditionality, and the bureaucratic structures (hierarchically organised bureaucracy, very limited budget, importance of informal contacts) on the transfer processes and the interactions between actors. In this part I adopt multiple perspectives, investigating the networks and interactions between state and non-state actors across different scales (Evans, 2010).

So far, norm promoters' adaptation to obstacles has received little scholarly attention. This part analyses how norm promoters choose their transfer methods and how they adapt them to norm addressees' resistance and structural obstacles. In particular, it sheds light on three dimensions of non-state actors' adaptation: contentious/non-contentious, formal/informal, and multi-scalar approaches. This research provides evidence of how, in the course of transfer endeavours, non-state and state actors negotiate their relative scalar positions.

CHAPTER 5

Policy Implementation in Practice: Political Power Struggles, Lack of Money, and Street-Level Bureaucrats

Introduction

> Sometimes the problem was in the law itself, sometimes one law said one thing and another law said the exact opposite [...]. Sometimes there was a law but there were no administrative procedures, sometimes there was a law and administrative procedures but no money. Sometimes there were all those things but there was someone in the hospital who just didn't want to receive them [the asylum seekers or refugees]. (Interview, head of a faith-based asylum NGO, 2014)

To what extent do state authorities put laws and policies into practice? Most transfer studies have found that implementation of the transferred formal norms is limited, often citing obstacles emanating from actors high up in the political hierarchy, that is, those who produce laws and policies.

Research on public policies has shown that laws are sometimes written without the intention of being implemented or of fulfilling their official function. A law may be written in a way so as not to be implemented, serving as a compromise between different positions (Blankenburg, 1986). In fact, some laws are written in a vague way so as to avoid conflict and to allow them to be voted in parliament without resistance. Transfer scholars such as Wade Jacoby have pointed to "Potemkin harmonization" through which reforms are undertaken on paper only to fulfil

I. Mützelburg, *Transferring Asylum Norms to EU Neighbours*, The European Union in International Affairs,
https://doi.org/10.1007/978-3-031-04528-8_5

EU demands (Falkner et al., 2008; Goetz, 2005; Jacoby, 1999). If the intentions of the lawmakers diverge from the official function of the law, institutional mechanisms are likely to impede the effective implementation. In addition, according to the "public service gap", the policy goals and means given to the authorities nearly always diverge (Hupe & Buffat, 2014, p. 555). Drawing upon this public policy and transfer research, I will examine how and why top-down obstacles hinder the implementation of asylum norms in Ukraine.

However, top-down approaches to understanding policy implementation need to be complemented with bottom-up approaches, focusing on street-level bureaucrats acting as policy co-makers (Dubois, 1999; Lipsky, 1980). I will show that street-level bureaucrats may remain passive, causing the absence of implementation, or may improvise or transgress rules and procedures in order to provide certain services foreseen by the law. When the transferred norms clash with domestic norms or interests, domestic actors can resist the practical implementation of the formal norms (Bache & Taylor, 2003; Kubicek, 2003; Saurugger & Terpan, 2013). Scholars have also highlighted the translation of the norms through which domestic actors adapt the international norms to the local context (Acharya, 2015; Kluczewska, 2019). These three visions of implementation following transfer processes are norm-centred; they expect the domestic actors to react to the transferred norms—with application, translation, or resistance.

However, as I will argue in this chapter, domestic policy implementers can also work independently of the formal norms. In other words, not all of the administrative staff's practices are reactions to the formal norms. Officials face practical situations where they make decisions and where they may decide whether and how to use a legal norm (Bourdieu, 1990; Israël, 2009; Lipsky, 1980; Maynard-Moody & Musheno, 2000).

Thanks to its multi-perspective and multi-scalar approach, this chapter contributes to transfer studies in explaining the frequently diagnosed "gap" between the formally adopted norm (policy document and law) and state practices. Combing findings and approaches from macro transfer research, public policy analysis, and sociological studies of the administration, I analyse the impact of politicians' choices and institutions on administrative practices, but also officials' everyday decision-making and coping with concrete situations. Put differently, I investigate how in the course of asylum policy making and norm transfer, regional and national scales are produced and how they affect each other.

No Implementation Without State Institutions: Political Power Struggles and Low Political Prioritisation

Macro perspective transfer studies often insist on the role of political interests, veto players, external incentives for domestic politicians, and institutional frameworks, which obstruct the practical implementation of transferred norms. When examining Ukraine's asylum policies from a macro perspective over the first 30 years, the most fundamental and visible obstacle to the implementation of laws was the absence of institutions capable of and responsible for it.

In the first two decades after Ukraine's independence, central state actors sought to build up the new state, to define the relations between national and regional scales, and to construct the national scale as the relevant and legitimate one to manage various policy areas, including asylum. The policy area being new to the young Ukrainian state, setting up functioning state bodies took time, especially as asylum was not a political priority. In Ukraine, after the elaboration of the first Law on Refugees in 1993, the executive was slow to build up administrative bodies in charge of asylum matters. The government gradually issued the decrees that established the responsible bodies and detailed their functions. Then, despite the formal creation of migration institutions, Ukrainian state bodies began examining asylum applications only in mid-1996. For more than two years, the Law on Refugees thus remained without implementation because of the absence of functioning institutions. Domestic political actors did not prioritise the practical implementation of the formally adopted international norms. In fact, the shallow legislative adoption, observed in the first part of this book, coincided with a slow and unclear formal distribution of responsibilities among the different institutions supposed to implement the laws.

What is more, political power struggles destabilised the asylum administration. Ukrainian asylum policies were shaped by incomplete and poorly enforced institutional rules and the disproportionately strong position of the President in the 1990s and early 2000s, followed by a major reshuffling of the power distribution between the President, the Prime Minister, and the Parliament in the aftermath of the Orange Revolution in 2004 (D'Anieri, 2007, pp. 60–61). Indeed, under President Victor Yushchenko (2005–2010), the power struggle between the President and the government undermined the vertical decision-making and the implementation process (Wetzel, 2016). Major political actors, such as the Ministry of Justice and the Ministry of Interior, struggled for power and sought to maintain their influence and their organisational, financial, and human resources (Boroda, 2008, p. 44; Tolstokorova, 2013, p. 109). The executive repeatedly reorganised the state authorities responsible for attributing the refugee status: control over migration matters was sometimes attributed to the Ministry of Justice, sometimes to the Ministry of Interior (Interview, former high official of the State Committee on Nationalities and Religion, 2014).

The reorganisations repeatedly paralysed the asylum administration. Owing to unclear competencies of the new institution, unclear hierarchies, and modalities of cooperation between different state bodies involved (e.g. central migration authorities and their regional offices, the Ministry of Interior, the State Border Guards, the Security Services, the Ministry of Labour and Social Policy), as well as lacking secondary legislation, the new institutions took a long time to begin working (Düvell & Vollmer, 2009, p. 18; International Centre for Policy Studies (Kyiv, Ukraine) & Institute for Public Affairs (Warsaw, Poland), 2006, p. 5; Kazmierkiewicz et al., 2009, p. 22; Tajibaeva, 2008; Vollmer et al., 2010, p. 29). The reorganisation meant, for instance, that files were temporarily inaccessible. During several phases, the authorities did not implement asylum policies at all, interrupting the refugee status determination and even the registering and accepting of asylum applications (Table 5.1). The restructuring of the authorities also entailed a budgetary vacuum which obstructed the state bodies' work. For instance, in 2011, institutional restructuring meant that it was unclear which body was responsible for funding the temporary accommodation centre for refugees in Odesa. Consequently, between January and April 2011, this centre was left without money and could not pay for food, water, electricity bills, and staff salaries (State Migration Service of Ukraine (MS Odessa) & Foundation for Assistance to Refugees and Displaced People 'Spivchuttya' (Compassion), 2011a, 2011b, 2011c, 2011d). Finally, the responsibility was attributed to the State Migration Service, which then resumed the payments. Furthermore, repeated institutional reforms often implied the regular recruitment of new, untrained staff, thus destabilising the functioning of the authorities. For instance, between December 2010 and summer 2011, during the process of removal of the previous central asylum authority, employees were dismissed and then partly hired again. As a consequence of this restructuring, the asylum administration interrupted its work. At several moments between 2000 and 2007, the recognition rate[1] dropped to 0 (Fig. 5.1). At the beginning of the restructuring, it dropped from above 50% to 0%, and then remained very low until the late 2000s. The migration authorities responded to the institutional instability in the 2000s by rejecting most asylum applications.

Stable formal executive institutions and a clear distribution of the responsibilities and relations between different bodies involved have been preconditions for the implementation of laws and policies. Since 2011, the formal set-up of the asylum authorities stabilised as fewer and less radical restructuring were undertaken and the relations between the State Migration Service (SMS) and other state institutions were clarified. Since then and until early 2022, the implementation of asylum laws by the migration authorities was overall uninterrupted. This stabilisation can be explained partly by the more authoritarian presidential leadership of Victor Yanukovych (2010–2014), which overcame the previous political power struggles. Moreover, as domestic politicians started attributing more importance to EU conditionality, they also attributed more importance to asylum policies and followed the EU request of establishing a unified and functioning State Migration Service (Tolstokorova, 2013, p. 110; Wetzel, 2016).

In short, as political actors made and unmade state bodies, caring more about their power over resources and policy fields than the practical implementation of asylum policies, the latter was chaotic and frequently interrupted over a long period. This initial lack of political prioritisation of this policy area also led to less visible but major and often persistent obstacles to implementation.

Migration Officers Between Inaction and Improvisation

Contradictory formal rules and the lack of material resources at the administration obstruct in a top-down fashion the implementation of laws. Yet, officials at the administration have some leeway to choose to remain passive or to improvise. Indeed, officials can use discretion in the

[1] The recognition rate is the number of asylum seekers granted refugee status or complementary protection status divided by the total number of applicants.

Table 5.1 The evolution of Ukrainian state bodies in charge of asylum matters (1993–2017)

Year	*Political measures affecting the asylum administration*
1993	Creation of the Ministry for Nationalities and Migration *No refugee status determination in practice*
1994	Creation of a national Migration Service *No refugee status determination in practice*
1996	Creation of the **State Committee for Nationalities and Migration** (SCNM), liquidation of the Ministry for Nationalities and Migration
1997	Creation of **regional Migration Services** which took the final refugee status decisions until 2001
2000	Abolition of the SCNM *Regional Migration Services kept working. Varying number of functional regional MS (in the first half of 2001, 21 out of 27 were active) Some with an important backlog (e.g.in Zakarpattya)*
2001	Creation of the State Department for Nationalities and Migration In summer, abolition of the newly created State Department for Nationalities and Migration, re-creation of the SCNM within the Ministry of Justice *In the second half of 2001, the Ukrainian authorities stopped accepting asylum applications* *The SCNM took one year to become operational. All asylum procedures suspended*
2002–2005	*Continuing political struggle over the migration authorities with changing chairmen* *For some periods, many regional Migration Services did not work (e.g. 2005)*
2006	Creation of the **State Committee for Nationalities and Religions** (SCNR) (merging the SCNM and the State Committee for Religions)
2007	*Suspension of the work of the SCNR on refugee status determination for eight months given that the body was deprived of the legal basis enabling it to take such decisions*
2008	Government resolution to delegate the responsibilities to the Ministry of Interior *Refugee status determination suspended* Then, suspension of the resolution by presidential decree
2009	Theoretical creation of the **State Migration Service** (SMS) as part of the Ministry of Interior *but could not work due to lack of secondary legislation*
2010	Abolition of the **SCNR** SMS officially in charge *but slow to start working due to unclear competences*

(continued)

Table 5.1 (continued)

Year	*Political measures affecting the asylum administration*
2011	*SMS not working fully for half a year; impossibility for many asylum seekers to apply for asylum. During the process of removal of the SCNR between December 2010 and summer 2011, employees were dismissed and partly hired again. During the transfer, files were not accessible*
2015	Reduction of the number of regional Migration Services from 27 to 13
2017	Further slight reduction of the number of regional Migration Services

Source Author's production

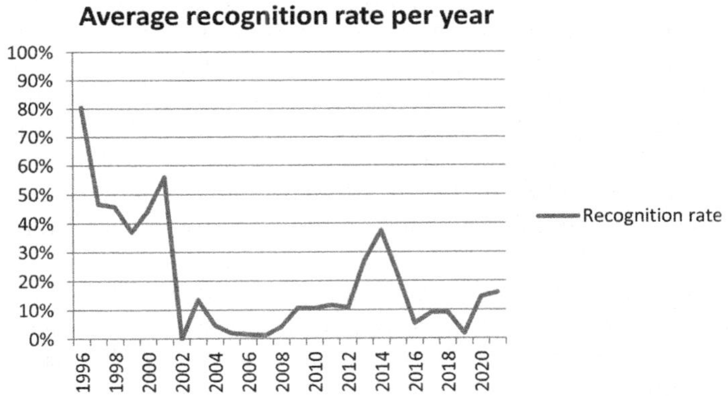

Fig. 5.1 Evolution of the average recognition rate, including the attribution of the refugee and complementary protection statuses

implementation of official laws and policies as a "coping mechanism to overcome barriers to job performance" (Gofen, 2014, p. 457; Lipsky, 1980).

Coping with Legal Obstacles and Lack of Information

Contradictions between laws and administrative procedures as well as the lack of secondary legislation made implementation difficult. For example, policy-makers did not translate asylum seekers' theoretical right to legal employment, introduced in a shallow way in the law on refugees from

1993, into other texts and procedures, which regulated the administration's work in practice. For instance, in order to work legally, an asylum seeker needed to obtain a tax number from the tax administration. However, the national tax administration usually refused to deliver a tax number on the basis of a temporary document, such as the asylum seeker certificate, instead of a passport. This rule according to which a temporary document was insufficient for obtaining a tax number was not enshrined in the law on the state registry of natural persons, but was invoked by most tax officials as an imperative principle of their work. Neither the Tax Administration nor the State Migration Service accepted to significantly modify their rules so as to allow asylum seekers to realise their legal right to formal employment (personal communication, senior official of the Central State Migration Service in Kyiv, 2015 and 2016).

Yet, desk officers enjoyed discretionary powers that made the implementation of laws possible. In certain regional offices, state officials accepted to transgress a formal procedure to allow for the implementation of another legal right. NGOs reported that in one city, the tax administration refused to attribute a tax number to asylum seekers without a national passport, whereas the tax administration in another city and a town accepted to do this. Street-level bureaucrats sometimes diverge from formal rules (bending, breaking, or ignoring them) to overcome barriers to their work and to provide justice to their clients out of a professional or ethical imperative (Carey & Foster, 2011; Gofen, 2014; Lipsky, 1980).

The lack of information at the administration can also hamper the implementation of certain legal provisions. For example, since the amendment to the Law on Refugees from 2001, recognised refugees theoretically had the same rights to employment as Ukrainian citizens. However, employment offices were often unaware of this and refused to register and to support them. Tax offices also sometimes refused to issue a tax number to refugees because they categorised them as foreigners. The administration's lack of information about the formal rules suggests that hierarchically higher levels of the executive did not inform the officials interacting with the refugees (e.g. producing circulars or organising internal training). The lack of consistent top-down information about laws among street-level bureaucrats at the administration caused heterogeneous practices—some officials being informed (e.g. by members of NGOs and IOs) or searching actively for information and others ignoring and refusing to implement the laws.

Coping with the Lack of Resources

Lack of resources impeded upon the officers' possibilities to implement laws, regulations, and action plans or even to ensure the functioning of their institution. While the Ukrainian administration was generally underfunded (Liebert et al., 2013, p. 12), severely underfunding specific state functions is also a way to sabotage the implementation of certain policies and laws (Barnhizer, 2013). Interviewees commonly and spontaneously brought up the under-equipment of regional Migration Services. Representatives of NGOs often reported a dramatic lack of basic material at state authorities (e.g. lack of printers, paper, computers, telephone, and internet connection). For example, a representative of an NGO told me in an interview that in 2013, the regional Migration Service did not pay its rent so that the employees suddenly found the entrance to their office blocked and had to move to another office. Migration officers also reported that they did not have an internet connection for three months in 2013 because of lacking budget (informal conversation, caseworkers at a regional migration service, 2013).

Temporary lack of equipment at state authorities led to difficulties in implementing basic services, for example, providing documents to asylum seekers and refugees. In 2013, for about six months, asylum seekers could not obtain the asylum seeker certificate ("dovidka"), the document proving that they had applied for asylum and therefore had a legal status in Ukraine. Furthermore, the migration authorities could not issue passport-like identity documents to people who were recognised as persons in need of complementary protection until spring 2014, three years after the introduction of the legal status into Ukrainian law. Until then, the documents had not been printed, according to NGOs, due to the lack of money and technical equipment.

However, officers were able to improvise some responses to such top-down and structural difficulties. Instead of a passport-like document, the Migration Services prolonged the asylum seeker certificate (dovidka) and added by hand that the person had obtained complementary protection. While this document was recognised as a proof of legal stay in Ukraine, it was not recognised as a passport by other authorities such as the employment office and the tax administration, so that the concerned people did not have access to certain economic and social rights. These improvised measures only partially solved the problems the concerned migrants encountered and only partially allowed for the implementation of certain legal provisions.

Domestic politicians elaborated policies and laws without foreseeing any funding for the implementation. I will analyse how street-level bureaucrats coped with this situation in two prominent cases which both state and non-state actors in Ukraine regularly brought up in interviews: the implementation of an action plan for the integration of refugees and the guaranteeing of interpretation during communication with asylum seekers, foreseen by law.

Central and regional state bodies partly resisted the implementation of policies or measures requested by international actors. In 2012, under the influence of the EU Visa-Liberalisation Action Plan, the Ukrainian government decided on a National Plan on Integration of Refugees and Persons in Need of Complementary Protection into the Ukrainian Society for the Period until 2020—but until at least August 2016 did not foresee any budget for its implementation. The plan envisaged numerous measures, among them cost-intensive ones such as the "development of a network of temporary accommodation centres for refugees in the regions of their highest concentration", the establishment of "social integration centres for refugees and persons in need of complementary protection in Kyiv, Kharkiv, and Vinnytsia", of "temporary accommodation centres" for asylum seeking minors, of an accommodation centre for refugee children in Kyiv region and of an accommodation centre for single refugee mothers in the Kyiv region. The plan foresaw that all of these measures should be undertaken until 2015 or 2016 but had not even been started by then. Central executive bodies could thus hinder imported or imposed policies by failing to foresee a budget for their realisation.

Street-level bureaucrats were supposed to implement certain policies even though the central authorities did not offer them the means to do so. The officers decided to improvise solutions or to remain inactive. For instance, regional state bodies were supposed to realise certain aspects of the action plan, such as the organisation of Ukrainian language classes for recognised refugees—but had no funding to do so. Facing this obstacle, migration officers reacted in different ways, ranging from zealous and experimental responses to "aloof and burden-shedding" ones (Moore, 1990, p. 194). While many officers remained passive, a few resorted to their personal network and tried to organise language classes with volunteers, for instance with students from the local university. Through "practical inventiveness", officers tried to compensate for the lacking state resources to "make the state work" (Hamani, 2014). These practices often diverged from and sometimes even contradicted formal norms but occasionally allowed state officials to fulfil their tasks despite the lack of resources. Such activities can be read as a form of volunteering at work. This shows the important role of street-level bureaucrats for the functioning of state services. Scholars have found similar practices in underequipped West African state bodies (Bierschenk & Sardan, 2014).

In brief, street-level bureaucrats responded heterogeneously to top-down obstacles, with responses ranging from passivity and rule upholding to volunteering, improvisation, and transgression of formal rules and procedures to allow for the implementation of laws.

Attempts to Control Policy Implementation

The extent to which central authorities control local practices of policy implementation plays a major role in the analysis of transfer of norms and policies. Indeed, while most transfer scholars have referred to aggregated factors such as weak state capacity (Schimmelfennig, 2015; Sissenich, 2010), weak administrative capacities and limited statehood (Börzel, 2011), the analysis of these factors and of the central institutions' control over the implementation has remained cursory.

To decide whether factors located at the level of central authorities, such as political interest or political adoption costs, are relevant for the analysis of policy transfer, it is necessary to understand to which extent central authorities determine policy implementation. Scholars such as Peter May and Søren Winter have suggested that street-level bureaucrats' discretionary powers are shaped, among others, by the organisational implementation machinery, and in particular the extent to which the organisation delegates decision-making powers to street-level bureaucrats or, rather, limits their discretion (May & Winter, 2009, pp. 454–455). In other words, implementation is influenced by the principal-agent problem according to which, due to asymmetric information, the principal has only limited control over the agent (Ellig & Lavoie, 1995). On the one hand, refugee status decision-making entails generally a high level of discretionary powers for the frontline bureaucrats as it requires "sensitive observation and judgment, which are not reducible to programmed formats" (Lipsky, 1980, p. 15). On the other hand, some states divide the labour of the asylum decision-making, which is officially justified as reducing corruption and discretion (Spire, 2008, p. 23). In this section,

I will investigate the Ukrainian top-down attempts to control local state practices in refugee status determination.

With the establishment of the Central State Migration Service in 2009, Ukrainian central authorities increasingly tried to exert top-down control over regional state practices. Newly established central institutions sought to construct the national scale as dominating the regional scale. Scholars have characterised the Ukrainian administration as strongly hierarchical (Condrey et al., 2013, p. 15; Langbein & Wolczuk, 2012, p. 870). Moreover, EU incentives and monitoring temporarily increased the attempts to control regional practices.

EU Conditionality as a Motor for Policy Implementation

How does the domestic politicians' wish to fulfil EU requirements under sector-specific conditionality affect policy implementation? Or, more precisely, how does the EU's supervision of the implementation affect the central domestic authorities' attempts to control policy implementation? While research has frequently highlighted that EU conditionality triggers formal and little practical norm adoption, it has paid little attention to the effects of this conditionality on administrative practices, and in particular, the domestic processes through which these effects take place. Yet, these domestic processes can mediate, strengthen, or block transfer of norms.

Between 2010 and 2015, the EU supervision in the framework of the Visa-Liberalisation Action Plan pushed the central authorities to control policy implementation more intensively. The government of Ukraine pressured certain central executive state bodies to obtain positive evaluations by the EU. For instance, the State Migration Service was responsible for the implementation of the integration plan for refugees, requested by the EU, in front of the Cabinet of Ministers. While at first the Cabinet of Ministers did not supervise the implementation of the plan, the EU incentives and monitoring triggered closer control by the government. Especially between 2014 and late 2015, the President of Ukraine demanded that different Ministries and Services fulfil the EU requirements, including implementing the integration plan. After the EU issued a report in which it criticised, among others, asylum policies in Ukraine, the Cabinet of Ministers questioned the State Migration Service. The high officials of the State Migration Service were under pressure from the President and the Cabinet of Ministers to fulfil the EU demands so that the subsequent evaluations of the asylum system would be positive.

Nevertheless, the government exerted its pressure heterogeneously on the different central state bodies. While the State Migration Service was under significant pressure because it was in charge of regular reports to the government on the integration plan's progress, other ministries were less directly pressured. The State Migration Service tried to pass the government's pressure on to the other involved ministries, requesting biannual reports on how they implemented the integration plan, which the SMS then transmitted to the Cabinet of Ministers. However, some central state bodies considered themselves less responsible for the implementation of the integration plan. For instance, the Ministry of Education, though mentioned in the plan, rejected any responsibility. The vice-director of the asylum department of the State Migration Service tried in vain to convince the Ministry of Education to participate in the fulfilment of the plan by organising Ukrainian language classes for refugees. Hierarchies meant that a state service could not force a ministry to contribute to the implementation. Unequal governmental pressure and the limited legal authority (Weber, 1922, pt. I) of the pressured state bodies over other executive bodies partly explain why the domestic authorities implemented the norms and policies requested by the EU heterogeneously.

However, the pressured State Migration Service was able to pass this pressure on to the regional Migration Services, over which it exercised legal authority. The State Migration Service required the regional services to report every six months on how they implemented the integration plan. These hierarchical control practices illustrate how EU conditionality participated in the production of scales. The EU managed to construct the European scale as vertically above the national Ukrainian one, which the Ukrainian policy makers accepted as they sought to obtain the EU incentives. In the course of the transfer processes, Ukrainian state actors renegotiated scales by accepting or refusing to report to and obey other state actors. Central state bodies in Ukraine constructed the national scale as vertically superior to the regional scale when requesting the regional services to report on their implementation.

Central State Bodies' Attempts to Control and Standardise Regional State Practices

While scales within the state apparatus were taken for granted by the actors involved, they were nevertheless constantly renegotiated in practice. The spatial scope of the scales was mostly accepted and reproduced through practices, but the vertical control was negotiated as central authorities struggled to fully control the local authorities' everyday practices.

In the context of EU conditionality, central authorities in Ukraine increasingly sought to control and standardise the policy implementation in the regions. Two types of central state bodies had the role of controlling and standardising the practices and decisions of regional Migration Services: the Central State Migration Service and the courts. These actors perceived themselves as acting on a national scale. Since 2000, the Central State Migration Service made the final status decision on the attribution of the refugee status, instead of the regional Migration Services. Indeed, the central SMS formally read all the recommendations written at the regional Migration Services and took the final decision.[2] In interviews, regional migration officers presented the acceptance or rejection of the local recommendation by the State Migration Service and courts as a legitimate evaluation of their work and claimed to take their criticism seriously to inform future practices. Once in a while, the central SMS attempted to standardise regional practices via direct contact with the officials. Officers of the Central Service were occasionally in direct contact with the regional caseworkers to give feedback or request additional information. The central organ sometimes sent the file produced by the regional body back, asking for an additional interview or revision of the text. This scalar organisation was accepted by the state actors as natural—both in terms of spatial scope and of vertical authority. The practices of control, feedback, and information requests or provision among regional and national authorities reperformed this scalar structure.

[2] I could not find out how frequently the Central State Migration Service overturned the regional Migration Services' recommendations. The internal statistics, obtained from an employee of the SMS, did not include this information. Moreover, while local state officials claimed in interviews in 2014 that the central organ supported most of their decisions, the central state officials underlined the importance of their role of supervision and correction vis-à-vis the local authorities, stating that they very often overturned the local recommendations.

However, the central authorities' attempts to standardise regional state practices through other channels than the proofreading of recommendations remained limited and occasional. In the 2010s, the Central State Migration Service gradually developed guidelines for the regional caseworkers, but these remained fragmentary. Newly recruited state officials received no official and centralised training. The central migration service only rarely gathered the staff from the regional services to spread information and procedures. Moreover, the high turnover of subordinate officials, though different depending on the regional office, undermined the central authorities' attempts to standardise their practices.

At a distance, the officials at the Central State Migration Service could not control regional officials' informal practices given that they only had access to the written traces of the procedure (principal-agent problem). The heads of regional asylum departments could control the migration officers more closely. Some of them read the caseworkers' draft recommendations and transcript of the interview, commented on formulations, and asked for modifications or for additional interviews. Yet, due to the heads' own differing trajectories, experiences, knowledge, beliefs, and judgments, this oversight at the regional scale did not lead to a national standardisation. According to the accounts of central migration officers and NGO workers, each of the regional offices had its own work practices. Actors with a national-scale identity presented this regional heterogeneity as problematic—it undermined the imagined scalar structure according to which central authorities should be able to control and standardise regional practices. In addition to the regional departments, practices of the individual caseworkers strongly differed.

Street-Level Bureaucrats' Discretionary Use of the Law: Social Norms, Personal Interests, Moral Judgments, and Emotions

> You should understand that we do not decide. This is all predetermined by the law. When we decide whether a person should be a refugee or not, we only follow the law. (Interview, caseworker at a local asylum department, 2014)

This migration officer claimed that the legal norms determine the status decision. Street-level bureaucrats deny their discretionary power and "hide" behind hierarchies and formal norms to avoid the questioning of their decisions (Bourdieu, 1990, pp. 87–88; Spire, 2008, p. 11). Yet, subordinate officials decide whether or not to use a legal norm and also how to use and interpret it in the specific case (Lipsky, 1980).

In many post-Soviet countries, the habit that laws are negotiable and can be used by state employees for their own profit undermines the implementation of law (Désert, 2006; Kurkchiyan, 2003). Research has shown that the effectiveness of a law depends on the domestic context and the attitudes towards law in general and towards the particular law. The implementing organisations and their staff pursue interests (e.g. taking bribes) diverging from the ones foreseen by the lawmakers so that the implementation differs from the legal text (e.g. which foresees free treatment). Social norms compete with state laws—often at the expense of the latter (Galligan, 2003). For instance, widespread bribe-giving at public hospitals obscured refugees' right to free healthcare. Formally, only sophisticated tests and treatments as well as drugs listed in a government decree were liable to represent costs for the patient. However, in addition to these official payments, unofficial ones were commonly expected, requested (by the staff), or offered (by the patient) for services that were officially free of charge. Moreover, as formulated by a representative of an NGO in Ukraine in 2014: doctors "only see that the person is a foreigner and they don't know that he is a refugee or what a refugee is. And they want money." Hospital staff used the asylum seekers' and refugees' situation to request bribes and refuse the treatment without payment. Nevertheless, in several accounts the initial refusal was not upheld and another doctor finally agreed to take over the treatment without any payment.Indeed, research on informal payments in the Ukrainian medical sector has shown that informal payments were not always "mandatory" and that the medical staff sometimes examined the patients' needs and wealth when determining the amount (or absence) of the informal payment (Morris & Polese, 2016, p. 491). When the medical personnel had known the patients for longer or evaluated them as poor and in serious need of treatment, it sometimes decided to refrain from requesting informal payments. Due to social norms of negotiable law and corruption as well as the officials' interest in diverging from the law, officials used formal rules heterogeneously.

The head of an asylum NGO in a big city in Ukraine commented:

> It's a big problem for refugees: Here everything depends on the person in charge. If the person is friendly then there is no problem. If the person is unfriendly or in a hurry, or lacking instructions, doesn't know the law, it's difficult. The law may be good but if the person at the desk doesn't want to help the refugee… (Interview, head of an NGO, 2014)

Officials adapted the formal rules to fit their liking or dislike of the applicant. For example, depending on the individual, they adapted the interpretation of how an interview was supposed to be conducted. Officers could decide to question a favoured applicant numerous times to collect the elements to justify a positive recommendation for a protection status. Less favoured applicants could be questioned only once and if they did not deliver the necessary arguments immediately and from their own initiative, the recommendation would be negative. Formally, the procedure was respected in both cases but the chances offered to the different asylum seekers diverged strongly. Ukrainian migration officers could request more documents from an applicant they liked or pitied, which allowed the applicant to have a more convincing file and was in turn more likely to be accepted at the central Migration Service. They could also choose to be less strict concerning certain procedures, such as letting the applicants translate the document themselves instead of requiring an official translation. Such discretion could make the applicants' submission of a document easier or even allow them to modify the content of the document to their advantage. A migration officer reported how she stretched the legal provisions in order to be able to grant a protection status to applicants who, according to her, could not return to their country of origin.

> It had been very hard before this additional [complementary] protection [status] was introduced. Many refugees are nominal, they didn't fit the conventional [refugee] status because they didn't have those five obvious conventional reasons. We dragged them in… There were girls whose parents were killed during those internal movements in the country. They were lost and somehow one of them was found by her aunt or uncle and got to Ukraine. It's clear that it is hard for her to go back – though she doesn't fit the conventional criteria. So we dragged it into the "separate social group" and in this way they were granted refugee status. Now [since the introduction of the legal status of a person in need of complementary protection] it's easier because if there is any violence and if there is some threat for the life – not necessarily personal persecution – it still gives a

> reason to give some protection. (Interview, caseworker at a local asylum department, 2014)

The vagueness of the legal criteria of "special social group" allowed migration officers to recommend the granting of a protection status. Rather than applying a norm, the officer used the norms to justify her decision.

Migration officers subjectively appreciated the applicants, whom they categorised intuitively as "good" or "bad" migrants, like many other street-level bureaucrats who attribute or refuse social benefits by distinguishing between the "deserving" and the "undeserving" based on moral judgments and emotions (Castel, 1995, p. 764; Fassin & Kobelinsky, 2012). Interviews conducted between 2013 and 2015 in various regional Migration Services show that migration officers were overall aware of the criteria foreseen in the law for the two Ukrainian legal protection statuses, the refugee status, and, since 2011, the status of a person in need of complementary protection. However, the translation of this abstract legal knowledge into concrete evaluations of individuals differed among the different migration officers and concerning different applicants.

Street-level bureaucrats evaluated the asylum seekers' deservingness and innocence. Deservingness refers to migration for socially legitimate reasons (e.g. voluntary vs. involuntary migrants, accepted flight grounds vs. unaccepted ones) but also to a meritocratic evaluation of the applicant outside of the migration grounds. Innocence involves, on the one hand, honesty, moral purity, and freedom of wrongdoing. On the other hand, it relates to vulnerability based on passivity, irresponsibility, and simplemindedness (Ticktin, 2015). It matters most when a person is to be judged based on passivity, namely women and children. Migration officers often cited children, especially orphans, and women when talking about deserving applicants who triggered their compassion. A caseworker explained:

> Of course there is this subjective factor when you evaluate the whole case. When you start asking, you already think from the viewpoint of a psychologist: Is it possible for this child to go back to his homeland? I understand that his mother has probably sent him out of his country to search for a better life. I understand that there is no personal threat for him. No one persecutes him. I had one case. There was a young guy, 15 years old. It is hard to identify their age because there [in the country of origin] they

> become grown-ups very early. After his father's death, he became the head of the family. His father perished. He has two options for his future: he will either be recruited to the army just like his father or be suspected of being a spy and followed by secret services. There they can be recruited at a very young age. Here our children play with toy guns and they play with real ones. So we tried to take this into consideration and to assume what is the risk upon his arrival. By the moment of his departure, I realised that there was actually no threat. I understand that his fate will be similar to that of his father. They have no job and no land... what will he do? He won't have the opportunity to study because he has his mother and four younger siblings. So, a human factor influenced us in that case. We cannot help the whole planet but we can help a specific person. (Interview, caseworker at a local asylum department, 2014)

From this example it can be seen that even though the applicant did not formally fulfil the refugee criteria, the situation he would face in case of return justified the migration officer's wish to "help" this person whom she perceived as innocent and vulnerable. In contrast, caseworkers did not present as innocent applicants who lied and who resisted the bureaucratic order.

The evaluation of the applicants' honesty affected the officer's appreciation of the applicants' vulnerability. During interviews, Ukrainian migration officers presented the control of the truth as crucial in their work and often proudly exposed their skills and techniques in testing the applicants to figure out if they are lying. The testing of applicants' knowledge to control the "truth" of their story was also a result of international circulation of state and UNHCR practices—for example of the "credibility assessment". Indeed, scholars have highlighted very similar practices in other countries (Wettergren & Wikström, 2013). These control activities affected the officers' moral judgment. Indeed, officers presented lying as a personal offence against them and morally condemned applicants whom they suspected of lying. A person who lied or withheld important information undermined the social order and questioned bureaucratic domination (Dubois, 1999, p. 313). Similarly to practices in other countries, such as France or Sweden, such a moral condemnation by a Ukrainian migration officer eroded the applicant's chances of being granted a protection status.

Caseworkers appreciated certain characteristics of asylum seekers. Applicants appearing as docile and innocent, submitting to the administrative order and readily sharing their private information as well as those who were perceived as deserving (building up a successful business, having completed or completing higher education, learning Ukrainian or Russian) were informally favoured in the procedure. The favouring of some categories of migrants by the state officials thus explains part of the "gap" between the law on the books and the law in practice.

To conclude, when state officials distinguished between undeserving migrants and genuine refugees they partly translated formal, often originally international, norms to the concrete situation. Partly they carried out personal evaluations based on moral judgments and emotions independently from formal norms and they justified their decisions a posteriori by reference to the formal norms. Street-level bureaucrats therefore made policies, instead of merely applying or translating them to the local context. These practices could not be controlled by central authorities but could be affected by national and international discourses and norms on deservingness.

Conclusion

In the area of asylum in Ukraine, state practices often diverged from laws and formal policy documents. As found by transfer scholars, there was indeed a gap between rule adoption and rule application (Delcour, 2016, p. 122). Like most transfer scholars, I first approached this gap from a top-down perspective. This way, I identified several major top-down obstacles to implementation, namely the frequent restructuring of the migration authorities until 2011, shallow legislative adoption of international norms, in particular legal contradictions, lack of information for subordinate officials, and lack of resources for the implementation. First, these top-down obstacles can be explained by general characteristics of the Ukrainian state institutions and political sphere such as phases of paralysing political power struggles, contradictory regulatory production, and generalised underfunding of the administration. Second, the low political prioritisation of asylum exacerbated these difficulties—but was also countered by the EU sector-specific conditionality between 2010 and early 2016, which caused the attribution of resources and a deeper legislative adoption of international norms. This confirms common analyses of transfer studies which have shown that the respective states undertake façade change, a form of hidden policy resistance to transfer, if they are not urged via international actors' conditionality and monitoring to actually implement the norms.

However, the role of top-down factors for the work of the state authorities needs to be qualified. While some top-down obstacles made the implementation of norms completely impossible, others seriously obstructed it. In the latter cases, regional authorities and their officers responded heterogeneously: Some regional services remained passive and ignored the formal norm; others tried to implement it by rule bending, improvising, and volunteering (Condrey et al., 2013, p. 13). This phenomenon of improvisation and volunteering at state institutions affects processes and outcomes of transfer undertakings and has so far been ignored by transfer research.

When seeking to understand the factors which shape the way executive bodies implement transferred formal norms, most transfer studies have focused on macro factors, such as normative fit or national political regimes. Arguing that local sectoral actors' differentiated role needs to be taken into consideration to understand policy implementation in the EU neighbourhood, Dandashly and Kourtelis maintained that local actors' normative convergence with the transferred norms and their involvement in the policy formulation shape policy implementation (Dandashly & Kourtelis, 2020). However, it remains largely unclear *how* local actors shape policy implementation in a context of norm transfer. This chapter has shown that Ukrainian central authorities increasingly tried to gain control over the implementation of policies in the regions, namely through top-down pressure from the government that was transmitted via the state hierarchies, the moving of prerogatives of final decision-making from regional to central state bodies, the provision of internal directives, central authorities' feedback, and training for regional officials. Nevertheless, control and standardisation via the state hierarchies remained limited, fragmentary, and occasional. Beyond contextual considerations such as the lack of state resources, of training for officials, and of precise guidelines, the capacity of central state bodies to fully control and standardise regional practices in general is questionable. This is due to the principal-agent problem and the need for street-level bureaucrats' interpretation of formal norms in many policy areas. In other words, while state officials discursively accepted the vertical domination of the national scale over regional scales, they constantly renegotiated it in practice.

The implementation of laws and policies depended on street-level bureaucrats' use of these formal norms. Street-level bureaucrats used formal norms and procedures to justify and implement the decisions they had made beforehand based on moral and affective judgments in regard to the applicants. This importance of the bureaucrats' appreciation meant that applicants able to trigger friendly emotions—those perceived as innocent and deserving—were favoured by the administration. Via their practices, street-level bureaucrats thus developed policies which were necessarily heterogeneous.

In addition to the analysis of how street-level bureaucrats react to the formal norms that are transferred (localisation, resistance, translation) (Acharya, 2015; Hadjiisky et al., 2017), it can be insightful to qualify the role of formal norms as the origin of state action. Research on transfer would benefit from focusing more directly on state practices rather than departing from the formally transferred norms. This would allow scholars to understand which moral judgments prevail in this area and shape state practices. Such an approach is especially relevant in organisational contexts in which street-level bureaucrats have important discretionary powers and personalised relations with the applicants, for example in the attribution of social benefits.

Given that street-level bureaucrats perform policies by interpreting the law according to social norms and moral appreciations, norm promoters try to influence norm application by directly targeting these officials—as will be analysed in the next chapter.

References

Acharya, A. (2015). The responsibility to protect and a theory of norm circulation. In R. C. Thakur & W. Maley (Eds.), *Theorising the responsibility to protect* (pp. 59–78). Cambridge University Press.

Ademmer, E., & Börzel, T. A. (2013). Migration, energy and good governance in the EU's eastern neighbourhood. *Europe-Asia Studies, 65*(4), 581–608.

Bache, I., & Taylor, A. (2003). The politics of policy resistance: Reconstructing higher education in Kosovo. *Journal of Public Policy, 23*(3), 279–300.

Barnhizer, D. (2013). *The implementation gap: What causes laws to succeed or fail?* Unpublished Paper from Cleveland State University. https://works.bepress.com/david_barnhizer/79/

Bierschenk, T., & Sardan, J.-P. O. de. (2014). *States at work: Dynamics of African bureaucracies*. BRILL.

Blankenburg, E. (1986). La recherche de l'efficacité de la loi. Réflexions sur l'étude de la mise en œuvre (Le concept « d'implementation »). *Droit et Société, 2*, 73–94.

Boroda, M. (2008). *Migration trends and policies in the black sea region: Cases of Moldova, Romania and Ukraine*. Institute for Public Policy, Institute for

Development and Social Initiatives "Viitorul", International Centre for Policy Studies. http://old.icps.com.ua/files/articles/50/33/Migration_ENG.pdf

Börzel, T. A. (2011). *When Europeanization hits limited statehood—The Western Balkans as a test case for the transformative power of Europe*. Working Paper KFG The Transformative Power of Europe, 30. http://www.polsoz.fu-berlin.de/en/v/transformeurope/publications/working_paper/wp/wp30/index.html

Bourdieu, P. (1990). Droit et passe-droit—Le champ des pouvoirs territoriaux et la mise en oeuvre des règlements. *Actes de La Recherche En Sciences Sociales, 81*(1), 86–96.

Carey, M., & Foster, V. (2011). Introducing 'deviant' social work: Contextualising the limits of radical social work whilst understanding (fragmented) resistance within the social work labour process. *The British Journal of Social Work, 41*(3), 576–593.

Castel, R. (1995). *Les métamorphoses de la question sociale*. Gallimard Folio.

Condrey, S. E., Slava-Prodan, S., Battaglio, R. P., & Palinchak, M. (2013). Ukrainian public management: Top-down or bottom-up reform? In S. Liebert, S. E. Condrey, & D. Goncharov (Eds.), *Public administration in post-communist countries: Former Soviet Union, Central and Eastern Europe, and Mongolia* (pp. 7–22). CRC Press.

Dandashly, A., & Kourtelis, C. (2020). Classifying the implementation of the EU's normative power in its southern neighbourhood: The role of local actors. *JCMS: Journal of Common Market Studies, 58*(6), 1523–1539. https://doi.org/10.1111/jcms.13051

D'Anieri, P. (2007). *Understanding Ukrainian politics: Power, politics, and institutional design*. M.E. Sharpe.

Delcour, L. (2016). *The EU's policy transfer to the post-Soviet space: Domestic responses, (post)-Soviet legacies and Russia's policies* (HDR). Institut d'études politiques de Paris.

Désert, M. (2006). Le débat russe sur l'informel. *Questions de recherche, CERI, 17*.

Dubois, V. (1999). *La vie au guichet: Relation administrative et traitement de la misère* (3 (2010)). Economica.

Düvell, F., & Vollmer, B. (2009). Irregular migration in and from the neighbourhood of the EU. A comparison of Morocco, Turkey and Ukraine. *Clandestino*, 1–44.

Ellig, J., & Lavoie, D. (1995). The principal–agent relationship in organizations. In P. Foss (Ed.), *Economic approaches to organizations and institutions: An introduction*. Darmouth.

Evans, M. (Ed.). (2010). *New directions in the study of policy transfer*. Routledge.

Falkner, G., Treib, O., & Holzleithner, E. (2008). *Compliance in the enlarged European Union: Living rights or dead letters?* Ashgate Publishing.

Fassin, D., & Kobelinsky, C. (2012). Comment on juge l'asile. *Revue française de sociologie, 53*(4), 657–688.

Galligan, D. J. (2003). Legal failure: Law and social norms in post-communist Europe. In M. Kurkchiyan (Ed.), *Law and informal practices: The post-communist experience* (pp. 1–23). Oxford University Press.

Goetz, K. H. (2005). The new member states and the EU: responding to Europe. In S. Bulmer & C. Lequesne (Eds.), *The member states of the European Union* (pp. 254–280). Oxford University Press.

Gofen, A. (2014). Mind the gap: Dimensions and influence of street-level divergence. *Journal of Public Administration Research and Theory, 24*(2), 473–493.

Hadjiisky, M., Pal, L. A., & Walker, C. (Eds.). (2017). *Public policy transfer: Micro-dynamics and macro effects*. Edward Elgar Publishing.

Hamani, O. (2014). "We make do and keep going!" Inventive practices and ordered informality in the functioning of the district courts in Niamey and Zinder (Niger). In T. Bierschenk & J.-P. O. de Sardan (Eds.), *States at Work: Dynamics of African bureaucracies* (pp. 145–174). BRILL.

Hupe, P., & Buffat, A. (2014). A public service gap: Capturing contexts in a comparative approach of street-level bureaucracy. *Public Management Review, 16*(4), 548–569.

International Centre for Policy Studies (Kyiv, Ukraine) & Institute for Public Affairs (Warsaw, Poland). (2006, June). *Ukraine's policy to control illegal migration*.

Israël, L. (2009). *L'arme du droit*. Les Presses de Sciences Po.

Jacoby, W. (1999). Priest and penitent: The EU as a force in the domestic politics of Eastern Europe. *East European Constitutional Review, 8*(1–2), 62–67.

Jacquot, S., & Woll, C. (2004, January 16). *Usage of European Integration—Europeanisation from a sociological perspective*. SSRN Scholarly Paper. http://papers.ssrn.com/abstract=485983

Kazmierkiewicz, P., Lvova, O., & Chumak, V. (2009). *Coordinating migration policy in Ukraine: Lessons from Poland*. Institute of Public Affairs, Warsaw & International Centre for Policy Studies, Kyiv.

Kluczewska, K. (2019). How to translate 'good governance' into Tajik? An American good governance fund and norm localisation in Tajikistan. *Journal of Intervention and Statebuilding, 13*(3), 357–376.

Kubicek, P. (2003). *The European Union & democratization: Reluctant states*. Routledge.

Kurkchiyan, M. (2003). The illegitimacy of law in post-Soviet societies. In D. J. Galligan & M. Kurkchiyan (Eds.), *Law and informal practices: The post-communist experience* (pp. 25–46). Oxford University Press.

Langbein, J., & Wolczuk, K. (2012). Convergence without membership? The impact of the European Union in the neighbourhood: Evidence from Ukraine. *Journal of European Public Policy, 19*(6), 863–881.

Lenschow, A., Liefferink, D., & Veenman, S. (2005). When the birds sing. A framework for analysing domestic factors behind policy convergence. *Journal of European Public Policy, 12*(5), 797–816. https://doi.org/10.1080/13501760500161373

Liebert, S., Condrey, S. E., & Goncharov, D. (2013). *Public administration in post-communist countries: Former Soviet Union, Central and Eastern Europe, and Mongolia*. CRC Press.

Lipsky, M. (1980). *Street-level bureaucracy: The dilemmas of the individual in public service*. Russell Sage Foundation.

May, P. J., & Winter, S. C. (2009). Politicians, managers, and street-level bureaucrats: Influences on policy implementation. *Journal of Public Administration Research and Theory, 19*(3), 453–476. https://doi.org/10.1093/jopart/mum030

Maynard-Moody, S., & Musheno, M. (2000). State agent or citizen agent: Two narratives of discretion. *Journal of Public Administration Research and Theory, 10*(2), 329–358.

Moore, S. T. (1990). Street-level policymaking: Characteristics of decision and policy in public welfare. *The American Review of Public Administration, 20*(3), 191–209.

Morris, J., & Polese, A. (2016). Informal health and education sector payments in Russian and Ukrainian cities: Structuring welfare from below. *European Urban and Regional Studies, 23*(3), 481–496. https://doi.org/10.1177/0969776414522081

Saurugger, S., & Terpan, F. (2013). *Resisting EU norms. A framework for analysis*. Sciences Po Grenoble Working Paper, n°2.

Schimmelfennig, F. (2015). Europeanization beyond Europe. *Living Revue European Governance, 10*(1). http://www.europeangovernance-livingreviews.org/Articles/lreg-2015-1/

Schimmelfennig, F., & Sedelmeier, U. (2005). Conceptualizing the Europeanization of Central and Eastern Europe. In *The Europeanization of Central and Eastern Europe* (pp. 1–28). Cornell University Press.

Sissenich, B. (2010). Weak states, weak societies: Europe's east-west gap. *Acta Politica, 45*(1–2), 11–40. https://doi.org/10.1057/ap.2009.28

Spire, A. (2008). *Accueillir ou reconduire: Enquête sur les guichets de l'immigration*. Raisons d'agir.

State Migration Service of Ukraine (MS Odessa) & Foundation for Assistance to Refugees and Displaced People 'Spivchuttya' (Compassion). (2011a). Gazeta Migratsiya February 2011a. *Migratsiya, 2*(108). http://en.migraciya.com.ua/upload/Migration_fabruaru_2011.pdf

State Migration Service of Ukraine (MS Odessa) & Foundation for Assistance to Refugees and Displaced People 'Spivchuttya' (Compassion). (2011b). Gazeta Migratsiya March 2011b. *Migratsiya, 3*(109). http://en.migraciya.com.ua/upload/Migration_march_2011.pdf

State Migration Service of Ukraine (MS Odessa) & Foundation for Assistance to Refugees and Displaced People 'Spivchuttya' (Compassion). (2011c). Gazeta Migratsiya April 2011c. *Migratsiya, 4*(110). http://en.migraciya.com.ua/upload/Migration_april_2011.pdf

State Migration Service of Ukraine (MS Odessa) & Foundation for Assistance to Refugees and Displaced People 'Spivchuttya' (Compassion). (2011d). Gazeta Migratsiya May 2011. *Migratsiya, 5*(111). http://en.migraciya.com.ua/upload/%D0%BC%D0%B0%D0%B9_%D0%9C%D1%96%D0%B3%D1%80%D0%B0%D1%86%D1%96%D1%8F6.pdf

Tajibaeva, N. (2008). Labour migration and home state responses in the post-Soviet area: The cases of Ukraine and Kyrgyzstan. In A. Güneş-Ayata (Ed.), *Challenges of global migration: EU and its neighbourhood* (Zeplin İleşim Hizmetleri, pp. 55–76). KORA—Center for Black Sea and Central Asia, METU—Middle East Technical University.

Ticktin, M. (2015, June 10). *Innocence: Understanding a political concept*. https://soundcloud.com/refugeestudiescentre/innocence-understanding-a-political-concept-annual-elizabeth-colson-lecture-2015

Tolstokorova, A. (2013). Evolution of institutional framework focussing on migration and asylum issues in Ukraine since 1991. In A. Bara, A. Di Bartolomeo, Z. Brunarska, S. Makaryan, S. Mananashvili, & A. Weinar (Eds.), *Regional migration report: Eastern Europe* (pp. 109–114). European University Institute.

Vollmer, B., Bilan, Y., Lapshyna, I., & Vdovtsova, S. (2010). *Ukraine country and research areas report*. EUMAGINE Imagining Europe from the Outside, 3.

Weber, M. (1922). *Wirtschaft und Gesellschaft – Grundriß der verstehenden Soziologie* (Economy and society—An outline of interpretative sociology) (G. Roth & C. Wittich, Eds.). University of California Press.

Wettergren, Å., & Wikström, H. (2013). Who is a refugee? Political subjectivity and the categorisation of Somali asylum seekers in Sweden. *Journal of Ethnic and Migration Studies, 40*(4), 566–583. https://doi.org/10.1080/1369183X.2013.830502

Wetzel, A. (2016). From halt to hurry: External and domestic influences on Ukrainian asylum policy. *Eurasian Geography and Economics, 57*(1), 66–88.

CHAPTER 6

A Multi-Scalar Transfer Chain: Capital, Control, and Contacts of Norm Promoters

Introduction

> We try to make authorities more sympathetic to refugees. They believe that all of them are abusing the procedure and for example that they are all adults and just pretend that they are children. It's difficult. It would be better to change staff. These old Soviet ladies should go away. It would be better for them and for the refugees. [...] There is ultra-nationalism and racism there. For example, these directors of shelters say: These people should not live with our children!" (Interview, junior Ukrainian employee of UNHCR in Ukraine, 2014)

Non-state actors in Ukraine judged state practices related to asylum seekers and refugees as problematic. They explained these problems to a large extent by the officials' lack of knowledge and beliefs diverging from their own. Stressing the importance of individuals implementing policies and laws, they depicted many state officials as untrained, uninformed, unmotivated, racist, and corrupt. According to the NGOs and IOs, this led to a gap between state practices and domestic laws or international asylum norms. Consequently, norm promoters tried to change the knowledge, norms, and practices of a maximum of subordinate and intermediary state officials through direct interaction. Direct interaction also allowed non-state actors to rescale the transfer process away from

I. Mützelburg, *Transferring Asylum Norms to EU Neighbours*, The European Union in International Affairs, https://doi.org/10.1007/978-3-031-04528-8_6

the national scale, so that they could promote norms independently from politicians' interest in asylum and central authorities' capacity to control everyday administrative practices.

Researchers have argued that interactions between norm promoters and norm addressees may change the latter's norms, interests, and identities (Brucker, 2007; Colineau, 2014; Finnemore & Sikkink, 1998; Freyburg, 2011; Sedelmeier, 2006). The norm promoters' legitimacy in the target context affects the outcomes of attempts to transfer norms (Flowers, 2008; Schimmelfennig & Sedelmeier, 2005, p. 19). However, empirical research has so far remained scarce, meaning that the extent and the ways through which changes occur are unclear. We also do not know how different modes of interaction between norm promoters and norm addressees affect the outcomes of transfer attempts.

To better understand the role that different modes of interactions play in norm transfer, we can benefit from approaches adopted by political sociology, especially with regards to the relations between state and non-state actors and the role of informality in post-communist contexts. Studies on social movements have pointed to the intertwined relations and the role of activists in state authorities (Banaszak, 2010; Katzenstein, 1999). NGOs make use of personal contacts, in particular in post-communist contexts (Grødeland & Aasland, 2011). In some cases, staff of NGOs and administration are composed of closed, informal networks that resist the formalisation of procedures (Osborne & Kaposvari, 1998). International assistance organisations fail in their efforts if they do not take into consideration informal processes and institutions in the post-communist setting in which they operate (Adamson, 2002).

Based on these insights, the present chapter[1] examines the principal links of the transfer chain: transfer from international organisations to Ukrainian NGOs who take over transfer activities, targeting domestic authorities. NGOs then turn certain domestic officials into allies and even brokers, who then further transfer norms to other officials. It shows how international transfer undertakings produce new transfer actors and networks, and affect relations between NGOs and authorities. It also addresses how norm promoters use their resources to build up contacts with officials. Further, it indicates how different modes of interaction—formal / informal, regular / unique, harmonious / contentious—affect transfer processes and outcomes. Finally, it suggests that direct interaction leads to norm transfer outcomes that are heterogeneous across actors and

[1] Some content from this chapter and the following one is in the process of being published here (Mützelburg, forthcoming).

space, and unstable over time. This is why norm promoters try to use their contacts among decision makers to influence the production of formal rules.

Creating and Controlling Domestic NGO Norm Promoters

Since the early 2000s, the European Commission financed various projects on asylum in Ukraine. Most funding was channelled via international organisations such as UNHCR, which in turn funded Ukrainian NGOs. Scholars have reached diverging conclusions regarding the effects of international influence via domestic NGOs. Some researchers, such as Ryhor Nizhnikau, have argued that foreign action may "empower" domestic actors to make political claims in harmony with the external actors' norms (Nizhnikau, 2015). It may shape domestic actors' incentives and capacities (Langbein, 2015, p. XVIII; Langbein & Wolczuk, 2012; Sedelmeier, 2006, p. 10) and allow some of them to benefit from international resources, so that they reach their political goals at the national scale (Dezalay & Garth, 2002; Langbein, 2015, pp. 155–156). In contrast, other researchers have shown that foreign funding influences the thematic and ideological orientation and activities of the NGOs, which then act in a donor-driven way (Henderson, 2002; Parks, 2008; Sampson, 2004). Drawing on the actor-centred research on development aid, I complement institutionalist transfer research, taking into account an often overlooked part of the transfer economy or networks: NGO-donor relations.

Following research on NGO-donor relations, I develop new questions for the analysis of transfer of norms and policies. First, which functions do donors want the funded NGOs to fulfil? Which services are NGOs expected to carry out in the donors' place? Are NGOs the final norm addressees, or are intermediaries supposed to transfer the norms to third parties (namely state authorities)? Second, what are the intended and unintended effects of the donors' intervention on the funded NGOs and the targeted non-state sector? Third, what are the reasons for the donor's influence on the funded NGOs?

To spread and establish their asylum norms in Ukraine, international organisations caused the emergence of NGOs (or donor-driven NGOs – DONGOs) to whom they delegated norm transfer activities. While a small number of organisations were funded by international donors other than

UNHCR, by far the biggest, the most powerful and most active group, the "UNHCR implementing partners", was exclusively or predominantly funded by UNHCR. These organisations were composed of paid staff of Ukrainian origin. Even if all the actors in Ukraine called them "UNHCR partners", I call them "UNHCR subcontractors" to reflect the power relations between the donor and the implementing organisations (Reimann, 2006, p. 49). These DONGOs, first targets of norm transfer themselves, were standardised and controlled by their donors.

UNHCR increasingly dominated the funding for asylum in Ukraine. International funding for asylum—and the number of asylum NGOs—increased in the years 2000. During that decade, the EU funded directly, apart from UNHCR, different international organisations and international non-governmental organisations which then organised asylum projects or funded NGOs in Ukraine (for example ECRE 2005–2011; Danish Refugee Council 2007–2013, Austrian Caritas 2004–2008, Chernihiv Public Committee for Human Rights Protection 2005–2007). Since 2013, when the funding for asylum-related activities of the Danish Refugee Council ended (until then the second major intermediary aid receiver/donor in Ukraine) the EU channelled its funding almost exclusively via UNHCR.

NGOs emerged or added asylum activities due to the availability of UNHCR funding. In contrast to situations in which international donors funded activities around an issue which had already mobilised domestic activism before the funding, asylum in Ukraine had barely triggered any domestic volunteering prior to and independently from the availability of international funding. External actors produced the non-state asylum sector in Ukraine.

Over time, UNHCR restructured its subcontractors, including the types of activities they carried out. In cities with larger refugee populations, following UNHCR's wish, NGOs split in two so that they could separate the work in two spheres. One organisation provided legal aid to asylum seekers (namely helping them prepare documents to apply for asylum and file court appeals after a rejection) and the other one offered social support (namely providing material aid such as money, clothes, mattresses, hygiene products, food and school material for children, Ukrainian language classes and computer classes, psychological support, advice and accompaniment for job search, administrative procedures, and schooling). UNHCR also caused the modification of the work areas of NGOs that had existed already before becoming subcontractors.

For instance, UNHCR asked a future subcontractor to add legal support activities to its work, which it did. The types of activities carried out by the NGOs classified as "legal partners", "social partners" or those covering both areas were also standardised. By comparison, NGOs which were not UNHCR subcontractors undertook more diverse activities in the field of asylum, diverging from the ones carried out by UNHCR subcontractors.

Following UNHCR principles, subcontractor NGOs standardised and seemingly rationalised their practices. In addition to complying with various reporting and accounting rules, NGOs which provided social support to asylum seekers and refugees adopted a point system: A commission attributed points to migrants, assessing their vulnerability and needs, to determine whether they should receive support for a few months.[2]

UNHCR spread its norms among the employees of its subcontractors. All UNHCR subcontractors adopted the UNHCR practice of distinguishing between legitimate refugees and illegitimate migrants. UNHCR subcontractors all carried out this evaluation and did not support migrants independently from the grounds for their migration—in contrast to some organisations that were not UNHCR subcontractors. UNHCR transferred to its subcontractors the standardised procedure and the criteria for the evaluation of legitimate refugees, based on the criteria of the international Convention Relating to the Status of Refugees. The similarity with the state practices of conducting a status determination interview was striking. The employees of the subcontractors, especially the lawyers, conducted refugee status determination interviews, questioning the applicants about their personal story but also testing their knowledge about the alleged country of origin, independently from the grounds of persecution. They judged the "truth" of the story, interpreting lacking knowledge about the indicated place of origin as a sign of lying—just as state officials did. UNHCR and its subcontractors defined what nationals from a certain country ought to know, for instance the name of a local football club. The employees of UNHCR subcontractors also adopted the asylum norms of UNHCR in their discourse, in particular the norm of the necessity of distinguishing between legitimate refugees and illegitimate migrants. Novice employees of UNHCR subcontractors learnt the appropriate work practices and norms through trainings organised

[2] For a more detailed analysis of neoliberal bureaucratisation of asylum NGOs in Ukraine see (Mützelburg, 2020a).

by UNHCR, for example, dealing with refugee status determination, interview techniques, administrative questions, and fundraising. They also adopted norms through everyday work interactions with UNHCR staff and the colleagues at the subcontractor-NGO.

The employees of UNHCR subcontractors did not have any activist background in the area of asylum nor prior knowledge or strong beliefs in this sphere. In contrast to asylum NGO workers in Western Europe who sometimes struggle with political dilemmas because their beliefs partly clash with their activities consisting of categorising migrants and drawing boundaries similar to state practices (Fischer, 2009), Ukrainian NGO workers accepted UNHCR norm transfer without questioning it critically (Mützelburg, 2018). UNHCR also benefited from its legitimacy in the area of asylum. In interviews, NGO workers recognised the knowledge and understanding of asylum of the employees of the UNHCR office in Kyiv.

UNHCR was able to impose its norms and work practices on its subcontractors because most asylum NGOs heavily depended on UNHCR funding for which they needed to reapply annually (Mützelburg, 2020a). UNHCR subcontractors reported quarterly on their activities and went through an annual UNHCR audit. In addition, the Kyiv office of UNHCR closely observed the NGOs' work. It produced a scale of UNHCR subcontractors that was vertically subordinate to the UNHCR scale and spatially more limited, most NGOs acting only in one city.

Despite this control and dependence on their donor, UNHCR subcontractors enjoyed some leeway in their work. Employees of asylum NGOs had discretion when they selected the migrants that they would support. Like street-level bureaucrats, members of NGOs categorised migrants as legitimate refugees or illegitimate migrants – a categorisation affected by moral judgements and emotions, even though this was hidden behind rationalised and standardised procedures. They chose to use or not to use certain organisational rules to help certain migrants they considered deserving and to exclude others whom they considered undeserving (Mützelburg, 2020a).

NGO workers also translated norms and activities defined by their donor to adapt them to their context, interests, norms, and emotions (Acharya, 2015; Clarke et al., 2015). Transfer across a chain was shaped by processes of translation, that is, the interpretation and adaptation of meaning to another context (Clarke et al., 2015, p. 35). I propose to distinguish between reframing and adaptation. I understand reframing as a largely rhetorical process to make a project, norm, or policy acceptable to different audiences—without changing its substance. For instance, by "decoupling" language and action, Russian disability NGOs use Western language when writing project proposals and final reports for their donors but keep their actions and communications towards domestic state officials organised according to traditional domestic norms (Fröhlich, 2010, p. 86). In contrast, adaptation involves substantial change.

The actors' position in the transfer network or chain can make translation necessary. Actors have several roles and interact with difference audiences between whom they translate. Less powerful actors translate to please more powerful actors, which can allow them to ensure their survival (Shutt, 1975) and gain some freedom. Non-state actors try to translate the activities they (wish to) carry out to their donors' expectations. In Ukraine, non-governmental organisations tried to fulfil UNHCR expectations; UNHCR tried to fulfil European Commission. In fact, the UNHCR subcontractors did not communicate directly with the European Commission and did not fulfil its complicated application and reporting requirements. UNHCR took over this work, which implied reframing concrete activities according to the categories and the discourse expected by the Commission. While the European Commission sought primarily "sustainable" and "systemic" change in the target state and rejected "charity", local NGO workers were often motivated by their emotions concerning individual migrants. UNHCR, at an intermediary position in the donor chain, presented its activities and those carried out by its NGO subcontractors as contributing to "sustainable" and "systemic" change when communicating with the European Commission—but discussed the problems faced by refugees and asylum seekers with local NGO workers (Mützelburg, 2020a). When possible, non-state actors tried to reframe their activities rhetorically.

However, in some cases non-state actors needed to adapt their activities substantially to meet the donors' expectations. For example, contrary to the NGOs' wish to support migrants, UNHCR decided that they should stop replacing state authorities as a means of forcing them to take over tasks. Until the early 2010s, UNHCR and its subcontractors organised and paid for healthcare, language classes, and interpretation at migration authorities even though the legislation or the government's plan on the integration of refugees foresaw that the state provided these services. UNHCR then decided that its subcontractors should stop ensuring these state tasks, hoping that this withdrawal would lead to changes in state policies. NGO workers disagreed with this decision because of the problems it created for individual asylum seekers and refugees. As this decision involved financial means provided by UNHCR, NGO workers had very limited leeway in this case and could only continue to support certain asylum seekers whom they considered the most vulnerable.

UNHCR strongly shaped the relations between the NGO norm promoters it had established and the Ukrainian state bodies in charge of asylum matters. First, UNHCR arranged institutional links between its subcontractors and authorities. For instance, employees of NGOs reported how they benefited from UNHCR's help especially initially when, in the organisation's early days, they lacked contacts in state bodies, how UNHCR increased the organisation's "authority" in regard to state authorities through "professional skills", training and personal contacts with state officials. Moreover, in Ukraine, only NGOs that were UNHCR subcontractors had access to detention facilities. The position of UNHCR in Ukraine in relation to the authorities conferred important advantages on its subcontractors. At the same time, it bound the NGOs even closer to UNHCR, because they would be unable to fulfil the same tasks without the support of the UN agency.

UNHCR controlled the contacts between subcontractors and authorities. For example, UNHCR expected its subcontractors not to formulate their criticism of the state authorities themselves but via UNHCR. The NGOs thus observed state practices and legislation and its application, and communicated their analysis and criticism to UNHCR, which then decided whether, how, and where to transmit this criticism. For instance, for a few years, UNHCR's strategy of pursuing harmonious relations with state authorities led UNHCR to discourage its subcontractor from undertaking contentious action against the state authorities. The head of a subcontractor reported that the NGO had prepared a complaint for the European Court of Human Rights (ECHR) and, in light of UNHCR's strong "recommendation", did not send it.

When UNHCR subcontractors had a problem with Ukrainian state authorities, they usually turned to UNHCR for advice and help. While UNHCR took the side of its subcontractors when they experienced difficulties with state authorities, it also imposed its way of dealing with the situation. For instance, the head of a UNHCR subcontractor explained that the regional Migration Service had sent them a letter asking them to report how they fulfilled the integration plan of the Migration Service.

The head of the NGO discussed this question with UNHCR, who decided that the NGO should reply in written form that they did not fulfil any plan of the Migration Service but of UNHCR, which was why the NGO was not accountable to the authorities. UNHCR told the NGO to further mention in the letter that the officials could ask UNHCR for information about the NGO's work. The head of the NGO carried out this solution, chosen by UNHCR, even though she pointed out that she did not want to reply this way because she expected it to deteriorate the relations with the regional authorities. UNHCR subcontractors, as "tools" for UNHCR norm transfer to the domestic state bodies, did not fully define their relations with the latter themselves but rather followed and largely accepted UNHCR control and determination of these relations.

In sum, international actors set up a transfer chain across scales. This transfer chain allowed for transfer activities at different scales depending on the state actors in charge and the scalar framing of the issues. UNHCR combined a national scale identity and a global scale identity. It produced and vertically dominated NGOs that were active on a city or regional scale and composed exclusively of Ukrainian staff. With their local scale identity, these NGOs appeared more legitimate to deal with domestic and local issues than big IOs. NGOs and their donor were related by power relations and relations of dependence and control. Yet, each actor also had some leeway to translate its activities between contexts and interlocutors so that each actor influenced the transfer process.

Seminars as a Vehicle to Spread International Asylum Norms' Legitimacy

In the context of weak political interest in the issue and limited top-down control over regional administrative practices, norm promoters tried to directly transfer norms to the state officials implementing the policies, including in formal settings, such as during seminars and study visits. These transfer practices were shaped by scales and participated in producing them. NGOs and IOs officially invited the participants via state bodies, senior state officials—often at a central institution—deciding which subordinate employees should take part. This way, NGOs and IOs produced the national state scale as vertically dominant to themselves and regional authorities. This procedure made it acceptable to officials that non-state actors taught state officials. Indeed, teaching state officials produced the hierarchical relations as dominated by the non-state actors. Scales and power relations between state and non-state actors were not fixed but constantly renegotiated. Non-state actors considered that it was more legitimate when employees of international rather than national organisations conducted the trainings for state officials, reflecting a scalar construction of NGOs as subordinate to state officials, whereas IOs would be superior to state officials. More specifically, an interviewee from UNHCR in Kyiv (2015) explained that staff of the country office could intervene as trainers but that employees – of UNHCR or other international organisations—who lived abroad were more legitimate. This is why UNHCR Kyiv sometimes invited such external experts, who were not necessarily more competent than the staff in Kyiv, but who were taken more seriously by Ukrainian officials. The scalar position of UNHCR Ukraine was therefore a shifting one; sometimes it was accepted as superior to the national authorities and sometimes it was not.

Through seminars, norm promoters sought to change officials' practices and beliefs. All interviewed state officials involved in migration policies participated in at least one, often more, seminar(s) organised by non-state actors. Trainings covered topics such as interviewing techniques, general asylum norms and Ukrainian legislation, the writing of status recommendations, unaccompanied minors and refugee children, and information about certain countries of origin such as Afghanistan and Syria. Norm promoters tried to affect officials' practices and beliefs by triggering certain emotions, including compassion for migrants. However, depending on the officials' normative frameworks, these emotional approaches, though increasing the audience's attention, did not always lead to the expected normative adherence and sometimes led instead to resistance or diverging conclusions. For example, during a seminar, the trainers showed photos of endless queues in refugee camps in Somalia and described situations of forced marriage and forced labour of minors in Somalia and Afghanistan. While some officials looked touched, others rejected these attempts to target their emotions, for instance claiming that in Ukraine children also worked and that therefore this was not a reason to flee. Another participant interpreted forced marriage and child labour as a sign of the lack of civilisation of Africans which seemed to reinforce her negative stereotypes. Officials listened to the norm promotion discourse through their own normative filters.

Non-state actors also organised study visits for Ukrainian state officials as a means of observing how asylum systems operated in other countries, considered models. These visits, for example to Germany, Poland, Sweden, Austria, and Slovakia, were supposed to leave stronger memories of exemplary practices than would, for instance, the mere description of these foreign practices during a seminar in Ukraine. However, the officials later mostly reported that in these countries more funding was available for asylum authorities. The lack of financial means in Ukraine, which became even more obvious through these trips, was the major justification for the differences between the Ukrainian practices and the ones observed abroad. This insistence on the material differences suggests that state officials saw these foreign "models" as unreachable and therefore as less practically inspiring than the organisers of these trips expected.

Finally, norm promoters tried to spread technical norms via argumentation, in particular by referring to broader international norms. However, when these broader international norms clashed with common ideas and practices, some participants reacted with contestation and resistance. For example, trainers tried to spread the international norm that unaccompanied migrant minors could be refugees and therefore could not be sent back to their place of origin automatically and against their will, even if their parents might live there. Some middle-aged participants of the seminar who had worked with mainly Ukrainian minors for a long time rejected this norm, claiming that minors were often unreasonable and needed to be brought back to their parents whenever possible. If the promoted norms clashed with the target actors' normative framework, they were less likely to be adopted (Börzel & Risse, 2000; Finnemore & Sikkink, 1998, pp. 914–915). But what does it mean for officials to "adopt" norms?

Scholars gain from distinguishing among the different dimensions of transfer, namely knowledge and understanding of the norms, discursive reactions reflecting the norms' legitimacy, and practices of using, translating, or resisting them. Through their interactions with state actors, the norm promoters spread the knowledge and the appropriateness of their norms, leading to their discursive adoption. I was able to observe this process first-hand during a seminar on unaccompanied minors. Participants who had not been aware of the existence of these norms and of the fact that international organisations considered them "right", freely contested them, stating their critical opinions at the beginning of the seminar. For instance, during the first hour of the training, several state officials vigorously questioned the newly introduced procedure for the age assessment of unaccompanied minors, voicing support for the former procedure of X-raying and the suspicion that unaccompanied minors wanted to avoid the X-raying to conceal that they were actually adults. However, once the trainers had discussed this question and contradicted the mentioned arguments, state officials stopped their criticism and took up the organisers' arguments; for example, the difficulty of correctly assessing age, the inaccuracy of the X-raying method, the potential gap between appearance and actual age, the benefit of the doubt. During an intermediary phase, some participants voiced their dissent with the promoted norms in small groups during breaks but refrained from formulating it in front of the entire group and the teachers. This suggests that the norm promoters imposed the legitimacy of their own ideas in the context they dominated, even if, at least temporarily, the norm addressees rejected the legitimacy in another context.

Over the course of the seminar, the participants increasingly adopted the organisers' discourse. During the final group work presentations and also in individual conversations with me, several participants repeated the organisers' ideas as if they were their own, even adding more radical positions which the organisers had not formulated explicitly. For example, an employee of a children's shelter told me in a private conversation that, given the imprecision of the age determination procedure, the state authorities could also simply recognise all applicants, who claimed to be minor, as such. All participants who intervened towards the end of the seminar, even those who had been very critical initially, reproduced the discourse promoted by the trainers. While it cannot be known to what extent participants were persuaded by these ideas, the trainers managed to spread the knowledge and the appropriateness of the norms. Through the norm promoters' assertive presentations of the legitimate norms, the norm addressees became aware of the fact that, at least in the context of the seminar and more broadly in contact with international and non-governmental organisations, the norm promoters' ideas were the legitimate ones and their own (initial) views were inappropriate. They therefore adopted the international asylum norms discursively.

I have also observed that the extent to which normative misfit (Börzel & Risse, 2000) leads to explicit resistance and contestation to the transfer strongly depends on the relations between norm promoters and addressees. The setting and the type of the interactions between the norm promoters and the norm addressees affected the formers' legitimacy and their capacity to establish their norms as the legitimate ones. In the formal setting of the seminars and trainings, the representatives of IOs and NGOs enjoyed stronger legitimacy (than for instance during interactions at Migration Services, where they were visitors in the officials' office), as they presented themselves as transnational experts and played the role of teachers. Moreover, being the organisers, they determined the agenda and invited additional participants, such as local asylum lawyers, to support their positions and thus increase their legitimacy.

The norm addressees' openness to the norm promotion depended on the (temporary) state of their relations with or attitudes towards the norm promoters. Indeed, in the observed seminar, harsh criticism and judging attitudes of the non-state actors led to counter-reactions among the state officials who then rejected the organisers' ideas. A struggle for legitimacy and recognition could be observed, over the course of which state officials requested the acknowledgement of their competences and efforts. When the non-state actors adopted a more conciliatory tone and recognised the state officials' work, the communication became peaceful again. The state officials then stopped defending themselves and attacking the organisers and instead recognised their legitimacy (Checkel, 2002). This illustrates the role of social factors such as the setting and the personal relations between norm promoters and norm addressees for the spreading of the norms' legitimacy.

Regular, Personalised Interactions and Their Influence on State Practices

NGOs made considerable efforts to build up and maintain harmonious working relations with state officials. Most IOs and NGOs cooperating with authorities stated that they initially faced mistrust and refusals to interact until they managed to establish relations of trust. During meetings and trainings, non-state actors gave out their mobile phone numbers and e-mail addresses and repeatedly encouraged state officials to contact them in the future. Indeed, the seminars served the purpose of networking.

NGO workers explained that they had become "friends" with certain state officials. This friendship blurred the boundaries between private and professional, between formal and informal, but remained instrumental (Kharkhordin, 2012, 2016; Voicu & Basina, 2005). The friendship between NGO workers and regional state officials gave the former means to informally influence state practices. The latter, however, needed to avoid the suspicion of corruption and biased practices due to their contact with NGO workers. Indeed, state officials never mentioned any friendship to non-state actors and instead spoke of "cooperation".

The norm promoters strategically sought to personalise their relations with the norm addressees. They offered resources that the state authorities lacked, such as financial and material means, interpreters, and knowledge about international asylum norms and countries of origin. By complementing the state (Clark, 1992, pp. 151–152), non-state actors managed to be seen by the officials as helpful, rather than as threatening. They thus corresponded to the late Soviet role of NGOs as supporters of the state.

This support became even more important in a political context in which regional state officials were expected to fulfil standards which they could not fulfil given their limited budget. UNHCR and NGO staff reported that during the VLAP and in particular after the Maidan protests officials from the State Migration Service became more cooperative, asking for advice and support, as they faced pressure from the Cabinet of Ministers to achieve a positive image among international organisations and to fulfil the EU demands of the VLAP. While central state officials did not openly acknowledge that they resorted to non-state actors' support to fulfil EU demands, regional state officials sometimes admitted that they were unable to fulfil them without the action and the funding of NGOs. Regional Migration Services were under pressure from the Central State Migration Service to report on their implementation of the plan for the integration of refugees. Given the lack of funding, the regional Migration Services were unable to implement the plan. In order to still satisfy the top-down reporting requirements, they asked the local NGOs about their activities for the integration of refugees. The regional Migration Services cited the NGO activities in their own report, claiming to have undertaken them or at least using vague formulations that made them seem like their own activities. Given that the state officials were dependent on the NGOs to obtain this information for their reporting, they also had an interest in maintaining cooperative relations with the NGOs.

Many norm promoters in Ukraine tried to transfer norms by blurring the boundaries between themselves and the norm addressees. First, they met individually with certain officials to discuss more general asylum questions. Staff of NGOs managed, by establishing personalised, noncontentious relations with state officials, to influence their knowledge and ideas about asylum seekers, persuading some of them to read asylum laws and information about the countries of origin.

Second, non-state actors also influenced state officials' norms and practices through regular presence at the state officials' workplace. This privileged access to the state authorities originated from informal contacts as well as from official agreements between the central authorities and a non-state actor. For example, a member of a Kyiv-based NGO explained that thanks to her being "mates" with several of the regional migration officers and being often present during the asylum interviews at the regional Migration Service she could tell the officer if she considered a question inappropriate. Her interference in the regional authorities' practices had no formal basis and was only possible due to her personalised relations with the relevant officials. In a more formal vein, UNHCR, the Danish Refugee Council, and a UNHCR subcontractor managed to post one or two of their employees several days per week at the asylum Department of the central State Migration Service, after having overcome the authorities' initial resistance—based on a formal agreement. These employees had their desks at the State Migration Service, interacted on an everyday basis with the state officials and thus managed to build up harmonious relationships with them. This allowed them to follow everyday work practices, comment and offer advice, which was highlighted in positive terms by the surrounding officials. This illustrates the mixing of formal and informal approaches: On the one hand, the posting was based on a formal agreement of the central authorities. On the other hand, a personal contact between the state and non-state "colleagues" preceded the set-up; and the everyday interactions blurred the boundaries between formal and informal, between state and non-state actors. In contrast to the official short-term interventions during seminars, regular and increasingly informal interactions allowed norm promoters to not only spread the knowledge and the appropriateness of international norms but also to exert direct influence on state practices.

However, due to this approach to transfer norms through informal personal interactions, norm promoters avoided tensions with the targets of their norm promotion. Non-state actors refrained from conflict and criticism of state officials in order to establish or maintain the contacts. According to them, a conciliatory approach was necessary to reassure state authorities. This rejection of contestation and the focus on peaceful and close relations with the state authorities confirms Steven Saxonberg's argument according to which non-state actors in post-communist countries adopt less overtly contentious strategies of activism (Saxonberg, 2016, p. 2). NGOs mostly tried to refrain from public criticism or channel their criticism through larger organisations or networks. State officials accepted and appreciated cooperating with employees of non-state organisations who showed their respect of the state authorities. In contrast, when NGOs chose public criticism or court appeals, for instance to counter the extradition of a potential refugee, they were "punished" by the loss or deterioration of their relations with the state authorities.

Though primarily "professionalised organisations", NGOs in Ukraine also resorted to methods typical for "government affiliates" (Henry, 2006). They built up personalised and non-contentious relations with state officials through regular informal interactions, favours, and the avoidance of (public) criticism. Through informal personalised relations, norm promoters were able to intervene directly in the state practices and to discreetly transfer norms to state officials. In fact, blurring the boundaries between state and non-state actors, the latter reassured the former and gained access to state prerogatives.

A Heterogeneous, Unstable Transfer Approach

How did these transfer attempts affect state officials' norms and practices? The knowledge of norms was usually a necessary but insufficient condition for their application. Migration officers became aware of major international asylum norms through trainings organised by international and non-governmental organisations and through communication with employees of these organisations as well as with colleagues from the Migration Services.

For instance, in trainings for Ukrainian state officials, international and non-governmental organisations underlined the importance of the confidentiality of the asylum seekers' information—in respect to people outside of the Migration Service. Representatives of IOs and a UNHCR subcontractor insisted on the fact that the officials of different state bodies should not divulge the information which the asylum seeker had shared with them, including during a training. Migration officers I interviewed throughout my study were aware of these confidentiality norms and the norms' legitimacy, as they mentioned these norms spontaneously during interviews. For instance, migration officers frequently insisted at the beginning of the interview that they could not divulge information about the applicants, even though I had not requested this. However, while some officers indeed anonymised the examples, many violated the confidentiality of the applicants' data in the course of the interview, telling me applicants' stories indicating the current place of residence, the country of origin, major elements of their life story, their profession, and occasionally even the name. The discursive adoption of the norms—when facing a European researcher—reflected the awareness of the norms and of their legitimacy among Western actors. But the norms' practical implementation remained heterogeneous.

In contrast, norms which were not included in non-state actors' active norm promotion were unknown to the state officials, for example the privacy of the refugee status determination interview. While also linked to the confidentiality of the applicant's information (and thus the person's safety), this rule shall also put the applicant at ease so as to obtain a truthful account of the applicant's life and potential threat in the country of origin. The norm generally promoted by UNHCR stipulates that the place of the asylum interview should be completely private and only people should be present who are involved directly in the interview (UNHCR, 1995, 2010, p. 100). In Ukraine, due to the material conditions and the officials' lack of awareness, this norm was virtually never respected. I observed that officers could listen to the interviews conducted by their colleagues, and that several interviews occurred in parallel in the same office, sometimes of applicants from the same country of origin. The interviewed officers never raised this as a problem and when questioned denied that this might be problematic.

> At the local Migration Service, three migration officers sit together in a tiny office where there is not more space than for the three desks and two additional chairs for the applicants. A family of applicants arrives accompanied by an interpreter, some people stand squeezed in a corner. When I later ask one of the migration officers about the conduct of the interviews in such a small room she seems almost offended, asking whether I dislike their office. When I explain that there are quite a few people in the room to conduct an interview there, she seems surprised and replies, "It's only us who are here. We all conduct interviews. When someone comes for an interview we close the door and the two others work quietly on their computers. There has never been an applicant who complained about that. There is no problem." (Observation and informal communication at a local asylum department, 2015)

The employees of a regional Migration Service offered me to listen to refugee status determination interviews but did not ask the applicants for their agreement. I was not asked to sign a document of confidentiality, nor to agree orally to confidentiality. The state officials were not aware of this international norm. UNHCR did not spread this norm through its trainings in Ukraine.

During interviews, state officials tried to convey the impression that they applied the newly acquired knowledge in their everyday work. They often kept the material they received during the seminars within reach of their desk and claimed to use and reread it. Yet, both the studied cases of confidentiality norms and the accounts of non-state actors suggest that the practical application of the discursively adopted norms was heterogeneous.

The officials' discursive adoption of the norms actively diffused by the norm promoters shows that the latter successfully spread the awareness and the legitimacy of the international norms through direct interactions. However, the gap between discourse and practice is noteworthy and can be explained in three ways. First, due to top-down obstacles, officials lacked the material means required to respect certain international norms. Second, the difference between "public transcript" and "hidden transcript" could originate from state officials' concealed resistance to the norms and the norm promotion activities (Scott, 1990). The officials, rejecting certain norms while being aware of their legitimacy in certain contexts, decoupled their rhetoric from their practices. Third, the officials could also have "learnt" the norm at a theoretical level, being able to reproduce it in their discourse, without integrating it into their practices so as to apply it automatically. Indeed, especially during the short interactions at seminars, officials had little time to transform the theoretical norms into routinised practices.

Another limit to the approach via direct interaction was the difficulty of reaching the entire subordinate staff at the implementing authorities. In order to systematically change state practices in regard to asylum seekers and refugees, it would be necessary not only to interact with all migration officers but also with all the subordinate state officials of a large variety of different state bodies. Non-state actors tried to influence the practices of employment centres, children shelters, schools, universities, and public hospitals in regard to asylum seekers and refugees—but were unable to fully reach such a large and diverse target group. Also, given the low number of asylum seekers and refugees in Ukraine, most of these state employees interacted very rarely with asylum seekers and refugees. As a result, they were more likely to forget the content of their trainings before having the opportunity to apply it in practice.

The largest obstacle to the approach of teaching a maximum of subordinate state officials via direct interaction lied in the high turnover of state employees. Frequent change in staff undermined non-state actors' advocacy given that officials changed jobs soon after the training. The spreading of ideas and the establishing of networks were heterogeneous across space and actors, and unstable over time. This is why, non-state actors tried to use personal contacts among state actors to spread norms across the state apparatus.

Turning Officials into Horizontal or Top-Down Norm Brokers

NGOs had different possibilities when it came to establishing personalised relations at state bodies. NGOs outside Kyiv mostly interacted with officials working for administrative units with a regional scale identity, while NGOs in Kyiv built up ties to both regional and national scale officials, which allowed them to shift between scales. Also, the longer an NGO had already been active in the area of asylum, the more contacts it had established among officials.

Yet, not all officials accepted to interact and be taught by non-state actors, as an employee of an NGO explained:

> It is one of the prerequisites to be close to state authorities and to catch up on all the new developments because the pace of the developments is very high [...] New people come. For example, the new head of the State Migration Service. He has a tax background, which has nothing to do with refugees so he is supposed to be taught as well but he doesn't care. So we have other people to work with and we work with them. (Interview, head of an NGO, 2013)

NGOs needed to adapt to the changes in personnel and identify staff that was open to their activities. The NGO mentioned above had been active in the field of asylum for many years and had built up a network from which it benefited, all the while constantly searching for new allies. NGOs adapted to personnel turnover among the officials and learnt to manage certain officials' resistance, cooperating with whoever was willing.

Through interactions and training, norm promoters identified certain allies among the state officials, some of whom they turned into brokers. Brokers transfer norms between different spheres thanks to their legitimacy, network, multipositionality, and command of social codes and languages (Charton, 2017; Guignard, 2016; Jobard et al., 2020; Mützelburg, 2020b; Rioufreyt, 2013; Sabatier, 1986). Indeed, they are both norm addressees and norm promoters. They can arrange meetings between other officials and the norm promoters, inform other officials about formal rules and standardised practices, recommend certain practices, request compliance with formal rules or produce them. Brokers can occupy any hierarchical position at the state institutions.

A few subordinate state officials remained at the same service for an exceptionally long time, attended seminars regularly, and increasingly adhered to international asylum norms. These state officials spread their ideas horizontally to their colleagues of the same scale. Indeed, a few officials I spoke to had worked for the asylum department for over ten years despite the low salaries and seemed affectively attached to their work. These long-standing employees spread some of the norms and practices they had learnt through interactions with non-state actors. The most experienced migration officer of the department was the contact person for all new colleagues and explained to them the work practices and common norms at the office. Some long-standing migration officers followed the non-state actors' wish and became their brokers within the state institutions. In the 2010s, non-state actors started to actively formalise and strengthen this role.

Non-state actors in Ukraine tried to delegate the dissemination of international asylum norms to Ukrainian subordinate state officials. For this purpose, in 2014, UNHCR selected four caseworkers whom it considered experienced and attached to international asylum norms.[3] After participating in a training on European and international asylum norms, these state officials became trainers for their colleagues, who

[3] This particular initiative originates from the Prague Process, funded by the European Union and led by Swedish Migration Board and the Federal Office for Migration and Refugees of Germany, as well as, to a lesser extent, by the Ministries of Interior of the Czech Republic, Hungary, Poland, Romania, and Slovakia (Prague Process, n.d.).

then underwent the same training.[4] Through this "training-the-trainers-method", non-state actors tried to turn subordinate state officials into brokers to spread international norms among other subordinate officials.

Mid- and higher-scale state officials also acted as brokers, in particular in a top-down way towards subordinate officials. In contrast to national political actors (e.g. the head of the State Migration Service, MPs, or ministers), non-state actors considered these actors as more accessible and less involved in major corruption or criminal affairs. Non-state actors also highlighted that these state officials dealt with concrete matters on a daily basis and were mostly informed about the questions that the NGOs wanted to discuss. The head of an NGO commented:

> We discussed one issue with the employment centre in one district but the other staff in other districts doesn't know about this. We need therefore the help of the State Migration Service [...] to inform all administrations. (Interview, head of an NGO, 2014).

This quote illustrates the role intermediary state brokers played in countering the lack of awareness about certain rules among subordinate state officials. While officials at regional bodies only disseminated information within their region, officials at central state bodies had the means to spread it among the regional bodies across the national territory. By turning to central authorities, NGOs shifted the issue to the national scale, producing it as vertically superior to the regional one.

However, in a context of high turnover among the administrative staff, the transfer approach via personal contacts was precarious. For example,

[4] For one month, these caseworkers participated in an online course about asylum standards and working techniques (e.g. refugee status determination, the Refugee Convention, interview techniques, etc.) of the EU's European Asylum Support Office. After the completion of this online course, the participants gathered for a final three days face-to-face training in Poland and Romania conducted by caseworkers from Germany and Sweden, where they met and exchanged with other participants, for example caseworkers from Poland, Romania, and six other countries from the Eastern Partnership. The participants were introduced to the "European approach to writing a decision, to evaluation, what to base on, how it is done in Europe, how they work." After having completed this training, these four caseworkers were attributed the role of "national trainers" in Ukraine. Other, mostly young, caseworkers passed the online EASO training and the newly trained "national trainers" were supposed to guide them in their learning process. Each "trainer" was in charge of four participants who did online exercises which the "trainers" corrected. In the end, a face-to-face training was conducted in Kyiv by the "national trainers" for the other Ukrainian caseworkers.

according to NGOs and IOs, while the first Ombudsman of Ukraine (Nina Karpachova, 1998–2012) actively supported them, the subsequent Ombudsman (Valeriya Lutkovska, 2012–2017) was passive on asylum matters. When the individual occupying the position of the Ombudsman changed, non-state actors lost their broker. Conversely, if an individual who was close to the norm promoters took up a strategic position in the state apparatus, they gained a broker. For instance, the representative of the Commissioner for the Observance of Children's Rights, Non-Discrimination and Gender Equality (commonly referred to as the Ombudsman for Children), Aksana Filipishyna, had been involved in various issues of unaccompanied minors in cooperation with NGOs and IOs. She used to work on children's issues at the Ministry of Social Policy and members of NGOs and IOs had known her since then. As a result, they described their relations as close. Before she took this position, the Ombudsman for Children had not cooperated with asylum NGOs and IOs. The personal contact with the individual occupying this position allowed NGOs and IOs to benefit from the institution's support. The head of an NGO summarised this unstable situation:

> The problem is that today the system works on individuals, on personal relations. It works because Mrs G. [superordinate employee at the Refugee Department of the central State Migration Service] and Mrs P. [the interviewee] meet. But when Mrs G. leaves then we will have to become friends with the new head. It's [implementing the laws] not an obligation for them but it's personal. People work – not the system. (Interview, head of an NGO, 2014)

Most interviewees from NGOs complained that due to the frequent rotation of staff, they often lost influence or access and tried to get acquainted with the new employees. The spreading of ideas and the establishing of networks were heterogeneous across space and actors, and unstable over time. Norm promoters therefore tried to achieve formalised and generalised changes in administrative practices.

From Informal to Formal Influence

> The law is the same but the person is different. The work stopped. [...] They [migration officers] only follow instructions. If the instruction is very concrete on what precisely they should do, then they do it, but if it's not precise, rather not. Because for all mistakes and problems they will

> be responsible. Better not to do something rather than to do something. This is a problem. (Interview, head of an NGO subcontractor of UNHCR, 2014).

This quote reflects the NGO workers' ambiguous perception of formal documents: They sometimes presented formal rules as purely theoretical, irrelevant vis-à-vis the individual state official's leeway, and sometimes as a precise constraint and order which forced state officials to comply. Even though NGO workers frequently criticised Ukrainian administrative staff for not respecting the law, they tried to push for formalised changes. They hoped that changes in formal rules or top-down instructions would affect everyday administrative practices to some extent. Also, NGOs referred to formal rules to legitimise their requests when interacting with state officials.

An Unsurprising Absence of Bottom-Up Influences

Scholars have stressed that implementing agencies participate in the elaboration of laws and policies (Blankenburg, 1986). In his research on Western states, Erhard Blankenburg claimed that the less a topic was politicised, the stronger the influence of the respective ministries on the elaboration of the laws. Asylum seekers' and refugees' rights were neither a political priority nor strongly politicised in Ukraine. Following Blankenburg, the influence of the State Migration Service should thus be expected to be important for the legislative process.

Hypothetically, norm promoters could exert indirect influence on the production of formal norms through a bottom-up process: They would transfer norms to regional state officials who would then turn to higher state scales, for example requesting the resources for implementation or amendments of the legislation. The head of the asylum Department of the central State Migration Service claimed to collect information from all the regional Migration Services on the difficulties they experienced when implementing laws. However, I could find no further hints to the administration's influence on draft laws and policies.

Indeed, Ukrainian actors did not expect any bottom-up influences on law and policy making. Regional state officials presented meetings between higher and lower scales of the State Migration Service as serving top-down objectives, for instance to discuss how the regional offices fulfilled the central body's orders and took into account its suggestions. Regional officials reported that their director attended meetings at which he was told "what to pay attention to" (Interview, caseworker at a regional asylum department, 2014). They did not envisage the possibility that their director might also use these meetings to influence political decisions. Rather, they adopted an attitude of either passivity or of adaptation to whatever their superiors decided, trying to improvise solutions to contradictory expectations and situations. Even though they complained about the difficult setting, such as the lack of resources or contradictory legislation, representatives of regional Migration Services never described any attempts to change this situation at a national scale.

Non-state actors presented the Ukrainian administration as very bureaucratic and top-down structured. According to employees of UNHCR, heads and deputy heads of the State Migration Service and of the asylum department made even minor decisions, such as which subordinate state officials should participate in a UNHCR training or which room could be used. NGOs observed that the administration discouraged regional state officials from being committed and actively involved in their work. In my 2013 interviews, street-level bureaucrats voiced the opinion that too much commitment was seen inside the administration with mistrust and could be interpreted as corruption. This perception was shared by the NGOs, who, to explain the dismissal of a regional state official, cited the person's too active commitment at work and her arguments with her boss (2014 interview). Representatives of NGOs complained that regional state officials were passive, criticising older employees for waiting for their superior's decision before taking any action even though the superior was rarely present. In short, neither state nor non-state actors expected bottom-up processes within the administration. State and non-state actors perceived and routinely reperformed scales of the executive state apparatus as strongly hierarchical and limited to horizontal and top-down processes.

Achieving Formalised Change Through Personal Contacts

NGOs and IOs tried to push hierarchically higher state bodies to change or introduce formal norms and rules to regulate the implementation of state officials' practices. Through direct interactions, norm promoters tried to encourage higher or intermediary state officials to develop formal documents and guidelines for lower scale staff. For instance, NGOs arranged meetings with representatives of the Administrative Supreme Court. For example, they included the head of the Supreme Court into the steering committee of an NGO. Thanks to these interactions, they managed to push the plenary of the Court to publish decrees for judges. Such decrees specified which decision-making principles should be followed in order to respect international norms on asylum.[5]

NGOs benefited from personal contacts among officials to favour the production of formal rules. In 2013, after having established a solid network of "friends" among regional decision makers, an NGO gathered them to counter the lack of formal administrative procedures and instructions at different scales, as this lack meant that laws were not implemented. During a meeting of the NGO with regional officials of different institutions (Hospital Administration, Border Guards, Migration Services, Social Service Department of the City Council, Oblast Health Administration) and the mayor's wife, who did not have an official position but "who was active on social questions and had a large network" (according to the head of the NGO), they created a document which listed the rules and solutions to common problems arising when asylum seekers and refugees tried to obtain a certain state service (for instance, healthcare). Following this, the relevant officials (for example the head of the Health Administration of the Oblast) sent this document to all the regional offices in the region that implemented this policy (for example to all the hospitals), stressing that a recognised refugee was entitled to the same rights and services as Ukrainian citizens. Thanks to this initiative, regional decision makers produced and spread instructions to subordinate state officials in line with the NGOs' norms.

[5] (Postanova pro Sudovu Praktyku Rozhlyadu Sporiv Shchodo Statusu Bizhentsya, Vydvorennya Inozemtsya Chy Osoby Bez Hromadyanstva z Ukrayiny Ta Sporiv, Povyazanykh Iz Perebuvannyam Inozemtsya Ta Osoby Bez Hromadyanstva v Ukrayini (Decree on the Court Practice in Disputes over Refugee Status, Forced Removal of a Foreigner or a Stateless Person from Ukraine and Disputes over the Stay of a Foreigner and a Stateless Person in Ukraine), 2009; Postanova pro Sudovu Praktyku Rozhlyadu Sporiv Shchodo Statusu Bizhentsya Ta Osoby, Yaka Potrebuye Dodatkovoho Abo Tymchasovoho Zakhystu, Prymusovoho Povernennya i Prymusovoho Vydvorennya Inozemtsya Chy Osoby Bez Hromadyanstva z Ukrayiny Ta Sporiv, Povyazanykh Iz Perebuvannyam Inozemtsya Ta Osoby Bez Hromadyanstva v Ukrayini (Decree on the Court Practice in Disputes over Refugee Status and of a Person in Need of Complementary or Temporary Protection, Forced Return and Forced Removal of a Foreigner or Stateless Person from Ukraine and Disputes Related to the Stay of a Foreigner and Stateless Person in Ukraine), 2014).

State brokers allowed non-state actors to introduce their norms into the production of state rules and standardised procedures. Norm promoters used informal means to achieve formalisation of practices (Désert, 2006, p. 4). Through their contacts, norm promoters in Ukraine were for example able to transfer their templates and guidelines to state bodies. The latter integrated them into their work processes and documents. Indeed, these documents and procedures outlasted changes in the staff that had produced or imported them. For instance, due to personal contacts and the lack of internal guidelines and expertise within state institutions, UNHCR managed to spread guidelines to intermediary state officials. It distributed brochures, informational documents, and its handbook among state officials. State officials referred to these UNHCR documents and stated that they used UNHCR resources to find information on asylum seekers' countries of origin. The UNHCR website, refworld.org, was translated into Russian by UNHCR and remained for many issues the only Russian-language source for country of origin information available to Ukrainian migration officers. The former head of the State Committee on Nationalities and Religion, a temporary predecessor of the State Migration Service, explained in 2014 that their internal work procedures originated from UNHCR. Based on the suggestion of UNHCR and together with this IO, the State Committee on Nationalities and Religion wrote its instructions for regional migration officers. These instructions specified which documents were required, according to which system the folders should be organised, what an asylum application should look like, and which points needed to be verified. State officials framed the norms and practices spread by UNHCR as part of their increasing standardisation and professionalisation. The Migration Services adopted UNHCR's template for writing refugee status conclusions; before doing so, they worked without a template. State officials presented the template as useful and accepted it as their own, a state template (2014 interview). They stressed that the template facilitated and standardised their work (before "everyone just wrote how he wanted") and prevented defeats in court.

Thanks to state brokers, norm promoters also managed to gain access to state processes in which formal norms were produced. Indeed, non-state actors directly intervened in the production of state instructions and guidelines. For instance, the Danish Refugee Council and a UNHCR subcontractor participated in the creation of procedures for the treatment of unaccompanied minors. According to an NGO employee involved in this process (2014 interview), state practices concerning unaccompanied minors became more regulated and aligned with international standards after the introduction of national guidelines. Before the introduction of such guidelines, the NGO had struggled to place UAMs into state institutions. Since then, this worked "smoothly".

However, when the documents created by state authorities under NGO influence were not precise enough, NGOs needed to rely again on the individual officials for an implementation in line with international norms. For example, the procedure on the treatment of unaccompanied minors, created in part by Danish Refugee Council and a UNHCR subcontractor, remained ambiguous and contradictory on some points. The NGO's contact person at the Ministry of Health, who had promised that the ambiguity of the document would be applied in line with the NGOs' norms, changed jobs and other officials interpreted the procedure differently. This example reveals that even after the formalisation of certain norms, non-state actors continued to depend on individual brokers among the officials to ensure that administrative practices correspond to their ideas.

Conclusion

The relations between the different actors involved in the transfer of international asylum norms to Ukraine can be schematised as a transfer chain. International donors such as the European Commission funded large international organisations, such as UNHCR, to transform asylum policies in Ukraine. UNHCR further delegated these tasks internally, from its headquarters in Geneva to the office in Kyiv. This national office of UNHCR then delegated transfer activities to domestic NGOs, its subcontractors, active in various cities of Ukraine and supposed to spread international norms among domestic authorities. At the same time, international organisations were also in contact with the Ukrainian state authorities trying to transfer their norms directly. UNHCR and the NGOs further relied on brokers among the state officials who participated in the transfer activities within the state institutions.

While research on transfer has so far paid little attention to the actor dynamics underpinning the transfer attempts from international organisations to domestic non-state actors, this chapter has shown that international donors tried to promote their norms by establishing and structuring a specialised domestic non-state sector. UNHCR produced specialised

NGOs in Ukraine to whom it transferred its norms through socialisation via work and training, imposition of rules and procedures, control, and financial dependence. NGOs, using UNHCR norms and enjoying some discretion, carried out aid tasks to compensate for the state authorities' deficiencies and to alleviate asylum seekers' and refugees' problems. Through these activities, the international and non-governmental organisations produced and confirmed an international scale that was superior to the national or local scale of the NGOs.

As a next step in the transfer chain, domestic NGOs and IOs tried to transfer international asylum norms to Ukrainian state officials. In the context of volatile political attention to the policy area, and in addition to a top-down approach, norm promoters directly targeted subordinate and intermediary state officials. While research on transfer has so far been vague on the modes of transfer via "socialisation" or "capacity building", this chapter distinguishes between short-term, formal transfer meetings (namely seminars, trainings, study visits), and less formal and more frequent interactions (for example, posted non-state actors at state authorities, habitual encounters at the officials' workplace, occasional invitations for dinner). While normative misfit (Börzel & Risse, 2000) favours norm addressees' resistance and contestation of the promoted norms, personal relations between norm promoters and addressees matter more.

Scalar relations between state and non-state actors were complex and constantly renegotiated. Administrative officials approved of transfer activities and discursively adopted the norms when norm promoters conformed to the social order and scalar hierarchies as viewed by the officials—NGO workers should behave in a submissive and supportive way to the state officials. Drawing on research on NGOs in post-communist countries to complement transfer studies, I have demonstrated that most non-state actors primarily adopted a transfer approach based on personalised relations with state officials—shifting between the roles of professionalised organisations close to IOs and critical of the government; and government affiliates supporting the state to fulfil its tasks (Petrova & Tarrow, 2007; Saxonberg, 2016, p. 2). The NGOs blurred the boundaries between state and non-state spheres to discreetly gain access to state prerogatives and directly influence state practises. They did so by regularly interacting with certain state officials, including informally, offering favours, and avoiding (public) criticism. Indeed, public criticism uncovered the blurred opposition between state and non-state actors and sometimes led to the loss of the personalised relations and transfer possibilities—a "geographical dilemma" for the norm promoters (Masson, 2009, p. 126). So far, transfer research has paid little attention to these informal transfer processes and the norm promoters' dilemmas.

Through interactions with norm promoters, officials became aware of international asylum norms as well as of their legitimacy in certain contexts, adopting them discursively. However, norm compliant discourse diverged from heterogeneous practical application, which can be read as resistance to the norms and their promotion ("public transcript" vs. "hidden transcript" or decoupling [Fröhlich, 2010; Scott, 1990]) or as shallow learning. In the case of shallow learning, knowledge of the norms remains at a theoretical level and is not integrated into routinised practices.

In addition, difficulties in reaching all relevant officials and high turnover at the administration meant that changes in norms and practices due to transfer via interactions were heterogeneous across space and actors and unstable over time. Non-state actors coped with these obstacles, adapting their approaches. When the approaches, presented in this chapter, failed, norm promoters resorted to confrontational multi-scalar approaches.

References

Acharya, A. (2015). The responsibility to protect and a theory of norm circulation. In R. C. Thakur & W. Maley (Eds.), *Theorising the responsibility to protect* (pp. 59–78). Cambridge University Press.

Adamson, F. B. (2002). International democracy assistance in Uzbekistan and Kyrgyzstan: Building civil society from the outside? In Sarah Elizabeth Mendelson & J. K. Glenn (Eds.), *The power and limits of NGOs: A critical look at building democracy in Eastern Europe and Eurasia* (pp. 177–206). Columbia University Press.

Banaszak, L. (2010). *The women's movement inside and outside the state* (1st ed.). Cambridge University Press.

Blankenburg, E. (1986). La recherche de l'efficacité de la loi. Réflexions sur l'étude de la mise en œuvre (Le concept « d'implementation »). *Droit Et Société, 2*, 73–94.

Börzel, T. A., & Risse, T. (2000). When Europe hits home: Europeanization and domestic change. *European Integration Online Papers (EIoP), 4*.

Brucker, M. (2007). Transnational actors in democratizing states: The case of German Political Foundations in Ukraine. *Journal of Communist Studies and*

Transition Politics, 23(2), 296–319. https://doi.org/10.1080/13523270701317562

Charton, H. (2017). De l'art de bien gouverner l'école en Afrique: Domination gestionnaire et élimination des résistances. *Education Et Societes, 39*(1), 101–117.

Checkel, J. T. (2002). Persuasion in International Institutions. *ARENA Working Papers, 02/14.*

Clark, J. (1992). Democratising development: NGOs and the state. *Development in Practice, 2*(3), 151–162.

Clarke, J., Bainton, D., Lendvai, N., & Stubbs, P. (2015). *Making policy move: Towards a politics of translation and assemblage*. Policy Press.

Colineau, H. (2014). Interroger la diffusion des normes dans l'aide européenne aux pays en transition. *Politique Européenne, 46*, 118–140.

Désert, M. (2006). Le débat russe sur l'informel. *Questions de recherche, CERI, 17*.

Dezalay, Y., & Garth, B. G. (2002). *La Mondialisation des guerres de palais. La restructuration du pouvoir d'État en Amérique latine, entre notables du droit et « Chicago Boys »*. Seuil.

Finnemore, M., & Sikkink, K. (1998). International norm dynamics and political change. *International Organization, 52*(04), 887–917.

Fischer, N. (2009). Une frontière « négociée ». *Politix, 87*, 71–92.

Flowers, P. R. (2008). Failure to protect refugees? Domestic institutions, international organizations, and civil society in Japan. *Journal of Japanese Studies, 34*(2), 333–361.

Freyburg, T. (2011). Transgovernmental networks as catalysts for democratic change? EU functional cooperation with Arab authoritarian regimes and socialization of involved state officials into democratic governance. *Democratization, 18*(4), 1001–1025. https://doi.org/10.1080/13510347.2011.584737

Fröhlich, C. (2010). Walking the tightrope. Russian disability NGOs' struggle with international and domestic demands. In S. Fischer & H. Pleines (Eds.), *Civil society in Central and Eastern Europe* (pp. 77–87). ibidem-Verlag.

Grødeland, Å. B., & Aasland, A. (2011). Civil society in post-communist Europe: Perceptions and use of contacts. *Journal of Civil Society, 7*(2), 129–156. https://doi.org/10.1080/17448689.2011.573667

Guignard, L. (2016). La construction d'une norme juridique régionale: Le cas des mutilations génitales féminines en Afrique. *Critique Internationale, 70*, 87–100.

Henderson, S. (2002). Selling civil society: Western aid and the nongovernmental organization sector in Russia. *Comparative Political Studies, 35*(2), 139–167.

Henry, L. A. (2006). Shaping social activism in post-soviet Russia: Leadership, organizational diversity, and innovation. *Post-Soviet Affairs, 22*(2), 99–124. https://doi.org/10.2747/1060-586X.22.2.99

Jobard, F., Geeraert, J., Laumond, B., Mützelburg, I., & Zeigermann, U. (2020). Sociologie politique des passeurs. Acteurs dans la circulation de savoirs, de normes et de politiques publiques. *Revue française de science politique, 70*(5), 557–573.

Katzenstein, M. F. (1999). *Faithful and fearless*. Princeton University Press.

Kharkhordin, O. (2012). The importance of the politics of friendship for contemporary Russia. *PonarsEuarasia - Policy Memos*. http://www.ponarseurasia.org/memo/importance-politics-friendship-contemporary-russia

Kharkhordin, O. (2016). Friendship and politics in Russia. *Common Knowledge, 22*(2), 220–236. https://doi.org/10.1215/0961754X-3464828

Langbein, J. (2015). *Transnationalization and regulatory change in the EU's Eastern neighbourhood* (Routledge / UACES Contemporary European Studies).

Langbein, J., & Wolczuk, K. (2012). Convergence without membership? The impact of the European Union in the neighbourhood: Evidence from Ukraine. *Journal of European Public Policy, 19*(6), 863–881.

Masson, D. (2009). Politique(s) des échelles et transnationalisation: Perspectives géographiques. *Politique Et Sociétés, 28*(1), 113–133. https://doi.org/10.7202/001727ar

Mützelburg, I. (2018). L'empowerment par des financements internationaux ? Comment les donateurs créent un secteur non étatique en Ukraine. *Revue Gouvernance, 15*(1), 63–85.

Mützelburg, I. (2020a). Remote management of the European neighbourhood policy. The neoliberal bureaucratisation of a non-governmental sector in Ukraine. *Revue D'études Comparatives Est-Ouest, 4*, 45–75.

Mützelburg, I. (2020b). Produire des passeurs: Une stratégie de transfert de normes internationales. *Revue Française De Science Politique, 70*(5), 595–615.

Mützelburg, I. (forthcoming). NGOs in Ukraine's multi-scalar asylum governance – Between influence and dependence on state authorities. *Journal of Intercultural Studies*.

Nizhnikau, R. (2015). Institutional change in the eastern neighbourhood: Environmental protection and migration policy in Ukraine. *Southeast European and Black Sea Studies, 1–23*. https://doi.org/10.1080/14683857.2015.1050274

Osborne, S. P., & Kaposvari, A. (1998). Non-governmental organizations and the development of social services. Meeting social needs in local communities in post-communist Hungary. *Public Administration and Development*, *18*(4), 365–380.

Parks, T. (2008). The rise and fall of donor funding for advocacy NGOs: Understanding the impact. *Development in Practice, 18*(2), 213–222.

Petrova, T., & Tarrow, S. (2007). Transactional and participatory activism in the emerging European polity: The puzzle of East-Central Europe. *Comparative Political Studies, 40*(1), 74–94.

Postanova pro sudovu praktyku rozhlyadu sporiv shchodo statusu bizhentsya, vydvorennya inozemtsya chy osoby bez hromadyanstva z Ukrayiny ta sporiv, povyazanykh iz perebuvannyam inozemtsya ta osoby bez hromadyanstva v Ukrayini (Decree on the Court Practice in Disputes over Refugee Status, Forced Removal of a Foreigner or a Stateless Person from Ukraine and Disputes over the Stay of a Foreigner and a Stateless Person in Ukraine). (2009). http://zakon4.rada.gov.ua/laws/show/v_001760-09/ed20090625

Postanova pro sudovu praktyku rozhlyadu sporiv shchodo statusu bizhentsya ta osoby, yaka potrebuye dodatkovoho abo tymchasovoho zakhystu, prymusovoho povernennya i prymusovoho vydvorennya inozemtsya chy osoby bez hromadyanstva z Ukrayiny ta sporiv, povyazanykh iz perebuvannyam inozemtsya ta osoby bez hromadyanstva v Ukrayini (Decree on the court practice in disputes over refugee status and of a person in need of complementary or temporary protection, forced return and forced removal of a foreigner or stateless person from Ukraine and disputes related to the stay of a foreigner and stateless person in Ukraine), Pub. L. No. v_001760-09. (2014). http://zakon4.rada.gov.ua/laws/show/v_001760-09/ed20140515

Prague Process. (n.d.). *Asylum and International Protection*. Retrieved 27 September 2016, from https://www.pragueprocess.eu/en/asylum-and-international-protection

Reimann, K. D. (2006). A view from the top: International politics, norms and the worldwide growth of NGOs. *International Studies Quarterly, 50*(1), 45–67.

Rioufreyt, T. (2013). Les passeurs de la « Troisième Voie ». Intermédiaires et médiateurs dans la circulation transnationale des idées. *Critique internationale, 2*(59), 33–46.

Sabatier, P. A. (1986). Top-down and bottom-up approaches to implementation research: A critical analysis and suggested synthesis. *Journal of Public Policy, 6*(01), 21–48.

Sampson, S. (2004). Too much civil society? Donor-driven human rights NGOs in the Balkans. In L. Dhundale (Ed.), *Revisiting the role of civil society in the promotion of human rights*. Danish Institute for Human Rights.

Saxonberg, S. (2016). *Beyond NGO-ization: the Development of social movements in Central and Eastern Europe*. Routledge.

Schimmelfennig, F., & Sedelmeier, U. (2005). Conceptualizing the Europeanization of Central and Eastern Europe. In *The Europeanization Of Central And Eastern Europe* (pp. 1–28). Cornell University Press.

Scott, J. C. (1990). *Domination and the arts of resistance: Hidden transcripts*. Yale University Press.

Sedelmeier, U. (2006). Europeanisation in new member and candidate states. *Living Reviews in European Governance, 1*. http://europeangovernance.livingreviews.org/Articles/lreg-2006-3/

Shutt, W. (1975). Organizational survival and educational adaptation in a technical college. *The Vocational Aspect of Education, 27*(66), 11–16.

UNHCR. (1995). *RLD4—Interviewing applicants for refugee status*. http://www.refworld.org/docid/3ccea3304.html

UNHCR. (2010). *Improving Asylum Procedures: Comparative Analysis and Recommendations for Law and Practice—Detailed Research on Key Asylum Procedures Directive Provisions*. http://www.refworld.org/docid/4c63e52d2.html

Voicu, B., & Basina, T. (2005). Social capital and civic participation in Ukraine and Romania. In H. Rusu & B. Voicu (Eds.), *European integration process from EAST to EAST: Civil society and ethnic minorities in a changing world* (pp. 75–96). Psihomedia.

CHAPTER 7

Contentious Approaches to Counter Resistance to Transfer: Multi-Scalar Complaints

Introduction

> Our state structures are all about nice reporting. There are no problems with the refugees because no one has written an official letter about the problems that they experienced. So, when it reaches the ministry, everything looks nice because it has passed through many, many filters of the reporting system. We have 2 500 refugees and only 10 have received proper medical treatment. And my persistence aims at spoiling their statistical image. Everything is documented and this information then goes to the higher authorities. We just want this information to reach the ears of higher officials: People do have problems and these problems should be dealt with on the legislative level! [...] When it comes to the district administration, all district organs are related to the city administration. We address the city administration when their subordinate organ doesn't fulfil its function. [...] We go to their directors, managers of departments, to someone who controls their work. (Interview, lawyer at an NGO, 2014)

When other, more harmonious approaches failed, NGOs and IOs tried to change the authorities' practices by complaining about them. According to this lawyer, implementing authorities tried to maintain a spotless image of their work and to prevent news of their failure to implement laws from reaching higher scales of the state apparatus. By

I. Mützelburg, *Transferring Asylum Norms to EU Neighbours*, The European Union in International Affairs, https://doi.org/10.1007/978-3-031-04528-8_7

reporting to higher scales, the lawyers claimed to change state practices, which diverged from the law. For officials to accept this transfer approach by reporting and complaints, they needed to recognise the officials, to whom the norm promoters turned, as hierarchically higher and legitimate to evaluate, control, and direct them. This approach both relied on the prior construction of scales and participated in the construction of scales among state officials.

Non-state actors' scalar positions in relation to state authorities were in constant renegotiation. Ukrainian authorities often saw NGOs as lower than the lowest state administration, claiming that they should not teach or criticise officials. Given this low position, NGOs promoting asylum norms tried to use multi-scalar approaches to push for changes in state practices. The scale to which non-state actors turned depended on various factors, including on the way they framed the problem. For example, when they considered that state officials discriminated against certain groups of asylum seekers, they framed this problem as a regional one, claiming that officers at a specific regional migration service held racist views and unfairly prevented some groups of asylum seekers from obtaining a protection status. Hence, they sometimes targeted the problem at the scale of this department (for example, they might try to convince the head of the department to inform or put pressure on the officers or they might organise a training for officials in the region), producing a regional scale. They sometimes also asked officials from the central State Migration Service to use their legal authority to request changes specifically at this regional department. This way, non-state actors participated in producing the national scale as superordinate to the regional scale. Alternatively, non-state actors could also frame the problem as a national one, arguing that it originated from national laws, (lack of) national top-down instructions, or nationwide racism among officials across Ukraine. Based on such framing, non-state actors turned to central authorities for national action, producing the national scale as the main one. However, for these scalar requests for interventions to be successful, the contacted actors needed to accept the framing of the problem. For instance, discriminatory everyday practices among subordinate staff in attributing social benefits were difficult to frame in such a way as to tackle them at an international scale. To be brought to the attention of actors with an international (regional or global) scale identity, such as the EU, issues needed to be framed as major violations of human rights or core asylum principles.

Scales of the Ukrainian state apparatus were generally accepted as given (Condrey et al., 2013, p. 15). Non-state actors relied on these scalar representations of the administration to obtain pressure from higher officials to change lower officials' practices. In specific situations, they also relied on and coproduced the European scale as superior to the Ukrainian one, triggering international actors' pressure on Ukrainian actors.

Complaining to State Brokers at Strategic Positions

Whenever possible, NGOs compensated for their own weak position by relying on their state contacts to solve migrants' problems and change state practises. Indeed, they preferred non-contentious and informal approaches, relying on personal contacts with officials with various scalar identities. State brokers in superordinate positions could benefit from their legal authority, legitimacy, and networks among other officials to recommend or request certain practices, including requesting that other state bodies comply with formal rules. For instance, during weekly as well as additional irregular meetings with a senior official of the department for foreigners and stateless persons of the central State Migration Service, an NGO complained about problems at the regional Migration Service as well as other regional state authorities, for instance the tax administration or public hospitals. The NGO asked its contact person at the State Migration Service to request specific changes from other state bodies.

What is more, brokers arranged meetings between the non-state actors and other senior officials, asking them to request compliance from lower scales of a state body. In both cases, the brokers' power depended on their capacity to directly exercise authority over the other official (Weber, 1922, pt. I; Chapter 3). For example, thanks to the above-mentioned contact person at the central State Migration Service, the NGO was able to obtain occasional meetings with intermediary or superior representatives of other ministries such as the Ministry of Health, the Ministry of Social Policy, and the Ministry of Education. During these meetings, the NGO and the representative of the State Migration Service discussed refugee issues with these ministries and asked them to change some of their institution's practices. Despite being scheduled, however, these meetings did not always take place. The representative of the Ministry sometimes failed to attend them, conceivably because the representative of the State Migration Service was too low in the state hierarchies and could not exercise legal authority over representatives of other ministries.

By comparison to senior officials at the State Migration Service, the Ombudsman was a more powerful broker thanks to its position in the Ukrainian state apparatus. Non-state actors presented the Ombudsman as hierarchically high-positioned in the Ukrainian institutional setting though placed outside of the main institutions. Indeed, the Ombudsman, if active and interested in the matter, could intervene at different scales. They had the right to intervene directly at the locally implementing body for specific change or at higher scales of state bodies that would then send a formalised order to the implementing bodies. Non-state actors claimed that these higher institutions, such as the Cabinet of Ministers, could not ignore the Ombudsman's requests and have to order change from the ministries. Indeed, research on the Ukrainian Ombudsman Office shows that, even though they did not exercise direct legal authority over other state bodies, which would allow them to enforce changes in practices itself, they played a major role in controlling the respect of human rights and national law by pointing out violations to various state authorities (Melnychuk & Melnychuk, 2018). A state broker with an independent, high position outside of the concerned state bodies could request that the government exercises its legal authority over the administration and intervenes in struggles with other state bodies. The first Ombudsman of Ukraine (Nina Karpachova 1998–2012) supported non-state actors in struggles with powerful state bodies. For example, she cooperated with UNHCR to prevent an asylum seeker's refoulement. However, when she left this position, the NGOs lost their broker, as the following one was reluctant to criticise the government. When non-state actors did not have the appropriate contact inside the right state body to support their complaint and put pressure on other officials, they needed to complain from the outside.

Denouncing State Practices Across Scales

For their complaints from the outside of the state apparatus, non-state actors adopted a multi-scalar approach. Often they framed a problem in individual terms, claiming that a specific official's practices are problematic. This reflected the non-state actor's immediate experience of the state practices and was a pragmatic way of supporting specific migrants.

NGO workers usually started at this individual scale: They first directly confronted street-level bureaucrats whose practices diverged from the NGO's expectations. To legitimise the confrontation, they frequently referred to formal rules, mostly national laws.

In case of resistance, they moved to semi-formal contestation at hierarchically higher scales. NGOs complained to street-level bureaucrats' superiors to counter resistance and violation of formal rules. For example, NGOs reported in 2014 how they intervened when state officials, such as police officers, requested bribes from asylum seekers. The NGOs threatened police officers to inform their head. Over time, police officers refrained from requesting bribes from asylum seekers when they mentioned the NGO's name. After repeated experiences, state officials anticipated that the non-state actors would complain to the superordinate officials, who had proven in the past that they exercised their legal authority and punished deviation from the formal rules. Moreover, NGO workers accompanied migrants to the administration to support them in the procedures and to make sure that their rights were respected. In some cases, subordinate state officials rejected the demand despite the NGO workers' presence and arguments. NGOs then complained to higher scales of the same institution—or threatened to do so. For instance, following a common practice of requesting money from families for school refurbishment or equipment, a school told a refugee child that if they did not pay 200 UAH (approximately 10€ at the time) for the reparation of the building like the other children, they could not attend the school. The NGO denounced the school at the school administration at the regional scale. As a consequence, the school stopped requesting money from the child. The school headmaster accepted his own local scale identity, subordinate to the regional scale identity of the school administration. Norm promoters turned to indirect semi-formal contestation, trying to shift the decision-making to higher scales of the same state structure.

NGOs switched between different approaches, observing the state authorities' reactions and adapting their strategies to them. When it became apparent that the targeted state actor did not exercise legitimate domination over the subordinate state actor, norm promoters turned to another state actor. For example, in 2013, an NGO tried to denounce the head of a homeless shelter to a higher state official from an institution with a national scale identity, the State Migration Service. According to the head of the NGO, this undertaking was ineffective. The contacted official, while enjoying a national scale identity, belonged to another state body and could therefore not exercise legal authority over the targeted official with a local scale identity. Consequently, the NGO adapted its approach and threatened the head of the homeless shelter to take the written proof of his violation of the law to court. This made him comply with the NGO's request.

Yet, this multi-scalar approach caused "geographical dilemmas" (Masson, 2009, p. 126). On the one hand, it often proved to be successful in countering the lower state officials' resistance. On the other hand, such confrontational approaches frequently deteriorated the personalised relations between norm promoters and norm addressees (or, when no such relations existed, made their establishment more difficult). The NGO commented that as a consequence of its complaint to the school administration, "the head of school hates us" (Interview, head of an NGO, 2013).

The norm promoters' semi-formal contestation at higher scales of the state apparatus often triggered further resistance. Indeed, officials considered non-state actors to be illegitimate to critically interfere in state practices. The approach was unstable over time given that most state officials only complied if they were directly controlled by the NGO or risked a direct threat of being denounced with their superiors. Following the threat of legal action, the aforementioned head of the homeless centre indeed complied with the NGO's request—but only when the NGO lawyer accompanied the asylum seekers. Furthermore, officials with a higher scale identity could decide to ignore the complaints and refrained from taking any action regarding the subordinate officials' practices. NGOs observed that officials, for example of the central State Migration Service, sometimes showed "not much reaction" when they reported law infringements by regional Migration Services (Interview, head of an NGO, 2015). When the representatives of the higher scale state body disagreed with the complaint (for example because they rejected the interference as inappropriate, because they benefited themselves from the denounced unlawful practices, or because they did not adhere to the respective norms, such as international asylum norms), such contestation was ineffective. NGOs also explained that they wrote complaint letters to senior officials at ministries but that they rarely received an answer or only "lots of blabla" (interview, head of an NGO, 2013). State officials also resisted requests by non-state actors whom they described as aggressive and pushy. Indeed, they perceived themselves as on a higher scale than NGO workers and thus expected non-state actors to formulate their requests in a way that respected the hierarchy.

To avoid a deterioration of the personalised relations and to uphold the possibility of having recourse to informal means of transfer, norm promoters also sometimes indirectly contested state practices. Indeed, NGOs occasionally passed their criticism on to higher state bodies via UNHCR instead of formulating it themselves. They hence shifted the task of communicating the criticism to an actor with a higher scale identity.

The semi-formal approach, while not relying on personalised relations but on official complaints to hierarchically superior officials, largely depended on the individual mid- or higher scale officials who could choose to exercise their legal authority or to ignore the complaints. The effects of this approach were hence heterogeneous. In addition to this semi-formal approach through hierarchical complaints, non-state actors also contested state practices in court.

Litigation

Researchers have shown that activists use litigation to strengthen the implementation of national laws and to extend migrants' access to rights enshrined in international law (Basok & Carasco, 2010). In Ukraine, NGO lawyers reported that they regularly appealed against the detention of asylum seekers, against negative decisions of the State Migration Service, and against all negative administrative court decisions concerning the NGOs' clients, as well as against general state policies which, according to NGOs, violated national law.

In some cases, norm promoters managed to overcome state officials' resistance by threatening legal action. For this reason, NGOs often informed the state authorities that they were preparing legal action concerning a certain state practice—leaving the authorities some time to react. For instance, when an NGO prepared to sue the Migration Service because it violated laws by communicating insufficiently with the detention centres, the Migration Service called the NGO workers to tell them that it had changed this practice. Similarly, in 2014, the Migration Services were unable to provide passport documents to migrants who had been recognised as persons in need of complementary protection. An NGO obtained a written explanation from the employment centre stating that they could not register migrants without a passport. The NGO then prepared a court case against the Migration Service arguing that their work practices led to a violation of the migrants' rights. The authorities solved the problem, and the NGO dropped the case.

Legal action sometimes affected state practices through mechanisms other than the capacity to formulate orders, which needed to be obeyed to avoid sanctions: Judges enjoyed legitimacy among the staff of the administration and of lower-scale courts whose reputation they could affect with their decisions. Some state officials presented the court decisions as an evaluation of their work, which affected their ensuing practices. In particular, if courts recommended a reconsideration of the case, caseworkers interpreted this as questioning their work. In several interviews it became clear that certain state officials remembered with apprehension how their decisions had been criticised in court or how they recalled proudly that their decisions had been confirmed. Similarly, an NGO lawyer said in a 2014 interview that lower-scale judges feared that the overturning of their decisions by higher-scale courts might shed negative light on their work, including in the statistics of their decisions.

However, in some cases the courts lacked legal authority over the administrative body. NGOs recognised the limited effects of, for instance, court contestation on the functioning of the institutions, calling the method of court appeals a "game" (Interview, head of an NGO, 2014). In the area of decisions to grant or refuse asylum, courts could only return the decision to the administrative body and formulate recommendations. NGOs commented that the administration did not always take their court appeals on asylum procedures very seriously—especially because the courts could not make a final decision on protection status and could only force the Migration Service to reconsider the case. NGOs used formal complaints and appeals as one of their methods. When semi-formal complaints and formal contestation through courts failed, norm promoters turned to actors with an international scale identity.

Causing International Pressure

Local NGOs benefited from actors with an international scale identity to counterbalance their weak position in relation to domestic state authorities. Margaret Keck and Kathryn Sikkink argued that NGOs in states that are reluctant to comply with international norms are able to influence state policies by activating transnational networks, which in turn exert pressure on the state from the outside (Keck & Sikkink, 1998). Even though the legal authority of international organisations over domestic authorities is uncertain, clashing with the norm of state sovereignty, research has shown that "most of the states follow most of the [transnational] rules most of the time" (Anders Nordström, 2008, p. 17; Devin, 2013). As discussed in the first part of this book, Ukrainian state actors accepted to comply with international actors' demands when they sought to obtain their recognition or incentives. Instead of being able to directly enforce punishments for disobeyed orders, international actors relied on shaming and the threat of withholding incentives.

When NGOs had exhausted all domestic channels, they turned to international actors for help. This was not possible for all types of problems. Rather it was limited to violations of major international human rights or asylum rights, for instance when Ukrainian authorities detained underage migrants, committed or planned refoulement, and denied potential asylum seekers access to the state territory or the asylum procedure. Non-governmental and international organisations first contested such undertakings directly among the Ukrainian authorities, for instance the State Migration Service, the General Prosecutor's Office, the Ministry of Justice, and the Ombudsman Office. In some cases, however, other interests such as cooperative relations with other CIS countries prevailed over non-state actors' requests and pleas for the respect of human rights and asylum norms.[1] International organisations repeatedly highlighted that CIS states, including Ukraine, prioritised regional cooperation and national security over their human rights obligations, for example the non-refoulement principle. In these cases, UNHCR subcontractors filed rule 39 requests to the European Court of Human Rights (ECHR) (Chubenko, 2014) in order to obtain an interim measure that would suspend the extradition procedure, followed by a full application against the state decision. The Ukrainian state usually complied with the ECHR's requests to suspend the extradition procedure (*Case of Abuyev v. Ukraine*, 2013; *Case of Bayasakov & Others v. Ukraine*, 2010; *Case of Kaboulov v. Ukraine*, 2009; *Case of Soldatenko v. Ukraine*, 2008; *Case of Svetlorusov v. Ukraine*, 2009; *Case of Kebe & Others v. Ukraine*, 2013). Between 2008 and 2015, the General Prosecutor's Office repeatedly started following

[1] Reports of international organisations and interviewees from IOs and the EU Delegation in Kyiv claimed that state officials in the Ministries of Interior, the State Border Guard Services, the General Prosecutor Office, and the state security agencies in the CIS region shared a culture and operational ties which facilitated unlawful extraditions (Amnesty International, 2013; ECRE, 2007).

the country of origin's request for extradition of an asylum seeker but then stopped the extradition and released the applicant from detention following the appeal to the ECHR (*Case of Abuyev v. Ukraine*, 2013; *Case of Kreydich v. Ukraine*, 2009; *Case of Svetlorusov v. Ukraine*, 2009). The head of an NGO claimed in 2013 that in the cases of the detention of minors, the complaint to the ECHR led to the release of the minors and no other minors had since then been detained. Through their appeals, UNHCR and its NGO subcontractors participated in constructing the ECHR scale as superior to the national scale of the General Prosecutor's Office. By following the ECHR decisions, the General Prosecutor's Office accepted and confirmed these scalar relations.

To justify the action in individual cases at the ECHR, UNHCR, NGOs, and the Secretariat of the Ombudsman Office referred to an expected learning effect among the state authorities. While the actual impact on state practices in the long term remained uncertain, the number of cases of refoulement documented by UNHCR indeed decreased over time.[2] Norm promoters claimed that these changes in practices originated from international criticism and domestic changes in the legislation, which became increasingly detailed concerning the prohibition of refoulement.

Furthermore, UNHCR and its subcontractors in Ukraine occasionally asked the EU to intervene on Ukrainian state decisions regarding individual migrants. For instance, to prevent refoulement, UNHCR asked the EU High Representative for Foreign Affairs and Security and the EU Delegation in Kyiv to criticise these extraditions. When the EU intervened, the extradition was stopped. It is methodologically difficult to disentangle which actor's intervention made the difference in these cases and pushed the Ukrainian authorities to reject the extradition request of the country of origin. It seems though that the outcry of bodies of international organisations, such as the EU, UNHCR, and the ECHR, motivated the Ukrainian politicians to reconsider planned extraditions.

Non-state actors' approach of issuing complaints to international organisations about domestic authorities' rule violations relied on several steps: First, non-state actors had to gain access to the organisations with

[2] See UNHCR reports (UNHCR, 2013, p. 25; UNHCR Ukraine, 2016, p. 2) and yearly UNHCR "Fact sheets" concerning the situation of refugees and asylum seekers in Ukraine. However, given the difficulties of documenting and proving refoulement, the number of documented cases of refoulement was low and uncertain for many years, thus making it difficult to verify the claim of generalised change.

an international scale identity ("jump scale" [Stubbs, 2005]), who then needed to accept to use their authority to criticise the Ukrainian authorities. Second, the highest domestic state authorities needed to accept the IO as legitimate to interfere in domestic affairs, that is, to accept the construction of the international scale as superior to the national one. When domestic politicians tried to achieve positive evaluations from international organisations, for instance in the context of conditionality, IOs were in a better position to push national authorities to give in in specific cases of particularly salient human rights violations. Third, national authorities had to exert their own legal authority over the lower scales of the Ukrainian administration, who had to accept the construction of the national scale as superior to their scale.

Conclusion

The existence of individual contacts shaped non-state actors' scalar practices of norm promotion. Indeed, whenever possible, non-state actors privileged the path via state brokers to issue complaints about other officials' practices and request changes. Thanks to personal contacts to specific officials, non-state actors jumped scales. However, non-state actors did not always manage to establish the necessary contacts at the different state bodies and scales and to persuade officials to actively support their cause. They then sometimes decided to use contentious approaches from outside the state apparatus.

When framing the problem in individual terms, NGO workers first confronted state officials, often subordinate ones who interacted with migrants, criticised their practices or decisions, and requested changes, all the while referring to national and international law. When this failed, as norm promoters had no legal authority over state officials, they shifted scales within the state apparatus, complaining to different superordinate state officials—who could choose to ignore the complaints—or to courts. In particularly salient cases of violations of human rights or asylum norms, non-state actors could cause pressure from international actors. Indeed, non-state actors could counter state resistance by activating transnational networks that exert pressure on the state from the outside (Keck & Sikkink, 1998). Given that international organisations had only uncertain authority over domestic state actors, their power depended on the domestic political context. When domestic politicians sought the recognition and incentives offered by international actors, this increased the latter's power. This research confirms the importance of EU conditionality, pointed out in the literature on transfer, but it adds a micro- and meso-perspective understanding of the ways that EU conditionality affects processes, relations, and scales within state institutions and between state and non-state actors. EU action needs to be analysed not only as promoting norms directly but also as affecting the domestic political context, the construction of scales, and the opportunities for norm promoters on the ground.

Conclusion to the Second Part

While most studies categorise the practical effects of transfer attempts according to their strength, the second part of this book shows that norm promoters' transfer activities caused heterogeneous and unstable changes in state practices. They struggled with structural obstacles and domestic actors' resistance, which often discreetly hindered change. Norm promoters adapted to these obstacles and used various approaches to transfer norms.

In this second part, I have demonstrated that in Ukraine the laws adopted under international influences (see first part) were implemented heterogeneously. Top-down obstacles to implementation (frequent restructuring of the authorities, legal contradictions, lack of information and of material resources) originated from the lack of domestic political interest, adoption costs, and general characteristics of the Ukrainian state apparatus. But some of them were gradually eliminated, particularly between 2010 and 2015 under EU conditionality.

Nevertheless, implementation remained heterogeneous. Indeed a combination of macro, meso, and micro perspectives has shown that implementation of transferred norms can only be understood when taking into account the diverse actors with different scalar identities and their cross-scalar interactions. Approaches that only look at national political elites and supposedly homogenous national norms overlook that numerous actors are involved in transfer and policy implementation, all enjoying leeway. Drawing upon the sociological and ethnographic approaches to study (primarily Western European) public policy implementation, I show that subordinate state officials responded heterogeneously to top-down obstacles, some of them improvising, for instance through volunteering at work, whereas others remained passive. Moreover, they interpreted and used laws differently depending on their ideas and their personal, moral, and affective appreciation of the asylum seekers. Even though the central authorities' attempts to oversee and standardise regional practices increased since EU conditionality, these attempts were limited by the distance, the lack of administrative resources, and the need for street-level bureaucrats to use discretion at work. While the superiority of the national scale over the local scale was generally accepted within the Ukrainian state apparatus, in practice the control of the national administration over the local one was far from complete.

Given that the practical application of legally transferred norms did not take place automatically and fully, norm promoters intervened directly to shape domestic authorities' practices. Norm promoters with an international scale identity delegated transfer activities to actors with a national or local scale identity. I propose the concept of a multi-scalar transfer chain on which international donors, such as the European Commission, gave money to large international organisations such as UNHCR to change asylum practices in Ukraine. UNHCR's national office produced Ukrainian asylum NGOs to whom it delegated transfer activities. Enriching the usual transfer analyses with the research on development aid and the relations between donor and aid recipients, I show that transfer can take the shape of delegation, control, and dependence. Furthermore, similar to subordinate state officials implementing laws, NGOs and their employees enjoyed a certain leeway when interpreting and applying UNHCR rules. NGOs also translated their activities between the donors' expectations and what the NGO staff considered desirable or feasible.

I then followed the transfer chain and investigated how norm promoters in Ukraine tried to transfer norms to implementing state officials. Norm promoters adapted to state resistance and structural obstacles to transfer, shifting between scales, formal and informal, contentious and non-contentious approaches. While scalar hierarchies between state and non-state actors were fuzzy and constantly renegotiated, officials usually saw NGOs as low in the hierarchy, illegitimate to criticise or teach even state officials with a local scale identity. Transfer scholars have theoretically discussed the scenario that actors can be "socialised" to change their norms and practices via direct interaction, yet little empirical research has explored this mode of norm transfer and its effects. Drawing upon research on social movements and on NGOs in post-communist contexts, which has revealed the interrelatedness between state and non-state actors, I argue that NGOs build up personalised relations with subordinate state officials. NGOs in Ukraine initiated meetings, provided material and service support, and avoided public criticism of state practices. They indeed managed to increase state officials' awareness of domestic and international law and its legitimacy, therefore spreading the discursive adoption of the norms. However, due to either shallow learning or resistance, state officials applied the norms heterogeneously. Furthermore, the approach via direct interaction was limited by the impossibility of teaching all subordinate state officials and by high turnover among officials. Norm promoters therefore tried to turn certain state officials into brokers who would spread the norms horizontally or top-down to other officials. Through some state brokers in strategic positions, non-state actors also shaped the production of formal rules.

When these transfer approaches failed or were unavailable, non-state actors tried to change state practices by issuing complaints. If possible, they denounced lower scale authorities to brokers at key positions. Thanks to such contacts they could "jump scales" (Stubbs, 2005) and benefit from the brokers' legal authority over certain subordinate state actors to recommend or request certain practices. If non-state actors did not enjoy such privileged relations with well-positioned officials, they issued complaints about officials' practices, usually starting from the lowest scale, directly confronting the implementing officials. In case of resistance they shifted across scales, complaining to superordinate officials or to courts. When a case could be framed as a particularly salient violation of human rights or asylum norms, norm promoters sometimes complained to international organisations to obtain their pressure on domestic politicians. However, contentious approaches often caused geographical dilemmas. They provoked resistance and limited the norm promoters' access to non-contentious transfer approaches. Given that norm promoters tried to keep as many transfer channels open as possible in order to be able to adapt and combine their strategies, they sometimes refrained from denouncing state practices. The combination of various imperfect, localised, and unstable methods explains why attempts to further the practical adoption of international norms led to heterogeneous effects.

This second part of the book provides evidence of the need to differentiate among the dimensions of practical application of transferred norms. While direct interactions between norm promoters and norm addressees largely increased the knowledge of international norms as well as their discursive adoption by the state officials, the practical implementation nevertheless remained heterogeneous. Top-down approaches, in particular via the international scale and especially in the context of political interest in the IOs' recognition or incentives could somewhat enhance the provision of information and resources for implementation, control, and pressure by higher state bodies. Despite these top-down changes, in light of the findings of public policy implementation research in Western European states, the central authorities' capacity to fully control the lower-scale implementation should not be overestimated.

References

Amnesty International. (2013). *Return to torture: Extradition, forcible returns and removals to Central Asia* (EUR 04/001/2013). https://www.amnesty.org/en/documents/eur04/001/2013/en/

Basok, T., & Carasco, E. (2010). Advancing the rights of non-citizens in Canada: A human rights approach to migrant rights. *Human Rights Quarterly, 32*(2), 342–366. https://doi.org/10.1353/hrq.0.0150

Case of Abuyev v. Ukraine. (2013). No. 11657/12.

Case of Bayasakov and others v. Ukraine. (2010). No. 54131/08.

Case of Kaboulov v. Ukraine. (2009). No. 41015/04.

Case of Kebe and others v. Ukraine. (2013). No. 12552/12.

Case of Kreydich v. Ukraine. (2009). No. 48495/07.

Case of Soldatenko v. Ukraine. (2008). No. 2440/07.

Case of Svetlorusov v. Ukraine. (2009). No. 2929/05.

Chubenko, A. (2014). The implementation of Strasbourg's judgments in Ukraine. *Scientific Library of the National Law university Iaroslav Mudry*, 24–26.

Condrey, S. E., Slava-Prodan, S., Battaglio, R. P., & Palinchak, M. (2013). Ukrainian public management: Top-down or bottom-up reform? In S. Liebert, S. E. Condrey, & D. Goncharov (Eds.), *Public administration in post-communist countries: Former Soviet Union, Central and Eastern Europe, and Mongolia* (pp. 7–22). CRC Press.

Devin, G. (2013). *Sociologie des relations internationales* (3rd ed.). La Découverte.

ECRE. (2007). *Belarus, Moldova, Russian Federation and Ukraine—Situation for refugees, asylum-seekers and internally displaced persons (IDPs)* (Country Report). http://www.refworld.org/docid/48e4a7c32.html

Keck, M. E., & Sikkink, K. (1998). *Activists beyond borders: Advocacy networks in international politics.* Cornell University Press.

Masson, D. (2009). Politique(s) des échelles et transnationalisation: Perspectives géographiques. *Politique Et Sociétés, 28*(1), 113–133. https://doi.org/10.7202/001727ar

Melnychuk, O., & Melnychuk, M. (2018). Open journal systems. *Society Integration Education*, 394–404. https://doi.org/10.17770/sie2018vol1.3166

Nordström, A. (2008). *The interactive dynamics of regulation: Exploring the Council of Europe's monitoring of Ukraine.* Stockholm University.

Stubbs, P. (2005). Stretching concepts too far? Multi-level governance, policy transfer and the politics of scale in South-eastern Europe. *South East European Politics, 6*(2), 66–87.

UNHCR. (2013). *Ukraine as a country of asylum. Observations on the situation of asylum-seekers and refugees in Ukraine.*

UNHCR Ukraine. (2016). *Ukraine Factsheet*.https://doi.org/www.reporting.unhcr.org/sites/default/files/UNHCR%20Ukraine%20Factsheet%20-%20July%202016.pdf

Weber, M. (1922). *Wirtschaft und Gesellschaft – Grundriß der verstehenden soziologie (Economy and society—An outline of interpretative sociology)* (G. Roth & C. Wittich, Eds.). University of California Press.

CHAPTER 8

Conclusion

Transfer is everywhere. Individuals, organisations, and states constantly try to influence what others do. Actors seek to spread their own norms, standards, ideas, beliefs, concepts, definitions, ways of doing, laws, and policy instruments. Despite the omnipresence and widespread academic interest in this phenomenon, transfer still lacks research that grasps its multi-scalar and multi-actor dimensions. In particular, transfer undertakings orchestrated by international actors, such as the European Union, the United Nations, and the World Bank involve numerous and diverse actors. These include individuals and organisations, state and non-state actors, and non-profit and for-profit organisations. The present research shows that various actors participate in shaping transfer processes and outcomes. Engaging in multi-scalar activities, these actors construct and renegotiate relations and scales, changing society and state beyond the normative effects of transfer. Analysing the case of transfer of international asylum norms to Ukraine in the three decades following the independence of the state in 1991, this book shows that scholars studying international transfer endeavours gain from taking into consideration all actors involved across different scales and examine them through different perspectives, from micro-interactions among individuals to the macro-dynamics of international relations.

I. Mützelburg, *Transferring Asylum Norms to EU Neighbours*, The European Union in International Affairs, https://doi.org/10.1007/978-3-031-04528-8_8

Based on a single case study, this book does not pretend to produce generalisable truth about all transfer phenomena. While the observations are necessarily specific to the case, this research demonstrates the need to complexify the study of transfer. It proposes new perspectives and analytical tools that can be usefully applied to understand other transfer phenomena.

Asylum Norms in Ukraine: Which Case of Transfer?

Norms travel differently depending on whether they are actively promoted and whether they fit social norms, and certain actors' beliefs and interests in the destination space. International asylum norms travelling to Ukraine were mostly promoted by the EU, UNHCR, and other international and non-governmental organisations. This active promotion of a specific set of norms is what I call transfer. International actors used various approaches, including international agreements, pressure, and conditionality, as well as funding and delegation to NGOs to spread and establish specific norms. The norms in question are enshrined in the 1951 Geneva Convention or EU Directives, or have been produced more recently by organisations such as UNHCR. These norms define the criteria and procedures according to which states should grant migrants various protection statuses and rights.

In contrast to Western Europe, asylum attracted little domestic interest in Ukraine, either from politicians or from activists. The small group of asylum seekers and refugees in Ukraine remained largely invisible from the public sphere. Among high-level political actors, asylum norms clashed with political interests, such as the upholding of cooperative relations with other regimes from the Commonwealth of Independent States (CIS) and the limiting of budgetary spending. They also lacked strong societal roots and support from the Soviet past, and clashed with prevailing xenophobia and with the growing attempts of the young state to control its territory and borders, establishing restrictive migration policies.

Because transfer scholars have increasingly highlighted the role of domestic actors as "filters" in transfer processes, asylum in pre-invasion Ukraine is an interesting case that makes it possible to identify more clearly the effects of external norm promotion activities (Dumoulin & Saurugger, 2010). Domestic actors, depending on their interests and norms, have been found to either use international actors' resources or to oppose their influence (Delcour, 2016). Transfer has usually been studied in policy areas in which powerful domestic actors (veto players) have strong supporting or opposing interests, for example concerning the fight against corruption, democracy promotion, energy, trade, and agricultural policies (Dimitrova & Dragneva, 2013; Langbein, 2015). The present research has investigated how transfer processes operate when domestic actors have little interest in the policy area, that is, when many state actors resist (slightly) and NGOs are open to transfer.

Norm Transfer Despite Disinterest and Resistance Among State Actors

Ukrainian legislators first integrated international asylum norms into domestic law for symbolic reasons. They displayed little interest in the practical consequences of these legislative changes and did not expect them to solve any public policy problems. Despite conflicting interests and beliefs, they adopted the norms in order to join international organisations, such as the Council of Europe, and so that they could show an international and national audience that they were democratising and Europeanising Ukraine. Yet, this legislative adoption remained shallow in many aspects, obstructing implementation.

Legislative adoption only deepened when the EU introduced its highly attractive sector-specific conditionality, linking the demand for asylum reforms with the incentive of abolishing visa requirements for Ukrainian tourists. Scholars have asserted that EU sector-specific conditionality can mitigate “preferential misfit” between the promoted policies and veto players’ interests and decrease opposition (Buzogány, 2013). The present research confirms this finding, even though it highlights that EU conditionality was not the only factor shaping norm transfer.

So far, research has overlooked the fact that in the presence of attractive external incentives, a lack of strong domestic political interest in the policy area can increase the international norm promoters’ capacity for transfer, especially concerning legislative adoption. The present case study suggests that such a situation allows the norm promoters to translate general demands into concrete steps and to define technical measures and legal formulations. In fact, when domestic officials were not directed by domestic veto players’ interests but were only under top-down pressure to fulfil external actors’ demands, they asked these actors to specify their expectations (here the European Commission), thus increasing the latter’s influence. Further research is needed to determine if this finding can be generalised.

Scholars still debate whether, after the end of EU conditionality, domestic norm adoption continues, stagnates, stops, or is even reversed (Dimitrova & Buzogány, 2014; Knill & Tosun, 2009; Pridham, 2008; Sedelmeier, 2008). However, these studies have focused on processes following EU accession. In these cases, EU institutions continue to influence the new member states (Steunenberg & Dimitrova, 2007), which is not the case at the end of EU sector-specific conditionality, for example in Ukraine. Gwendolyn Sasse argued that the continuation of compliance and reforms might indicate the role of socialisation, as opposed to purely rationalist explanations (Sasse, 2008). My research shows that when in April 2016, the European Commission proposed to grant Ukrainian tourists visa freedom, and the Council of the European Union and the European Parliament accepted this proposal, the EU also ended its less visible activities to promote asylum norms in Ukraine. It did not maintain monitoring and organised no follow-up activities surrounding asylum. In the first years after the end of the EU conditionality, Ukrainian law-makers neither reversed legal asylum reforms nor did they further harmonise domestic law with international asylum norms. More research is needed to study the developments of transfer processes after the end of EU conditionality, including in terms of practices and relations between state and non-state actors.

The Absence of "Empowerment" of Domestic NGOs

The investigated case differs from many other analysed ones in terms of domestic non-state actors' commitment and agency. Some scholars have claimed that through "capacity building" and support of existing domestic NGOs, external actors can enhance their own capacity to transfer norms (Buzogány, 2013). In Ukraine, there were barely any domestic actors who had defended similar asylum norms before the arrival of external influences and who could have benefited from international support to realise their activist objectives (Mützelburg, 2018). Instead, norm promoters produced most of the asylum NGOs in Ukraine, delegating to them the further diffusion of international norms. The diffusion of feminism in post-communist European countries bears certain similarities with asylum in Ukraine, for example concerning the limited communist heritage and the major role of international donors, platforms, and seminars for the formation of the non-state sector (Cîrstocea, 2015). Yet, Eastern European feminists display more agency and critical activism, benefiting from international resources and arenas but asserting what they frame as their own version of feminism. In contrast to this, Ukrainian asylum NGOs largely followed and spread their donors' norms—but only as long as they received international money. On the one hand, international norm promoters can more easily transfer their version of the norms when there is little pre-existing or emerging activism in the same area. On the other hand, such donor-driven norm promoters stop their transfer activities once the international funding stops.

Norms which also enjoy little support among domestic activists in post-communist countries are gender-neutral language, the rights of Roma communities, and anti-discrimination principles protecting sexual minorities (Teteriuk, 2015). These cases have so far attracted little attention from transfer scholars. Comparison of these cases to asylum norms in Ukraine could be a fruitful way of more systematically assessing how the lack of pre-existing domestic norms and interests shapes norm transfer.

Smooth Circulation of Norms That Fit Domestic Interests and Beliefs

While international actors tried to promote pro-asylum norms, restrictive migration-related norms also travelled to Ukraine. International actors actively promoted them in part, but otherwise only passively spread them, leaving Ukrainian actors to actively import them. In both cases, restrictive migration norms circulated more smoothly than pro-asylum norms.

Restrictive migration norms circulated due to EU external policies—some of which can be considered active transfer undertakings. For instance, EU member states and, subsequently, the EU signed readmission agreements with Ukraine, including Ukraine into an international migration regime and pushing it to adopt more restrictive migration and border policies. The EU actively encouraged Ukraine to lengthen detention periods for migrants caught while trying to irregularly cross the border to the EU.

Through their external and internal anti-migrant policies as well as their political and media discourse on migration, the EU and its member states spread the perception that most migrants are undesirable and dangerous and that borders need to be tightly controlled against human mobility. For example, in November 2021, when Poland and Lithuania built fences and violently pushed back migrants brought to the border by the Belarusian regime, the Ukrainian military also trained to push back migrants who could potentially cross the Belarusian border. For decades, international organisations had tried to spread international asylum norms in Ukraine, such as protection seekers' right to cross the border irregularly to apply for asylum and the prohibition of refoulement. However, Ukrainian authorities quickly followed Poland's model (or more largely the EU's model) of disrespecting these principles and fighting off migrants who might qualify as refugees. Material is not available to assess through which channels this model travelled to Ukrainian decision makers: Did Polish actors interact with Ukrainians and consult them? Or were the images of Polish pushbacks in the media sufficient for Ukrainians to imitate them? In any case, these practices circulated quickly, without the long training sessions and conditionality clauses that were necessary for asylum norms to be adopted.

Ukrainian legislators imported restrictive instruments, such as safe third country provisions and restrictive deadlines for filing asylum applications, from EU member states, even before these instruments were included in EU Directives. When for the same issue diverging norms co-existed, Ukrainian legislators selected the restrictive one. For example, UNHCR promotes the principle of not penalising migrants for violating immigration laws, but many European states practise the opposite. Ukrainian law penalises the attempt to enter Ukrainian territory without proper documentation as well as the irregular presence on Ukrainian territory—irrespective of the reasons for migrating. Even when international actors did not promote these restrictive norms—and instead criticised Ukraine for adopting them—Ukrainian decision makers chose the restrictive norms.

This smooth circulation of restrictive migration norms reflects the lack of credibility of the EU in promoting pro-asylum norms abroad without fully respecting them within its own borders. It also suggests that restrictive migration norms and instruments, thanks to their fit with Ukrainians social norms and politicians' interests, travelled more easily, possibly more through imitation than active transfer, than international asylum norms. Future research could investigate these questions more systematically and with a comparative research design.

Despite the specificities of transfer of asylum norms in Ukraine, this case study contributes to broader debates on transfer. In particular, this book has elaborated a new multi-perspective, multi-scalar, and multi-actor approach to study transfer processes which could be applied to further research projects on transfer phenomena.

Studying the Role and Leeway of All Actors Involved in Transfer

All actors involved in transfer shape its processes and normative outcomes. This study contributes to the current efforts to break up the common binary categories of norm promoters and norm addressees by showing that many intermediary actors play a role in the selection, dissemination, and transformation of norms and can be both norm addressees and norm promoters. Going beyond macro-perspective theoretical models of lesson drawing, imitation, socialisation, and persuasion that presuppose empirically inaccessible knowledge about actors' minds, this research proposes to study actors' expressions of awareness, support, or contestation (verbal or non-verbal) as well as their discreet or open practices of selecting, supporting, using, resisting, and translating norms.

European Union actors select norms that they try to transfer and translate them into benchmarks, requirements, and recommendations for third states. They choose the instruments for transfer, for example attaching incentives or threats to their demands, and choose how to control the norms' implementation. Depending on their interests, EU actors decide to insist on the fulfilment of these requirements or decide to ignore them, for instance when other political interests, such as showing support to the third country's regime, become more important than the norm transfer. Different actors within the EU participate in these decisions, some insisting on norm transfer when others prioritise other objectives. Different actors within the European Commission also negotiate how much money to spend on specific transfer undertakings, from whose budget, for which measures, under whose control, and via which implementing organisations—usually large international organisations. Officials from DG DEVCO at the Commission and from the EU Delegation formulate tenders, select, control, and evaluate the implementing organisations, spreading practices, procedures, technical standards, and norms to these organisations and their subcontractors.

Large international organisations, such as UNHCR, apply for these EU funds. Thanks to their offices in major cities (Geneva, Brussels, Kyiv), they translate between different contexts, for example between EU institutions, authorities in the target state, and subcontracting NGOs. UNHCR frames the activities carried out in Ukraine to fit the expectations of the European Commission, for instance presenting them as contributing to sustainable and systemic change. UNHCR selects the norms that it tries to transfer to its different interlocutors and presents them in different ways. Thanks to its knowledge production, UNHCR shaped the way EU actors perceived the asylum situation in Ukraine and the instruments they considered appropriate. UNHCR in Kyiv also selected NGOs to become its subcontractors. It shaped and controlled their work spheres, activities (including transfer activities), norms, procedures, as well as their relations to the domestic authorities. When communicating with local NGOs, UNHCR adapted its discourse. Indeed, NGO workers cared specifically about the situation of the migrants whom they wanted to help. When interacting with UNHCR, NGOs sometimes presented their activities as contributing to a more generalised change in the authorities' practices. Sometimes rhetorical reframing was not sufficient and NGOs needed to adapt their activities substantially to meet their donor's demands. UNHCR and NGO employees' understanding of asylum norms was shaped by their pre-existing beliefs and norms. When evaluating migrants' deservingness as refugees according to UNHCR criteria, NGO workers used discretionary powers in the same fashion as street-level bureaucrats, affectively and morally judging the asylum seekers.

UNHCR and its NGO subcontractors in Ukraine translated the norms and adapted their transfer practices to their state interlocutors. During EU conditionality, the office of UNHCR in Kyiv presented its norms as EU norms to facilitate transfer when communicating with Ukrainian officials and politicians. It also adapted its work practices to local norms and habits; in Ukraine, UNHCR and NGO staff sought to establish personalised contacts with politicians and officials to shape policies and practices informally. NGOs and UNHCR selected the norms to spread among which domestic officials. They chose which practices to criticise and which to ignore; they chose whether to prioritise imposing their normative objective (for instance saving a migrant from refoulement) or maintaining harmonious relations with state officials.

Domestic state actors reacted differently to norm transfer activities. Political actors occasionally contested norm transfer activities, questioning the norm promoters' legitimacy as a normative model (pointing to its incoherent policies in the area), and criticising egoistic interests underlying the transfer attempts (Saurugger & Terpan, 2013, pp. 23–25). Yet, most resistance and translation occurred discreetly. At all scales of the state institutions, politicians and officials chose to interact (or not) with international and non-governmental organisations and to get informed (or not) about asylum norms and migrants in Ukraine. Officials and politicians circumvented transfer by ignoring norm promoters' requests for reforms. For instance, parliamentarians sometimes failed to mention criticism and demands formulated by international norm promoters.

Domestic legislators do not only choose between adopting or not adopting international norms. Even in the case of international asylum norms, a policy of low salience and politicisation in Ukraine, legislators shaped the adoption in crucial ways:

1). Selection:
   a. Legislators choose among alternative international norms: When different international norms co-exist concerning the same issue, for instance one promoted by UNHCR and one by EU member states, Ukrainian legislators chose the one that fit their interests and beliefs best.
   b. Legislators select foreign models and policy instruments that do not have the status of a compulsory international norm according to international law, but that fit domestic law-makers' interests or beliefs. Domestic legislators imitate these models without international norm promoters' pressure, and without campaigns to inform or persuade.
2). Translation: Legislators translate an international norm to adapt it to the domestic context and to their own beliefs and preferences. In the present case, they mostly chose to import the model selectively, for instance by interpreting it narrowly, by leaving out part of a norm, or by adding a restricting clause or condition that limited the scope of the norm.
3). Shallow adoption: In parallel to the existing concept of "shallow application", shallow adoption means that the norm is integrated into a very "visible" (i.e. monitored) law, often in a vague way, but is not or not coherently integrated into related laws, nor into secondary legislation necessary for implementation. Legal contradictions or obstacles to the application of the apparently adopted norm remain. Scholars have overlooked the phenomenon of shallow legislative adoption, which can hinder rule application or which can be a preliminary step in the process of rule adoption.
4). Timing: Legislators may adopt norms more or less quickly (in comparison with the first law in the policy area, in comparison with the emergence and the establishment of the norm in international

or other model states' law, or in comparison with international norm promoters' requests for changes).

Further research could explore whether domestic legislators exercise even more leeway or other forms of leeway in other cases of policies and contexts in which domestic political actors pursue stronger and better defined interests. Other studies could analyse under which conditions legislators translate international norms more freely or invent new principles or formulations in their law.

Members of the government can hinder or interrupt policy implementation by repeatedly restructuring relevant administrative bodies. Government and highly positioned central executive officials shape norm transfer and implementation by foreseeing resources for the implementation of laws and action plans—or by failing to foresee them. They also decide whether training and information on the transferred norms will be provided to lower scales of the executive. By failing to foresee a budget and information about certain rules, higher scale decision makers hinder the implementation of laws and policies. They also shape administrative practices through top-down control, pressure, and instructions.

Administrative staff reacts differently to non-state actors' transfer attempts. Depending on their own norms and interests, as well as on their relations with individual norm promoters and the latter's behaviour (perceived as appropriately submissive or inappropriately arrogant), officials reject the interference and resist or adapt their own practices, put pressure on officials over whom they can exercise legal authority, spread information horizontally or top-down across the state institution, and use their network to transfer norms. Officials can become brokers and norm promoters themselves or (mostly passively) resist.

Acting as policy co-makers, subordinate state officials also exercise leeway in their direct interactions with the applicants. Officers' practices can be shaped by their affective and moral judgements of applicants according to which they ignored, used, and interpreted formal rules. Facing the obstacles produced by their superiors and legislative and executive decision makers, subordinate officials can choose to transgress formal rules, to improvise and volunteer in order to compensate for shallow legislative adoption or for lack of material resources to implement laws and policies—or to remain passive.

A fruitful avenue for future research could be to explore how a policy's target population participates in the transfer of norms and policies. In the present case, migrants played only an indirect role in the transfer process. As objects or tools of the norm promoters, NGOs and IOs, who declared themselves their spokespersons (Callon, 1986), migrants were expected to contribute passively to the transfer process, for instance by exhibiting favourable characteristics (appearing as suffering and deserving, attracting empathy and recognition among state officials), supporting the supervision by non-state actors (e.g. informing them about requested bribes), making the direct interaction between NGOs and state officials possible (e.g. at the occasion of a migrant's request to access a certain right), and legitimising the necessity of norm transfer. Yet, migrants exercise agency in many spheres of their life and shape migration policies through their practices (Genova, 2016; Mezzadra, 2010). Asylum seekers in Ukraine shaped asylum policies through their interactions with street-level bureaucrats, among whom they could trigger compassion, mistrust, and interest in asylum or situations in countries of origin. However, migrants in Ukraine did not seek to transfer international asylum norms to Ukraine—neither the newly arrived nor those who have settled in and organised in "diaspora organisations". They focused on how to best cope with existing laws and policies, rather than actively and consciously seeking to change them. Indeed, transfer of international asylum norms was not necessarily in the interest of all migrants in Ukraine. Migrants' lack of involvement in law and policy making can be explained by their dire socio-economic situation, (for some groups) limited interest in staying in Ukraine, limited legal and linguistic competences, as well as very limited political opportunities, as illustrated by the overall lack of bottom-up processes in the legislative processes.

However, in other contexts, bottom-up policy—and law-making processes are more relevant than in the observed Ukrainian context (Blankenburg, 1986). In these other cases, target populations could affect transfer processes by directly interacting with subordinate state officials who could then shape the law—and policy-making process in a bottom-up way. Certain types of target populations also organise interest groups to promote the import of favourable international norms or to lobby against the import of unfavourable norms. For instance, LGBT activists use transnational resources and norms to further their political struggles in the domestic arena (Ayoub, 2013). Future research could explore how a policy's target groups, as part of a large and diverse transfer network, participate in shaping transfer processes. Instead of being used as a mere passive object in the hands of other professionalised norm promoters, target groups could intervene actively, possibly pursuing normative objectives diverging from those of their professionalised spokespersons.

Multi-Scalar Analysis of Transfer Processes

This book developed the analytical tool of the multi-scalar transfer chain, which shows that actors are related by power relations and relations of delegation, (inter-)dependence, and control. The EU channelled its funding for asylum projects via UNHCR's office in Ukraine. UNHCR presented itself sometimes as an international actor and sometimes as a national one, via its office in Kyiv. Relations between UNHCR and the EU, namely the European Commission, were complex and shaped by interdependence. While the EU provided funding, it relied on UNHCR knowledge production and monitoring. UNHCR benefited from EU conditionality to push for changes in Ukrainian laws and policies.

UNHCR delegated some of the transfer tasks to NGOs in Ukraine. UNHCR funded and controlled these NGOs' work, and reoriented their activities. It produced seemingly local norm promoters. Scalar relations between UNHCR and the NGOs were clear, as NGOs acted on a more limited geographical scope, depended on UNHCR for funding, legitimacy, and access to certain state facilities. NGO workers mostly presented UNHCR as legitimate to teach them and make decisions about their work and relations to the authorities. While NGO workers enjoyed limited discretion in their everyday work, this did not fundamentally upset the clearly defined scalar relations between donors and subcontractors.

Scales within the state apparatus had been institutionalised and were taken for granted by all actors. These path-dependent scalar fixes (Brenner, 2001, pp. 606–607) were reflected in various actors' expectations of top-down orders and acceptance of higher actors' legal authority over lower scale officials. Neither state nor non-state actors expected bottom-up processes within the administration in law and policy making. State and non-state actors perceived and routinely reperformed scales of the executive state apparatus as strongly hierarchical and limited to horizontal and top-down decision-making and transfer processes, for instance when asking national scale officials to request changes in practices from regional scale officials.

Scalar relations between state and non-state actors were less clear. They were constantly renegotiated by the actors and affected by the domestic or international political context. International organisations such as UNHCR were often seen as legitimate to teach and train Ukrainian officials. In contrast, most state officials, even those with a local scale identity, saw Ukrainian asylum NGOs as located on a lower scale, considering it inappropriate for NGO workers to teach them or criticise their work. NGOs nevertheless wished to change state officials' practices, which clashed with their scalar relations. NGOs outside of the capital constructed a largely regional scale identity by interacting primarily with officials from regional authorities. They rarely shifted issues to a national scale, for example through opening court cases. NGOs in the capital interacted with state actors with both regional and national scale identities, hence shifting between the scales.

NGO workers escaped scalar hierarchies and expanded the range of their scalar transfer strategies by establishing informal, sometimes friendship-like, informal relations with individual state officials. They did so gradually by interacting repeatedly, offering favours, and avoiding criticism. In this way, they could intervene across scales, providing advice and information to state officials. NGOs could also ask their allies among the state officials to issue instructions, recommendations, or orders to lower scale officials. When these officials were willing and in a legitimate position to exercise legal authority over other officials whose practices they were supposed to change, changes were likely to take place—at least temporarily. Such contacts allowed NGOs to "jump scale" (Stubbs, 2005). Yet, these scalar practices depended on the NGO's network and on the individuals who occupied certain state positions.

When NGOs did not have the needed privileged relations with officials in the right position to solve a migrant's problem or support transfer activities, they needed to resort to other, more confrontational multi-scalar approaches. They denounced certain practices to the official directly responsible. In case of resistance, they shifted upwards across the administrative or judicial scales. In cases that they could frame as particularly serious violations of asylum or human rights, NGOs also shifted the issue to an international scale, namely to the EU or the European Court of Human Rights. This triggered top-down pressure onto state actors with a national scale identity.

The political context also affected scalar relations. After the Maidan protests in 2013–2014, NGOs temporarily considered that they had gained power in relation to the authorities. Officials who had worked under the previous president, Victor Yanukovych, feared to be removed from their positions under the lustration campaign and NGO workers felt that they could control the authorities and participate in law and policy making. Yet, after a few months, the relations changed and officials began rejecting NGOs' interventions again as illegitimate interference from lower scale non-state actors.

EU conditionality also shaped scalar relations. EU sector-specific conditionality and monitoring had direct effects on politicians, triggering deeper legislative adoption. Domestic politicians passed the pressure to obtain positive evaluations by the EU on to the administration. Officials had to report upwards across scales to the Cabinet of Ministers, detailing their fulfilment of the EU's expectations. Subordinate officials relied on NGO resources and activities in their reports, which affected their scalar relations with the NGOs.

Instability, Contingency, and Heterogeneity of Transfer

The claim formulated by many macro-perspective transfer scholars, according to which target governments do not implement the transferred norms, requires qualification. In general, public policy research has shown that governments do not fully control policy implementation, which means that the effects of top-down transfer attempts are always to some extent contingent and heterogeneous. In the absence of strong political support of the transfer endeavour and policy implementation, administrative staff lacks resources, information, control, and coherent legislation. Policy implementation therefore depends, more than usual, on individual officials. Often, it even depends on individual officials' willingness to improvise and volunteer to overcome top-down obstacles to their work—willingness that cannot be generalised.

In the analysed case, norm promoters used multiple transfer approaches, involving numerous actors who all shaped the transfer process. Indeed, the different actors involved in transfer resisted, supported, and translated, so that transfer outcomes were necessarily heterogeneous. Many of the transfer activities relied on personal contacts between norm promoters and norm addressees. Norm promoters could not interact directly with all state officials to "teach" them personally, meaning that awareness and legitimacy of the norms differed among officials. Moreover, NGO workers established personalised relations with some officials, some of whom became brokers and norm promoters themselves, so that the transfer practices and effects varied across actors and space. In addition, relations sometimes deteriorated and people left their jobs, causing instability over time. EU sector-specific conditionality shaped transfer processes and effects but ended in 2016. The effects in the long term remain to be explored. Because overall transfer effects are unstable over time, transfer gains from being analysed as a series of processes rather than as fixed results.

Asylum Regimes in Western Europe and Ukraine

Migration research gains from paying attention to the way multi-scalar dynamics affect migration policies (Lacroix, 2022). While this book focuses on a single nation state, it shows that migration policies are fundamentally transnational and multiscalar. Various types of actors with different scalar identities, such as the EU, IOs, international and local NGOs, as well as national and local state authorities, participate in migration policies at different scales. International organisations, the EU and its member states, pursuing their own interests in migration matters, seek to increase their reach (their capacity to make themselves present "at-a-distance" (Allen & Cochrane, 2010)),[1] including via partnerships. Hence, they rescale measures to control migration by cooperation across scales. For instance, the EU and its member states cooperate with third states to externalise migration control and extend their reach beyond their borders (Lacroix, 2022, p. 6). UNHCR enrols and produces allies and brokers (NGOs and individual state officials) with a national or local scale identity in Ukraine to extend its reach in Ukraine and spread its asylum norms. Ukrainian politicians and state officials across scales shape asylum policies according to their different hierarchical positions, interests, and beliefs—some interested in EU incentives, some sharing UN asylum norms, some individually judging asylum seekers they encounter, and some disagreeing with and resisting the promoted norms. To understand seemingly national asylum policies it is therefore essential to take into consideration multi-scalar and multi-actor dynamics.

Comparing asylum regimes, public policies, and state and non-state practices in Western Europe and Ukraine sheds light on the particularities

[1] While Allen and Cochrane (2010) criticise scalar approaches, opposing to them their concept of "reach", I consider that scales and reach can be complementary (Lacroix, 2022, p. 4).

of both.[2] In particular, it reveals the role of the bureaucratisation of the authorities and the institutionalisation of the non-state sector, including in its relations with the administration.

First, relations between the domestic state and non-state actors differ. While in Ukraine international donors funded and shaped all the (funded) work of asylum NGOs, in France or Germany the state is responsible for a large share of the NGOs' funding (Halluin-Mabillot, 2012, p. 89). This appears so normal to Western scholars that the funding of the asylum NGOs is rarely discussed in their research. However, because international donors strongly influenced the structure and practices of the Ukrainian non-state sector, it might be useful to explore the impact of state funding on Western European non-state sectors.

In Western European states, despite reliance on state funding, NGOs' practices are shaped by their members' activist backgrounds (Fischer, 2009b). NGO employees thus struggle with their role of implementers of state policies, a role in which they often coproduce state borders by distinguishing between deserving and undeserving migrants. In contrast, most Ukrainian NGO workers had no activist background. As a result, they largely accepted the norms their donors taught them. The short history of asylum in Ukraine, the low number of asylum seekers, and the existence of other social problems, often perceived as more important, meant that there was very little activism in this area. To understand the role and practices of NGOs it is therefore important to consider the history of activism and of politicisation of the policy area.

What is more, the relations between NGOs and state authorities in Western Europe differ strongly from those in Ukraine. For instance, French NGOs' access to detention facilities has been strongly institutionalised since the 1980s; it is their official work to support migrants' appeals against state decisions and to control and report violations of laws by the authorities (Fischer, 2009a). Ukrainian organisations, by contrast, could rarely access detention facilities and when they could, they depended on the authorities' good will to do so. As such, NGOs in Ukraine had to present their work as harmless and apolitical; they could not openly

[2] As this book is a case study of multi-scalar transfer processes before being a study of asylum policies in Ukraine, it covered a large variety of actors. This means that it does not offer the same depth and detail on specific phenomena as research that focused specifically on a single site, actor, or issue of a national asylum regime, such as Spire (2008) or Fischer (2009a, 2009b).

publish their observations and criticise state practices because they would risk losing access to the facilities. Overall, the relations between Ukrainian NGOs and authorities relied much more on personalised relations than in France. This comparison underscores how much the NGOs' capacity to criticise and counterbalance state practices depends on institutionalised or legal relations and NGOs' rights and tasks with regards to the authorities. It also confirms that authorities in many post-communist states function more on the basis of personalised relationships than Western European ones (Grødeland & Aasland, 2011).

Second, the comparison sheds light on the differences in work practices of Western European and Ukrainian states. Studies about Western European asylum policies highlight that the political will to restrict unwanted immigration has strongly affected state practices (Miaz, 2017; Spire, 2007). In Ukraine, given the lower number of asylum seekers and the weak politicisation of the issue, politicians made less effort to push for more restrictive practices among migration officers. Yet, domestic politicians' interest in the incentives offered by the EU and thus in positive evaluations led to more asylum seeker-friendly policies in the 2000s—in contrast to the restrictive European trends.

The number of asylum seekers also plays a role in the regional caseworkers' practices. While in France, "a policy of numbers" (*politique du chiffre*) put pressure on officials to deal with a set number of files per day and thus contributed, combined with a division of labour, to restrictive practices and the de-individualisation and dehumanisation of the applicants (Spire, 2008, Chapter 4), Ukrainian migration officers faced only a small number of applicants with whom they sometimes established personalised relations. This reinforced the importance of officers' affective and moral judgements of the asylum seekers. Nevertheless, the factors shaping these judgements are very similar across the countries, for example the appreciation of submissive behaviour and of innocence associated with women and children, the condemnation of lying, of attitudes judged too self-confident, or of refusals to uncover personal details (Darley, 2014; Fassin & Kobelinsky, 2012; Kobelinsky, 2012). This calls attention to internationally widespread types of judgement and of upholding of the state order. Only the Ukrainian officials' utilisation of meritocratic arguments concerning asylum seekers differed from French officials' arguments. This could originate from Ukrainian caseworkers' limited training. Indeed, in contrast to their French counterparts, Ukrainian officials were less aware of the dominant international norm according to which the asylum decisions should not be influenced by meritocratic types of reasoning.

Finally, the role of stability and resources of state bodies becomes visible. The stability of Western European state bodies comes into sight only when looking at the frequent restructuring of the Ukrainian ones. Moreover, even if scholars studying French migration authorities point to the scarce resources made available to asylum departments (Spire, 2008, p. 18), the Ukrainians ones were by far less equipped, sometimes rendering their work impossible. Under conditions of severe under-equipment, subordinate officials may improvise to implement laws and policies, such as in West African bureaucracies (Bierschenk & Sardan, 2014). It would be interesting to explore whether under certain conditions Western European bureaucrats also improvise to compensate for lack of resources or whether they do not improvise—and for which reasons. In Western political contexts, scholars have studied improvisation and discretion as granted top-down to cope with crises and other rapidly changing problems (Ansell et al., 2010; Eckhard et al., 2020). It remains to be investigated whether Western street-level bureaucrats also improvise in ordinary contexts and without top-down encouragement.

While studying Ukrainian state practices and comparing them with Western European ones contributes to our understanding of the latter, it also highlights how little we know about the functioning of post-communist states, including the Ukrainian state.[3] Indeed, Western European bureaucracies, especially in France, have been extensively studied in political sociology and anthropology with a focus on subordinate officials' everyday practices. In contrast, post-communist bureaucracies are largely under-researched. Even though I have begun to apply micro perspectives to the Ukrainian state apparatus, much research is still needed before its modes of functioning may be fully grasped. My research suggests that the Ukrainian state bodies are shaped by lack of resources, strong hierarchies, improvisation, bribe-taking, and personalised relations. However, the lack

[3] With growing academic criticism of the category of a supposedly homogenous post-communist, post-socialist, or post-Soviet space (Müller, 2019; Sucală, 2022; Thelen, 2012), increasing time passed since the end of the Soviet Union, and the strong orientation of Ukraine towards the EU and North America especially since 2014, research should not limit itself to comparing the Ukrainian administration to other former Soviet republics but include comparisons to other states. Rather than presupposing persisting similarities among the former Soviet republics this is an open question that needs to be studied.

of in-depth micro-scale research in other policy areas makes these findings difficult to generalise. Ethnographic fieldwork, including long-term participatory observation at the administration, similar to what has been conducted in France (Spire, 2008), would be a fruitful contribution to the lacking research on the administrations in the region.

References

Allen, J., & Cochrane, A. (2010). Assemblages of state power: Topological shifts in the organization of government and politics. *Antipode, 42*(5), 1071–1089. https://doi.org/10.1111/j.1467-8330.2010.00794.x

Ansell, C., Boin, A., & Keller, A. (2010). Managing transboundary crises: Identifying the building blocks of an effective response system Chris Ansell, Arjen Boin and Ann Keller managing transboundary crises. *Journal of Contingencies & Crisis Management, 18*(4), 195–207.

Ayoub, P. M. (2013). Cooperative transnationalism in contemporary Europe: Europeanization and political opportunities for LGBT mobilization in the European Union. *European Political Science Review, 5*(2), 279–310. https://doi.org/10.1017/S1755773912000161

Bierschenk, T., & de Sardan, J.-P. O. (2014). *States at work: Dynamics of African bureaucracies*. BRILL.

Blankenburg, E. (1986). La recherche de l'efficacité de la loi. Réflexions sur l'étude de la mise en œuvre (Le concept «d'implementation»). *Droit Et Société, 2*, 73–94.

Brenner, N. (2001). The limits to scale? Methodological reflections on scalar structuration. *Progress in Human Geography, 25*(4), 591–614. https://doi.org/10.1191/030913201682688959

Buzogány, A. (2013). Selective adoption of EU environmental norms in Ukraine. *Convergence á La Carte. Europe-Asia Studies, 65*(4), 609–630. https://doi.org/10.1080/09668136.2013.766039

Callon, M. (1986). Éléments pour une sociologie de la traduction: La domestication des coquilles St-Jacques et des marins pêcheurs dans la baie de St. Brieuc. *L'Année Sociologique, 36 numéro spécial La sociologie des Sciences et des Techniques*, 169–208.

Cîrstocea, I. (2015). «Se faire une voix». La production internationale du féminisme est-européen des années 1990–2000 *L'homme & La Société, 198*, 73–94. https://doi.org/10.3917/lhs.198.0073

Darley, M. (2014). Les coulisses de la nation. *Sociétés Contemporaines, 94*(2), 19–40.

Delcour, L. (2016). *The EU's policy transfer to the post-Soviet space: Domestic responses, (Post)-soviet legacies and Russia's policies* [HDR]. Institut d'études politiques de Paris.

Dimitrova, A., & Buzogány, A. (2014). Post-accession policy-making in Bulgaria and Romania: Can non-state actors use EU rules to promote better governance? post-accession policy-making in Bulgaria and Romania. *JCMS: Journal of Common Market Studies, 52*(1), 139–156. https://doi.org/10.1111/jcms.12084

Dimitrova, A., & Dragneva, R. (2013). Shaping convergence with the EU in foreign policy and state aid in post-orange Ukraine: Weak external incentives. *Powerful Veto Players. Europe-Asia Studies, 65*(4), 658–681.

Dumoulin, L., & Saurugger, S. (2010). Les policy transfer studies: Analyse critique et perspectives. *Critique Internationale, 48*(3), 9–24. https://doi.org/10.3917/crii.048.0009

Eckhard, S., Lenz, A., Seibel, W., Roth, F., & Fatke, M. (2020). Latent hybridity in administrative crisis management: The German refugee crisis of 2015/16. *Journal of Public Administration Research and Theory*. https://doi.org/10.1093/jopart/muaa039

Fassin, D., & Kobelinsky, C. (2012). Comment on juge l'asile. *Revue Française De Sociologie, 53*(4), 657–688.

Fischer, N. (2009a). Jeux de regards. Surveillance disciplinaire et contrôle associatif dans les centres de rétention administrative. *Genèses, 75*, 45–65. https://doi.org/10.3917/gen.075.0045

Fischer, N. (2009b). Une frontière «négociée» *Politix, 87*, 71–92.

Genova, N. D. (2016). The incorrigible subject: The autonomy of migration and the US immigration stalemate. In A. Oberprantacher & A. Siclodi (Eds.), *Subjectivation in Political Theory and Contemporary Practices* (pp. 267–285). Palgrave Macmillan UK. https://doi.org/10.1057/978-1-137-51659-6_14

Grødeland, Å. B., & Aasland, A. (2011). Civil society in post-communist Europe: Perceptions and use of contacts. *Journal of Civil Society, 7*(2), 129–156.

Halluin-Mabillot, E. (2012). *Les épreuves de l'asile. Associations et réfugiés face aux politiques du soupçon*. EHESS - En temps & lieux.

Knill, C., & Tosun, J. (2009). *Post-Accession transposition of EU law in the new member states: A cross-country comparison*. SSRN Scholarly Paper, ID 1562628. https://papers.ssrn.com/abstract=1562628

Kobelinsky, C. (2012). 'Sont-ils de vrais réfugiés?' Les tensions morales dans la gestion quotidienne de l'asile. In D. Fassin (Ed.), *Economies morales contemporaines* (pp. 155–173). La Découverte.

Lacroix, T. (2022). The transnational state and migration: Reach, flows and Policies. *Political Geography, 94*, 102571. https://doi.org/10.1016/j.polgeo.2021.102571

Langbein, J. (2015). *Transnationalization and regulatory change in the EU's Eastern neighbourhood* (Routledge/UACES Contemporary European Studies).

Mezzadra, S. (2010). The gaze of autonomy: Capitalism, migration and social struggles. In *The contested politics of mobility* (pp. 121–142). Routledge.

Miaz, J. (2017). *Politique d'asile et sophistication du droit: Pratiques administratives et défense juridique des migrants en Suisse (1981–2015)*. Strasbourg. http://www.theses.fr/2017STRAG010

Müller, M. (2019). Goodbye, postsocialism! *Europe-Asia Studies, 71*(4), 533–550. https://doi.org/10.1080/09668136.2019.1578337

Mützelburg, I. (2018). L'empowerment par des financements internationaux ? Comment les donateurs créent un secteur non étatique en Ukraine. *Revue Gouvernance, 15*(1), 63–85.

Pridham, G. (2008). The EU's political conditionality and post-accession tendencies: Comparisons from Slovakia and Latvia. *JCMS: Journal of Common Market Studies, 46*(2), 365–387. https://doi.org/10.1111/j.1468-5965.2007.00780.x

Sasse, G. (2008). The politics of EU conditionality: The norm of minority protection during and beyond EU accession. *Journal of European Public Policy, 15*(6), 842–860.

Saurugger, S., & Terpan, F. (2013). *Resisting EU norms. A framework for analysis*. Sciences Po Grenoble Working Paper, *n°2*.

Sedelmeier, U. (2008). After conditionality: Post-accession compliance with EU law in East Central Europe. *Journal of European Public Policy, 15*(6), 806–825. https://doi.org/10.1080/13501760802196549

Spire, A. (2007). L'asile au guichet: La dépolitisation du droit des étrangers par le travail bureaucratique. *Actes De La Recherche En Sciences Sociales, 169*(4), 4.

Spire, A. (2008). *Accueillir ou reconduire: Enquête sur les guichets de l'immigration*. Raisons d'agir.

Steunenberg, B., & Dimitrova, A. L. (2007). Compliance in the EU enlargement process: The limits of conditionality. *EIoP, 11*(5). https://papers.ssrn.com/abstract=995976

Stubbs, P. (2005). Stretching concepts too far? Multi-level governance, policy transfer and the politics of scale in south-eastern Europe. *South East European Politics, 6*(2), 66–87.

Sucală, V. I. (2022). Is post-communism still relevant today? *Post-Communist Economies*, 1–4. https://doi.org/10.1080/14631377.2022.2028479

Teteriuk, M. (2015). Gay rights and Europeanization processes in Eastern Europe: The case of bill 2342 "On amendments to some legislative acts of Ukraine concerning the prevention and combating of discrimination in Ukraine". *Emecon Employment and Economy in Central and Eastern Europe, 1.* http://www.emecon.eu/current-issue/1-2015/maria-teteriuk/

Thelen, T. (2012). Economic concepts, common grounds and 'new' diversity in the anthropology of post-socialism: Reply to Dunn and Verdery. *Critique of Anthropology, 32*(1), 87–90. https://doi.org/10.1177/0308275X11430874

Glossary

1951 (Refugee) Convention Convention Relating to the Status of Refugees
CIS Commonwealth of Independent States
CoE Council of Europe
DG DEVCO Directorate-General for International Cooperation and Development (of the European Commission)
DG HOME Directorate-General for Migration and Home Affairs
ECHR European Court for Human Rights
EEAS European External Action Service
EASO European Asylum Support Office
ENP European Neighbourhood Policy
EU European Union
HIAS Hebrew Immigrant Aid Society
IDP Internally Displaced Person
IO International Organisation
MP Member of Parliament
MS (Regional) Migration Service
NGO Non-Governmental Organisation
SCNR State Committee on Nationalities and Religion (predecessor of the SMS)
SGUA Support Group for Ukraine of the European Commission
SMS (Central) State Migration Service

I. Mützelburg, *Transferring Asylum Norms to EU Neighbours*,
The European Union in International Affairs,
https://doi.org/10.1007/978-3-031-04528-8

UNHCR United Nations High Commissioner for Refugees
USSR Union of Soviet Socialist Republics/Soviet Union
VLAP Visa-Liberalisation Action Plan

Index

I. Mützelburg, *Transferring Asylum Norms to EU Neighbours*,
The European Union in International Affairs,
https://doi.org/10.1007/978-3-031-04528-8

The manufacturer's authorised representative in the EU is Springer Nature Customer Service Centre GmbH, Europaplatz 3, 69115 Heidelberg, Germany. If you have any concerns regarding our products, please contact ProductSafety@springernature.com

Printed and bound by CPI Group (UK) Ltd, Croydon, CR0 4YY
30/09/2026
02225490-0008